# CULTURES OF
# CURRICULUM

STUDIES IN CURRICULUM THEORY
*William F. Pinar, Series Editor*

# CULTURES OF CURRICULUM

**Pamela Bolotin Joseph**
*Antioch University Seattle*

**Stephanie Luster Bravmann**
*Seattle University*

**Mark A. Windschitl**
*University of Washington*

**Edward R. Mikel**
*Antioch University Seattle*

**Nancy Stewart Green**
*Northeastern Illinois University, Emeritus*

2000

LAWRENCE ERLBAUM ASSOCIATES, PUBLISHERS
Mahwah, New Jersey                    London

Lawrence Erlbaum Associates, Inc., Publishers
10 Industrial Avenue
Mahwah, NJ 07430

Cover design by Kathryn Houghtaling Lacey

**Library of Congress Cataloging-in-Publication Data**

Cultures of curriculum / Pamela Bolotin Joseph ... [et al.].
    p.  cm.
   Includes bibliographical references and index.
   ISBN 0-8058-2274-7 (alk. paper)
   1. Curriculum planning—United States. 2. Education—Curricula—Social aspects—United States.  I. Joseph, Pamela Bolotin.
   LB2806. 15.C73   1999
   374'.001—dc21                                     99-28725
                                                        CIP

Books published by Lawrence Erlbaum Associates are printed on
acid-free paper, and their bindings are chosen for strength and
durability.

Printed in the United States of America
10  9  8  7  6  5  4  3  2  1

*In honor of our parents*

Claire and Jack Bolotin
Dorothy and Mort Luster
Valerie and Clete Windschitl
Margaret and Meryle Mikel
Laura Payton Stewart and Blair Stewart

Now it is Jessica's turn. "I have a number of goals for this class," she says. "I want you to pass the Regents. I want you to appreciate American literature. And I want you to come to your own conclusions about things, to have confidence in your own abilities."

—Samuel G. Freedman, 1990, *Small Victories: The Real World of a Teacher, Her Students, and Their High School*

Ivar's university, over the years, had made serious noises to all sorts of constituencies. Students would find good jobs, the state would see a return on its educational investment, business could harvest enthusiastic and well-trained workers by the hundreds, theory and technology would break through limits as old as the human race (and some lucky person would get to patent the breakthroughs). At the very least, the students could expect to think true, beautiful, and profound thoughts, and thereafter live better lives.

—Jane Smiley, 1995, *Moo*

The first antinomy is this: on the one hand, it is unquestionably the function of education to enable people, individual human beings, to operate at their fullest potential, to equip them with the tools and the sense of opportunity to use their wits, skills and passions to the fullest. The antinomic counterpart to this is that the function of education is to reproduce the culture that supports it—not only reproduce it, but further its economic, political, and cultural ends.

—Jerome Bruner, 1996, *The Culture of Education*

# Contents

# Preface

We wrote this book to foster awareness, examination, and deliberation about the curricula planned for and carried out in classrooms and schools, hoping that it inspires conversations about theory and practice, as well as political, social, and moral issues. We imagine that it will engage readers in a variety of levels or pathways —from the naming of orientations, to the recognition of the encompassing idea of culture represented by curricular orientations in classrooms and schools, to inquiry about the nature of curriculum that dominates American classrooms, and to exploration of possible visions. Although we wrote our book as a resource for graduate students (experienced educators and administrators) and new practitioners in courses of curriculum theory, curriculum studies, and the history and philosophy of education, we also believe that *Cultures of Curriculum* can enter the public discourse as readers bring its ideas and issues into their schools and communities.

Our purpose here is to expand critical consciousness about individuals' approaches to curriculum and practice. Using *Cultures of Curriculum* as a platform for inquiry, we encourage readers to consider if their curriculum work reflects a mélange of unarticulated methods and purposes, a struggle to maintain a coherent vision amidst many competing pressures, or an overarching aim enacted daily and embodied within a congruous set of practices.

We have developed a framework of inquiry that accomplishes these specific goals:

- To elucidate the concept of curriculum as culture—a revealing system of implicit and explicit beliefs, values, behaviors, and customs in classrooms and schools that are deliberated within communities and other public spheres.

- To acquaint our readers with patterns of curricular thinking that have influenced the development of the concept of cultures of curriculum.
- To give historical insight about shifting educational and social priorities that have influenced the course of curriculum in American schooling.
- To integrate moral and political discourse into recognition and discussion of curriculum.
- To encourage metaphoric thinking that enables new ways to perceive commonplace assumptions and embedded belief systems.
- To deepen awareness of dilemmas of practice inherent in curriculum work.
- To hold each culture of curriculum up to critical inquiry of its assumptions, purposes, and claims.

After such scrutiny, we hope our readers will give serious attention to issues raised for them and join with their colleagues, students, and communities in considering how to create curricula with purpose and congruent practices. For our readers who find affirmation of their beliefs and practices in reading this book, we hope also that they reflect about their visions as they consider dilemmas of practice and critique of cultures of curriculum. Furthermore, they might consider how they can provide leadership to others who feel overwhelmed by curricular forces and practices that leave them feeling fragmented and aware that they are "just getting by."

We think that the knowledge presented in this book, and the discussion it may stimulate, will help prepare teachers "who reflect on, and understand, the broader human and social purposes of what they do" and "make decisions about what and how they teach in the light of their commitments to attain these purposes"—to have "consciousness and conscience about the fundamental values that [they are] trying to initiate in the classroom" (Purpel & Shapiro, 1995, pp. 109–110). As well, we believe that reading this book may help prepare administrators or community members to reject simplistic solutions and thoughtfully and holistically frame their thinking about curriculum.

Also, our ideas may inspire examination of the beliefs concerning the purposes of education and the means to achieve them held by others, (including colleagues, administrators, school board members and the community, public officials, parents, and children). Through discussions with students, colleagues, and community members, our readers may find some fascinating commonalities about their beliefs about practice and the purpose of education. They may also discover disturbing dissonance in which they find that they have drastically different goals; they may learn that not all ideas and practices adhered to by others are acceptable to them. This book may help our readers to "draw lines"—deciding what ideas about curriculum could be negotiated and what positions cannot be compromised.

This book has three sections. In the first section, the first and second chapters set the theoretical background in which we delineate previous ideas about curriculum and the concept of culture that have informed our understanding of curriculum. The next section (chaps. 3 through 8) contains what we call the six content chapters that examine each curricular culture according to a framework of inquiry; each of these six chapters includes: a quote that captures much of the essence of its curricular orientation; a portrayal of a classroom in which theory is put into practice; a synthesis of the vision held by advocates of this curriculum; historical background of this curriculum within American schooling; assumptions within this curriculum about students, teachers, content, context (the classroom environment), planning, and evaluation; and discussions about dilemmas about practice and critique, when applicable, of both theory and practice within the culture of curriculum. The third section (chap. 9) is a reflection about inherent difficulties with the concept of curricular cultures and how it can be a springboard for inquiry, discussion, and school reform.

The six content chapters begin with two curricular orientations with the fundamental goals of the inculcation of cultural values, but with ultimate visions of the educated individual that have profound differences. The first is the curricular orientation most influential in schooling in contemporary American society, "Training for Work and Survival"; the following chapter, "Connecting to the Canon," describes the liberal arts tradition that advocates a vigorous intellectual education stemming from Euro-American classical sources. The next two chapters describe orientations that focus on individual learning; "Developing Self and Spirit" and "Constructing Understanding" explore child-centered education and constructivism. The final content chapters are curricular orientations with strong social visions. "Deliberating Democracy" explains democratic education and its goals for preparing students to understand the possibilities of living in a democratic society; "Confronting the Dominant Order" depicts the liberatory theories and practices of multicultural, feminist, and critical pedagogies.

Lastly, we would like to tell our readers about the development and process of writing this project. It began when David Purpel, our friend and a superb critical curriculum scholar (University of North Carolina, Greensboro), suggested to Pam Joseph the idea of writing about curricular orientations; her conversations with David and his creative thinking helped her to conceptualize several of the cultures of curriculum. David Purpel's other wonderful contribution to this project was to keep saying to Pam that "you really ought to meet Stevie Bravmann—you two really think alike." After several fascinating and laughter-filled lunches, it made a great deal of sense that this would become a project for Pam and Stevie to do together. Through these discussions, Pam and Stevie drew on their interest in culture as their way to "explain the world" and modified the project from curricular orientations to cultures of curriculum.

Pam then spoke with her colleague and friend, Ed Mikel, who has such passion and expertise in democratic education. He was delighted to have an opportunity for sustained writing and discussion. When Nancy Green, Pam's graduate-school friend and teaching mentor, retired from Northeastern Illinois University and moved to be with family in Seattle, the project was strengthened enormously because of Nancy's work in the history of women's education and her research in vocational education. Finally, when attending a conference on constructivism at which her friend, Mark Windschitl, presented a paper on dilemmas of constructivist teaching, Pam asked him to become an author and Mark eventually became a mainstay of the project, writing the chapter dealing with constructivism, the major portion of the chapter relating to critical pedagogy, and a good deal of the concluding chapter.

Writing this book as a collaborative project, we thoroughly enjoyed our exciting conversations about premises and conclusions. Our dialogue has been a tremendously interesting part of this project as we've challenged each other's ideas about what constitutes a culture of curriculum, what properly belongs in one, or what should be excluded. We've all been "stretched" as we have defended our positions, made changes, and shared the knowledge from each other's research.

## ACKNOWLEDGMENTS

First, we want to recognize the educators—our students—for ideas and feedback about this book as we shared versions of these chapters; our students at Antioch University, Seattle University, and the University of Washington have brought conceptual pieces and excerpts into classes for the past several years. We have learned a great deal from our students and are grateful for their willingness to offer their ideas to all the authors, especially about dilemmas of practice. Excerpts from students' journals, class activities, and interviews have been incorporated into several of our chapters.

We thank the teachers and colleagues who contributed their words, ideas, and excellent sources to this project. We especially want to acknowledge: Charlie Burleigh, Mark Smith, Stacy Scoles, Sue Kawakubo, John Moen, Matthew Page, Mickie Gunderson, Leigh Knapp, Mary Ann Simpson, Cindy Catalano, Cecile Eastman, Gary Greene, Tom Ingalls, Shelly Lacy, Dawn Simpson, Dennis Macmillan, Paul Brahce, Michael Sylvan, Susan Longstreth, Connie Saari, Jim Beane, Barb Brodhagen, Sunny Pervil, Carol Lieber, Mike Magrath, Jori Martinez, Jean Ann Hunt, Tom Kelly, George Wood, Stan Hiserman, Doris Brevoort, Robbie Barnes, and Sylvie Kashdan.

We are grateful to David Purpel for initiating this book and having the confidence in us to write it. We appreciate our editor, Naomi Silverman, for her patience and encouragement of this project; as life and work continued to interfere with our writing, her assurance that "this will be a wonderful book" kept us going. We also appreciate the help of Bryan Deever, who read our manuscript and made suggestions that clarified our thinking about curriculum and culture.

We also want to acknowledge our educational and intellectual debts. Harold and Ann Berlak have been mentors and colleagues in the arena of democratic education. Joe Park taught how to apply philosophy to "real life." Paul Bohannon inspired application of the lens of culture to think about education, systems, values, and actions; so many years after his exciting seminar at Northwestern University, the ideas learned there continue to be compelling.

## REFERENCE

Purpel, D. E., & Shapiro, S. (1995). *Beyond liberation and excellence: Reconstructing the public discourse on education.* Westport, CT: Bergin & Garvey.

# 1

# Conceptualizing Curriculum

**Pamela Bolotin Joseph**
*Antioch University Seattle*

*A theory that works is altogether a miracle: it idealizes our varying observations of the world in a form so stripped down as to be kept easily in mind, permitting us to see the grubby particulars as exemplars of a general case.*
—Jerome Bruner, 1996, *The Culture of Education*

The notion of curriculum as enveloping patterns of norms, endeavors, and values seems particularly lacking in these times, both within public discourse and in schools. Interest in curriculum too often involves narrow discussions about specific programs, outcomes, and effectiveness, as procedural perspectives of educational outcomes dominate curriculum development. Public debates about curriculum appear as politically motivated diatribes calling forth simplistic notions of what is wrong with schools or what sure-fire curriculum will save them. Few educators participate in public deliberation with vigorous discourse about purposes and practices of education. We seldom hear teachers, curriculum specialists, and administrators reflect on, question, and challenge curricular aims and actions by examining dominant patterns of curricular beliefs and their immediate or unforeseeable influences upon schooling.

Much of this failure to see and question the "big picture" is rooted in recent history. We note the increased reliance on "teacher-proof" programs or curriculum packages in which teachers become the "delivery system" by following scripts or recipes and providing copies of prepared handouts to their students. The teaching profession holds decreasing power to control curricular decisions in the wake of attacks on schools and the demands for accountability to uniform educational goals. And, despite the sincerity of many teachers who try each day to do right by their students, educators often are too immersed in the difficulty or complacent familiarity of their particular circumstances to note, to name, and to question the most dominant structures of school culture and what is taught to young people.

Moreover, for many people (including many of the new and experienced educators whom we teach) the nature of curriculum as a course of study embodies a narrowly specialized set of skills with the emphasis upon "technique" over "substance":

> We are referring here to the transformation of curriculum theory and practice from a concern about *what* should be taught and *why* we should teach it to those problems associated with *how to* organize, build, and above all now, evaluate curriculum and teaching. The difficult ethical and political questions of content, of what knowledge is of most worth, have been pushed to the background in our attempts to define technically oriented methods that will "solve" our problems once and for all. (Beyer & Apple, 1998, p. 3)

Overall, the contemporary state of discussion does not foster critical inquiry; people involved with curriculum often do not have the language or patterns of thought that would allow them to question dominant perspectives and purposes and imagine alternatives.

Neither broad attacks on schooling (from social reformers or conservatives) nor stultifying emphasis on outcomes and assessment allow educators or the public to have vigorous discourse about moral and social visions for education. We rarely know of public debate about the possibilities of education as a catalyst for the transformation of individuals or for social reform; limited expectations and cynicism have displaced hope and idealism.

## SEEING CURRICULAR PATTERNS

Our one cause for hope for critical inquiry and moral discourse about curriculum comes from the field of curriculum theory or curriculum studies. For educators who work in those areas, the study of curriculum is closely connected to qualitative research that seeks meaning rather than control or an ultimate version of truth.

> [T]he general field of curriculum, the field interested in the relationships among school subjects as well as issues within the individual school subjects themselves and with the relationships between the curriculum and the world, that field is no longer preoccupied with development.... [T]he field today is preoccupied with *understanding....* [I]t is necessary to understand the contemporary field as discourse, as text, and most simply but profoundly as words and ideas. (Pinar, Reynolds, Slattery, & Taubman, *1995, p. 6, 7*)

Curriculum as understanding allows educators to become more aware of possibilities for education. Thus, they learn to inquire into the embedded metaphors, assumptions, and visions within curriculum and to comprehensively critique their assumptions and practice and theoretical and instructional premises and goals.

As we work with teachers, adult educators, administrators, community activists, and curriculum specialists, our paramount purpose is realized when these educators expand their consciousness in their ways of viewing and understanding curriculum. This consciousness-changing seems evident in the words of a middle-school teacher participating in an introductory curriculum theory class: "We all need to know ... what *are* we talking about here?" Theories, frameworks, and images are the means for us to explore curricular meaning.

We wrote this book because of our desire to share patterns of meaning that have helped us to better understand the curriculum field. Previously constructed frameworks for revealing and deliberating curriculum have informed our efforts here; our inquiry joins an ongoing conversation about ways of understanding curriculum.

This chapter portrays the powerful approaches to conceptualizing curriculum in the past and in contemporary times that have contributed to our work with educators and our eventual consideration about curricular cultures. We conclude this chapter by briefly introducing our pattern of understanding curriculum.

## MULTIPLE CURRICULA

Perhaps no other discussion of curriculum has grounded our idea of cultures of curriculum as meaningfully as Eisner's (1985) conception of "three curricula that all schools teach." Eisner's heuristic allows educators to examine curriculum that is explicit (obviously stated), implicit (not official, often referred to as "hidden"), and null (nonexisting—the curriculum that schools do not teach).

The *explicit* curriculum is manifest in publicly stated goals of education—for example, teaching students American history or health. Explicit curriculum can be found in the school's presentation of itself to the public, in official curriculum guides, and in academic or behavioral outcomes in courses and lessons.

The *implicit* curriculum is the learning and interaction that occurs that is not explicitly announced in school programs. Implicit curriculum may be intentionally taught— for example, a teacher, fearful of confrontation from the very conservative community in which she works, continually tries to teach critical thinking but never announces these goals to parents or students. Implicit curriculum also may be inadvertent, such as when teachers may not realize how classrooms or schools teach competition as a social value.

The *null* curriculum deals with what is systematically excluded, neglected, or not considered. Thus, teachers create a null curriculum when they teach history as "the true story" but do not present the perspective of peoples from nondominant cultures—or choose as "the greatest literature" only works written by European males. (A caveat to the concept of null curriculum is that not all excluded curricula fall into this category; educators always make choices but what they do not choose is not necessarily null curriculum, e.g., selecting one textbook over another because of preference for an author's writing style.) The concept of null curriculum is compelling—as a reminder of the choices teachers made or did not even think about—as they examine their own practice as curriculum workers.

Cuban (1993) also proposes a framework of multiple curricula for curriculum investigation. He suggests that we view curricula in four categories: *Official* curriculum can be found in curriculum guides and conform with state-mandated assessment. *Taught* curriculum is what individual teachers focus on and choose to emphasize—often the choices represent teachers' knowledge, beliefs about how subjects should be taught, assumptions about their students' needs, and interests in certain subjects. *Learned* curriculum encompasses all that students learn; learned curriculum may be what teachers planned or have not intended, such as modeling teachers' behaviors or what students learn from other students. The fourth curriculum Cuban calls *tested curriculum*; these tests—whether derived from the teacher, the school district, state, or national testing organizations—represent only part of what is taught or learned.

As does Eisner, Cuban warns us not to be captivated by curriculum that is symbolic (how the school or state represents itself) but not necessarily indicative of what takes place in classrooms. Cuban explains that we need to consider these multiple versions of curricula if we really care about educational reform; changes in official and tested curricula may be meaningless unless we attend to the taught and learned curricula. The multiple curricula approach to curriculum inquiry reminds us that whenever we speak of curriculum, we must ask, "which curriculum?" We cannot engage in curriculum deliberation without reflecting upon curriculum as many-sided meanings and experiences.

## CURRICULUM AS TEXT

When we understand curriculum as having diverse meanings, we develop lenses to "see" curriculum as multiple layers of phenomena. We might also imagine curriculum as a multitude of discourses. Pinar, Reynolds, Slattery, and Taubman (1995), writing extensively about the historical and contemporary field of curriculum, teach us how to "hear" various curricular voices or to recognize different "languages":

> To understand the contemporary field it is necessary to understand the curriculum field as discourse, as text, and most simply but profoundly, as words and ideas. By discourse we mean a particular discursive practice, or a form of articulation that follows certain rules and which constructs the very object it studies. Any discipline or field of study can be treated as discourse and analyzed as such. To do so requires studying *the language of the field.* Yes, the curriculum field is about what happens in schools, but in being about schools it employs and is comprised by the language which both reflects and determines what "being about schools" means. (p. 7)

Conceiving curriculum as text or discourse compels us to listen to and make sense of the words, phrases, and patterns of language that characterize curriculum and to be aware of how this language itself shapes curriculum. We are encouraged to consider not only the ways that people talk about curriculum, but to seek understanding of its inherent themes and structures.

Pinar and his co-authors (1995) depict curriculum as various discourses: historical, political, racial, gender, poststructuralist/deconstructed/postmodern, autobiographical–biographical, aesthetic, theological, and institutional. Each discourse has its own premises and foci; each creates a particular "reality" of phenomena. For instance, aesthetic text represents curriculum as art and artistic experience; it features the teacher (curriculum worker) as artist, the appreciation of curriculum as connoisseurship, and the curriculum as a creative process—for example, as tempo, dance, or theater. Curriculum as institutionalized text concerns the structure of schools, curricular planning and design, implementation, supervision, evaluation, and technology. Each discourse contains particular language, patterns of thoughts, and norms about what is appropriate and valuable. Curriculum as text illustrates the continual dialogue of culture—the conversations and themes that are important to people who "live" in the culture or who portray it.

## CURRICULUM COMMONPLACES

Another avenue for understanding curriculum is the framework of curriculum commonplaces developed by Schwab (1973), who discusses "five bodies of experiences" (p. 502) necessary to consider for curriculum revision. When people come together to revise curriculum, they need to be familiar with knowledge about (in Schwab's order): subject matter, learners, milieus, teachers, and curriculum making.

*Subject matter* refers to knowledge of curriculum materials, the discipline of study and its underlying system of thought. For instance, Schwab would say that for a science curriculum to be revised, one of the people involved in this curriculum work must have expertise in science—specifically in the area of the curriculum (e.g., biology), and likewise, must know what it is to be a scientist and biologist.

Knowledge of *learners* involves familiarity with the children who will be learning the subject matter. Such knowledge includes awareness of their developmental abilities, "what aspirations and anxieties which may affect learning" (p. 502), the unique qualities of the children, and understanding about their probable "future economic status and function" (p. 503). Certainly, Schwab focuses more on "what is" and far less on the possibilities of education for social mobility and transformation.

The *milieus* refer to the school and classrooms—for example, the social structure in those environments. Schwab also wants to know what are the influences upon the classroom and school; he asks, "what are the conditions, dominant preoccupations, and cultural climate of the whole polity and its social classes, insofar as they may affect the careers, the probable fate, and ego identity of the children whom we want to teach?" (p. 504). Thus, Schwab asks about a multitude of values and attitudes stemming from the community and culture surrounding the school, such as those from religions, social classes, and ethnic backgrounds.

Knowledge about *teachers* means what "these teachers are likely to know and how flexible and ready they are likely to be to learn new materials and new ways of teaching" as well as their possible biases, political stances, personalities, and "prevailing moods" (p. 504). Schwab does not assume that those who revise curriculum would automatically have such knowledge of teachers because he does not suggest that teachers themselves are involved in curriculum revision.

The final "body of experience" is knowledge of the *curriculum-making* process. The person who has this knowledge is the curriculum specialist.

> It is he who reminds all others of the importance of the experience of each representative to the (curriculum-making) enterprise as a whole. It is he, as chairman, who monitors the proceedings, pointing out to the group what has happened in the course of their deliberations, what is currently taking place, what has not yet been considered, what subordinations and super-ordinations may have occurred which affect the process in which all are engaged. (p. 505)

To Schwab, it is the curriculum specialist who has the "big picture" and is the person who should guide the process of curriculum revision. It is the specialist who is in charge and has the power to influence curriculum; the voices of teachers, students, parents, or community members for the most part are not personally represented.

Schwab's scheme of commonplaces denotes a science of curriculum planning that is in opposition to the concept of lived curriculum, in which verities of daily life and myriad decisions teachers make to shape curriculum are acknowledged. Notwithstanding, his insistence upon the unique nature of each classroom (which flies in the face of the belief that only standardization can create good curriculum) and his awareness of the numerous influences on curriculum inside and outside of the classroom is a scaffold for imagining curriculum revealed within classrooms cultures.

Others have utilized Schwab's commonplaces to ground their thinking about curriculum. Connelly and Clandinin (1988) strongly emphasize the commonplaces for analyzing curriculum, giving it meaning, and understanding one's own stance as a curriculum worker (pp. 84–86). To them, commonplaces serve as a frame of analysis to uncover the "logic" or emphasis in a given rationale for curriculum as expressed by teachers, parents, or in national debate. This framework seeks answers to questions such as: what assumptions are held about learners—how they learn and what they need to learn? What expectations are made about the role of teachers? Who should have power over curriculum making? However, unlike those who advocate scientific curriculum making controlled by specialists, Connelly and Clandinin understand curriculum planning as fluid narrative, often stemming from the teacher's sense of self and place.

Exploration of the commonplaces reveals the metaphors that undergird belief systems about curriculum (see Foshay, 1980). We might ask ourselves: What content and methods shall we consider if we believe that the learner is an empty vessel rather than a dynamic maker of knowledge? How shall we structure the classroom if we conceive of the teacher as a fellow learner rather than as the transmitter of knowledge? Such metaphors indeed are "commonplace" in that they often are not perceived or considered—and yet they are omnipresent and function as strong influences on norms or expectations when people debate and decide curriculum.

Bruner (1996) likens such metaphoric thinking to folk pedagogies—deeply embedded cultural knowledge about education.

> Folk pedagogies, for example, reflect a variety of assumptions about children: they may be seen as willful and needing correction; as innocent and to be protected from a vulgar society; as needing skills to be developed only through practice; as empty vessels to be filled with knowledge that only adults can provide; as egocentric and in need of socialization. Folk beliefs of this kind, whether

expressed by laypeople or by "experts," badly want some "deconstructing" if their implications are to be appreciated. For whether these views are "right" or not, their impact on teaching activities can be enormous. (Bruner, 1996, p. 49)

Thus, as people (parents, teachers, politicians, etc.) act on these folk pedagogies, they accept their reasoning as normal, or true, or the best way of thinking about learners or education.

Commonplaces offer one set of powerful analytic tools. We gain deeper understanding of what is taking place when we pay attention to the rationale behind curriculum choice and notice which commonplace receives the greatest emphasis. This framework allows us to scrutinize the assumptions, beliefs, and values we hold and to discern what matters most to other people as we work within educational and political arenas to affect curriculum.

## CURRICULUM AS COMPLEX QUESTIONS

When there are the means to reflectively examine curriculum, we can get beyond superficial and unexamined meaning and think with complexity about curriculum as aims and experiences. The strength of the commonplaces heuristic is its facility for generating questions for understanding curriculum. The field of curriculum studies seeks to examine and challenge everyday assumptions, including those beliefs that both educators and the public implicitly hold. A framework for examination of curriculum is a starting point, but not sufficiently complex, for curriculum scholars who hold that curriculum deliberation and inquiry should stem from a diverse and complex set of questions.

Beyer and Apple (1998) provide a set of questions that contributes a sophisticated approach to curriculum inquiry. Beyer and Apple insist that "no list can ever do justice to the complexity of curriculum deliberations"; rather, they utilize this set of questions as a guideline, and we are encouraged to imagine what questions also are important for understanding curriculum. Beyer and Apple (1998) pose questions in eight categories: epistemological, political, economic, ideological, technical, aesthetic, ethical, and historical:

1. *Epistemological*: What should count as knowledge? As knowing? Should knowledge be considered a process or separate divisions of cognitive, affective, and psychomotor areas?
2. *Political*: Who shall control the selection and distribution of knowledge? Through what institutions?
3. *Economic*: How is the control of knowledge linked to the existing and unequal distribution of power, goods, and services in society?
4. *Ideological*: What knowledge is of most worth? Whose knowledge is it?
5. *Technical*: How shall curricular knowledge be made accessible to students?

6. *Aesthetic*: How do we link the curriculum knowledge to give personal meaning to students? How do we practice curriculum design and teaching in artful ways?
7. *Ethical*: How shall we treat others responsibly and justly within the realm of education? What ideas of moral action and community ground our stance toward student and teachers?
8. *Historical*: What traditions help us to understand curriculum and to answer the above questions? (p. 5–6)

These curriculum scholars add political, economic, and aesthetic dimensions to our conceptions of curriculum through a critical examination of issues of power and control. Moreover, Beyer and Apple explicitly place curriculum inquiry into the realm of moral discourse by recognizing inherent moral visions and the importance of ethical debate. They compel us to not only question if curriculum is effective but to ask, is it moral?

## CONFLICTING CONCEPTIONS OF CURRICULUM

The naming of curricular orientations has a long tradition in curriculum scholarship from the fields of the philosophy of education and curriculum theory. Schemes for conceptualization continue to be part of the dialogue on curriculum and the goals of schooling. This line of inquiry focuses on the ultimate aims of education and the means of reaching those aims.

Emphasizing the contested worth of kinds of knowledge, philosophers of education postulate educational theories or alternatives in education. George Kneller (1971) divides educational philosophy—and corresponding practice such as the teacher's role—into five major categories: perennialism, progressivism, essentialism, reconstructionism, and existentialism.

1. *Perennialism*: the belief in unchanging human nature and the need to teach knowledge of eternal truths.
2. *Progressivism*: modifying education in the light of new knowledge and social conditions, a focus on the interests of students, and learning in a democratic environment.
3. *Essentialism*: focuses on subject matter; advocates of this orientation do not suggest teaching eternal truths, but they believe that there is a variable body of knowledge or expertise that learners must obtain.
4. *Reconstructionism*: teaching about serious social and economic problems and to work toward developing a new social order of political and economic democracy.
5. *Existentialism*: reflects a worldview emphasizing the choices individuals make and individual responsibility; by connecting existentialism and education, the teachers must respect their students' freedom and urge their

students to recognize their freedom—to become actors in the drama of learning, not spectators. (Kneller, 1971, pp. 42–84)

John Goodlad, a curriculum scholar and reformer in teacher education, also emphasizes the aims of education, seeking to understand "what schools are for." Goodlad (1979/1994) explains that "goals for schooling emerge through a sociopolitical process in which certain sets of interests prevail over others for a period of time" (p. 43). He generates twelve goals that can be placed within four categories:

1. *Academic*: emphasis on sufficient schooling to learn the principles of religion and the laws of the land (functional literacy)
2. *Vocational*: readiness for productive work and economic responsibility
3. *Social and civic*: socialization for participation in a complex society
4. *Personal*: the goal of personal fulfillment. (pp. 43–44)

Goodlad views the goals not only as reflections of what researchers have seen in schools, but also as ideals (p. 45). He believes that listing goals serves as "a beginning point in a dialogue about education" and a way for communities to evaluate what is going on in schools (p. 45).

A classic work in the curriculum field by Eisner and Vallance, *Conflicting Conceptions of Curriculum* (1974), also points to the existence of five different curricular orientations "in terms of the goals and assumptions embedded within them" (p. 2). Eisner and Vallance see these orientations not just as ultimate aims but as systems of thought, values, and actions around curriculum, such as the nature of learning. These orientations are:

1. *Development of Cognitive Processes*: concern with the refinement of intellectual operations; it refers only rarely to curriculum content, focusing instead on the *how* rather than the *what* of education; it sees the central problem of curriculum as that of sharpening the intellectual processes and developing a set of cognitive skills that can be applied to learning virtually anything. (pp. 5–6)
2. *Curriculum as Technology*: it is also concerned with the *how* rather than the *what* of education; it conceptualizes the function of curriculum as essentially one of finding efficient means to a set of predefined, nonproblematic ends. It is concerned with the technology by which knowledge is communicated and "learning" is facilitated, it makes little or no reference to content, it is concerned with developing a technology of instruction. (pp. 5–8)
3. *Self-actualization, or Curriculum as Consummatory Experience*: strongly and deliberately value-saturated, this approach refers to personal purpose and to the need for personal integration, and it views the function of the curriculum as providing personally satisfying consummatory experiences

for each individual learner. It is child-centered, autonomy and growth-orientated, and education is seen as an enabling process that would provide the means to personal liberation and development. (p. 9)

4. *Social Reconstruction-Relevance*: with this orientation there is a strong emphasis on the role of education and curriculum content within the larger social context; stressing of societal needs over individual needs, social reform and responsibility to the future of society are primary; an approach in which social values and (often) political positions, are clearly stated; social reconstructionism demands that schools recognize and respond to their role as a bridge between what is and what might be, between the real and the ideal. It is the traditional view of schooling as the "bootstrap" by which society can change itself. (pp. 10–11)

5. *Academic Rationalism*: primarily concerned with enabling the young to acquire the tools to participate in the Western cultural tradition and with providing access to the greatest ideas and objects that humans have created. The curriculum should emphasize the classic disciplines through which [humans inquire] since these disciplines, almost by definition, provide concepts and criteria through which thought acquires precision, generality, and power; such disciplines exemplify intellectual activity at its best. (p. 12)

Eisner and Vallance declare the need for professional educators and lay people to understand that:

Controversy in educational discourse most often reflects a basic conflict in priorities concerning the form and content of curriculum and the goals toward which schools should strive; the intensity of the conflict and the apparent difficulty in resolving it can most often be traced to a failure to recognize conflicting conceptions of curriculum. Public educational discourse frequently does not bother to examine its conceptual underpinnings. (pp. 1–2)

Vallance (1986) takes a second look at "conflicting conceptions" a decade later, considering which orientations held steady or declined and raises questions about whether the scheme could "adequately describe curriculum discourse today" (p. 26). She also reflects upon the nature of these orientations, remarking that four orientations concern the goals of education and one (the technological conception) is an anomaly in that it does not deal with purposes but with means (p. 25). Vallance then describes two new orientations: The first is *personal success* and its accompanying study of business, computer science, and engineering—with the discouragement of courses in humanities and social sciences (p. 29). The second added orientation is *personal commitment to learning*, "an underlying passion for the hard work and joys of intellectual exploration" (pp. 27–28).

Curriculum conceptualized as orientations gives theorists and practitioners a meaningful strategy for comprehending the field of curriculum. The naming of curricular orientations provides a platform for awareness, analysis, and critique that allows for interpretation of a broad and perplexing field and for the encouragement of dialogue about curricular intentions and consequences. Recognition of diverse purposes of education and the means of accomplishing them is an important springboard for educational dialogue. Educators cannot help but make discourse more insightful and vigorous by clarifying their beliefs and experiences around curriculum, finding commonalities with others, and learning about what they truly value.

## CULTURES OF CURRICULUM

By writing this book, we have entered the curricular conversation by posing the concept of curricular cultures. We believe that perceiving *cultures of curriculum* is a way to engage in systematic inquiry and to change consciousness about the curriculum field and the curriculum manifest in classrooms. Moreover, we believe that this framework encourages thinking more about curriculum as overlapping systems—sometimes sharing significant commonalities; the concept of conflict is not always useful for explaining curricular orientations.

Informed by previous delineations of curriculum, we generated a classification of curricular orientations influenced especially by "conflicting conceptions of curriculum" (Eisner & Vallance, 1974). We affirm the relevance of conceptions of curriculum as an effective way to classify curriculum, especially because of the possibilities as a springboard for discussion, so that people may better understand their commonalties of beliefs and visions as well as their assumptions and values that are in conflict. However, our awareness of both changing classroom cultures and theoretical perspectives beckoned us to consider revision of Eisner and Vallance's scheme. Our discussion as authors increasingly demonstrated to us that individual curriculum orientations share assumptions about learners, instructional practices, and curriculum content, such as the need for integrated curriculum.

The following are the names we have chosen for these cultures of curriculum and a brief descriptions of their ultimate goals:

I.  *Training for Work and Survival*: To gain the basic skills, habits, and attitudes necessary to function in the workplace and to adapt to living within contemporary society.

II. *Connecting to the Canon*: To acquire core cultural knowledge, traditions, and values from the dominant culture's exemplary moral, intellectual, spiritual, and artistic resources as guidelines for living.

III. *Developing Self and Spirit*: To learn according to self-directed interests in order to nurture individual potential, creativity, and knowledge of the emotional and spiritual self.
IV. *Constructing Understanding*: To develop fluid, active, autonomous thinkers who know that they themselves can construct knowledge through their study of the environment and collaborative learning with others.
V. Deliberating Democracy: To learn and to actually experience the deliberative skills, knowledge, beliefs, and values necessary for participating in and sustaining a democratic society.
VI. *Confronting the Dominant Order*: To examine and challenge oppressive social, political, and economic structures that limit self and others and to develop beliefs and skills that support activism for the reconstruction of society.

We portray curricula as six cultures that depict how educators, and often the public, can make sense of curriculum in theory and practice. We name these orientations "cultures" because of our understanding of how they are revealed in belief systems, everyday behaviors and interactions, the artifacts that participants create, the use that people make of time and space, and the allocation of decision-making power. These curricular orientations comprise visions and practice—including assumptions about the needs and nature of learners, the role of teachers and instruction, norms about subject matter, learning environments, curriculum planning, and evaluation; in addition, we consider dilemmas of practice and critique of the inherent visions within these curricula.

And yet, in most instances, this book is not about the normal life of classrooms nor the culture of the school. Such a book would portray a world of curriculum making and implementation as a slice of life, a process often influenced by many fragments: curriculum guides, worksheets, district goals, state mandates, holidays, assemblies, available textbooks and videos, commercial curriculum kits, teachers' personal objectives and expertise, students' interests, and parents' requests. Ethnographic study undoubtedly would give our readers insight into the culture of their own classrooms and schools because it would cast light upon the norms—the usual and expected—patterns of thinking and behaving around curriculum.

To make sense of curriculum, we must do more than perceive composites of activities and interactions. We must understand the visions and belief systems that support the norms of classrooms and schools as individuals, groups, and communities make choices about the curriculum. We learn about what ideas and values are influential by examination of the known as well as unmindful assumptions in daily practice and policy. Moreover, consideration of archetypes containing congruent beliefs and practices allows a standpoint for reflection, even if there are few instances in schooling in which practice strictly conforms to philosophical or pedagogical ideals.

It is our hope that readers begin their study of curricular cultures by taking into account the curricular process in "real life"—the norms that influence curriculum in their own practice. Eventually we hope that they will analyze their curriculum work, consider their existing curricula (including, e.g., content, learning environments, and the role of teachers), and to deliberate about their aims of education. We encourage readers to question whether classroom practice supports their goals. Do teaching, content, and learning experiences together convey a clear purpose so that students know that schooling has meaning and an ultimate vision? Or do curricular purposes and practices give students irreconcilable messages, leaving them with a sense that schooling is fragmented and meaningless?

We ask our readers to imagine what their classrooms and schools might be like if all (or most of) the curriculum work taking place there had congruence—a deliberate pattern of planning, practices, and evaluation that would affirm their vision of how and why students should be educated. We want our readers to think deeply about curriculum as a coherent set of aims, beliefs, and practices so that all involved in or knowing about their curriculum work could say, "This is what education is about and how it is experienced here."

## REFERENCES

Beyer, L. E., & Apple, M. W. (1998). *The curriculum: Problems, politics, and possibilities.* (2nd ed.) Albany: State University of New York Press.

Bruner, J. (1996). *The culture of education. Cambridge, MA: Harvard University Press.*

Connelly, F. M., & Clandinin, D. J. (1988). *Teachers as curriculum planners: Narratives of experience.* New York: Teachers College Press.

Cuban, L. (1993). The lure of curricular reform and its pitiful history. *Phi Delta Kappan, 75,* 182–185.

Eisner, E. W. (1985). *The educational imagination: On the design and evaluation of school programs.* New York: Macmillan.

Eisner, E. W., & Vallance, E. (1974). *Conflicting conceptions of curriculum.* Berkeley, CA: McCutchan.

Foshay, A. W. (1980). Curriculum talk. In A. W. Foshay (Ed.), *Considered action for curriculum improvement.* Alexandria, VA: Association for Supervision and Curriculum Development, 82–94.

Goodlad, J. I. (1979/1994). *What schools are for* (2nd ed.). Bloomington, IN: Phi Delta Kappa Educational Foundation.

Kneller, G. F. (1971). *Introduction to the philosophy of education.* (2nd Ed.). New York: Wiley.

Pinar, W. F., Reynolds, W. M., Slattery, P., & Taubman, P. M. (1995). *Understanding curriculum: An introduction to the study of historical and contemporary curriculum discourses.* New York: Lang.

Schwab, J. J. (1973). The practical 3: Translation into curriculum. *School Review, 79,* 501–522.

Vallance, E. (1986). A second look at *Conflicting Conceptions of Curriculum. Theory Into Practice, 25*(1), 24–30.

# 2

# Understanding Curriculum as Culture

**Pamela Bolotin Joseph**
*Antioch University Seattle*

*[Culture] is in fact a prison unless one knows that there is a key to unlock it. While it is true that culture binds human beings in many unknown ways, the restraint it exercises is the groove of habit and nothing more. [Humans] did not evolve culture as a means of smothering [themselves] but as medium in which to move, live, breathe, and develop....*
—Edward T. Hall, 1959/1970, *The Silent Language*

To perceive curriculum as culture, we must start with an essential grasp of the nature of culture. Anthropologists describe culture as "that complex whole which includes knowledge, belief, art, morals, law, custom, and any other capabilities and habits acquired by [a human] as a member of society" (Tylor, in Herskovits, 1967, p. 3). Within this complex whole are shared ways in which people perceive, learn, categorize, prize, employ language, think about reality or common sense, show emotion, utilize time and space, work, play, and deal with each other (Geertz, 1983; Hall, 1959/1981; Hall, 1977).

Accordingly, culture influences epistemological beliefs: do people consider knowledge as authoritative, unchanging, or sacred? Or as fluid, personal, or open to question?

Culture essentially means sense-making. It becomes the system in which people organize their perceptions of their environment and their lives. Culture is

> the meaning which people create, and which create people, as members of societies.... *Homo Sapiens* is the creature who "makes sense." She literally produces sense through her experience, interpretation, contemplation, and imagination, and she cannot live in a world without it. The importance of this sense-making in human life is reflected in a crowded conceptual field: ideas, meaning, information, wisdom, understanding, intelligence, sensibility, learning, fantasy, opinion, knowledge, belief, myth, tradition.... (Hannerz, 1992, p. 3)

Although individuals will not have identical understandings, the existence of a culture suggests that there are shared systems of meanings as revealed in ideas and public expression.

Culture also can be interpreted as symbols and rituals. Symbols represent cultural values and have mutual meanings to individuals and may even provoke similar responses such as awe or devotion. Symbols are woven into activities that have significance to members of the culture; these rituals (as opposed to mere habits) "form the warp on which the tapestry of culture is woven" (McLaren, 1986, p. 36). Symbols and rituals socialize individuals and help them to articulate their understandings of their lives and values.

Individuals learn their culture and internalize its complex system of values and behaviors throughout infancy, childhood, and adolescence. Child-rearing embodies a multitude of messages about what it means to become an adult—from appropriate nonverbal communication, to the specific rules and beliefs that should be transmitted to the next generation, to the ways in which a culture defines itself or what it strongly emphasizes—for example, whether it values individuals, the tribe, or the nation, the young or elders, artistic expression or economic output. Complex patterns of knowledge and interaction are learned through formal and informal means of cultural transmission (e.g., parenting, role-modeling, religion, story and myths, art, media, and schooling).

These patterns include "action chains" (Bohannon, 1995; Hall, 1977) in which a fairly predictable series of actions, one followed by another, take place and thus "common understandings emerge" (Bohannon, 1995). We see culture as action chains of daily behaviors—get up, get dressed, go to work—or how people within a culture commonly respond to a problem, such as when you call your family to help you or you call representatives of government or you work out collaborative situations or you respond with aggressive behavior. When people are involved in acting out these cultural action chains, their behavior seems completely ordinary to them; only alternative patterns would seem odd or jarring.

In addition, we can understand culture is as "a continuing dialogue that revolves around pivotal areas of concern in a given community" (Spindler & Spindler, 1987, p. 153). For instance, in the dominant Euro-American culture in the United States, this dialogue often has focused on the theme of individuality; it is a motif in history, arts, in the selection of cultural heroes and heroines, in advertising, in political and everyday conversation, and in the way schools customarily assess the behaviors and work of students. Continual dialogue could also center on a problem, such as declining standards of morality in popular culture or public life.

## BECOMING AWARE OF CULTURE

Anthropologists caution that people usually are unaware of the culture that surrounds them because culture appears as usual life, what seems normal or natural. "If a fish were to become an anthropologist, the last thing it would discover would be water" (in Spindler, 1982, p. 24). This saying, attributed to anthropologist Margaret Mead, warns us that familiarity with the surrounding environment makes it terribly difficult to perceive the medium in which we live. In the normal, undisturbed course of living, we seldom recognize that it is our culture that influences what we take in and pay attention to, what choices we consider to be normal, and what we intend to do about those choices (Hall, 1977). Likewise, it is not obvious how cultural knowledge becomes communicated or internalized; directives about how to live one's life often remain unconscious or, at the very least, unexamined.

Why do we have such a problem perceiving and examining our culture? We are hampered because culture is our lens, our way of seeing and reasoning. "[We] cannot even think about culture except through the categories of thought that we have learned from the culture we grew up in and the one in which we have been trained." In order to see differently so that we can understand our own culture, "we must make gigantic efforts to step outside our culture-laden views" (Bohannon, 1995, p. 4).

How, then, can we see our culture? One way to perceive the culture in which we live is to experience disequilibrium (culture shock) by living in another culture. Only after extensive travel or staying for years in another culture do individuals come back to their native culture, recognize behaviors or customs, and properly attribute these familiar patterns as belonging to the culture. Previously, before experiencing another culture, what seemed natural, ordinary—"normal"—was indistinguishable. "We must struggle to examine our own culture in the same framework as every other culture" (Bohannon, 1995, p. 4).

Another way to see our culture is to discipline ourselves to use a systematic means of analysis. An insightful approach to understanding culture is to study the "primary message systems" within any given culture, "a complex series of activities interrelated in many ways" (Hall, 1959/1981, p. 58). We thus can pose a series of questions, such as: How is society organized and structured? How do people think about and deal with the environment? What activities are considered work and which are considered play? Thus, we can learn about a culture's implicit and explicit rules for appropriate behavior in such realms as social interactions, use of space, the rhythm of life and activities, gender, and humor (Hall, 1959/1981). An analytic classification helps us to understand how a culture has its unique characteristics and how its organization reflects a pattern of innumerable complex interactions that, in totality, make it unlike others.

Still, the task of perceiving a distinct culture is made more complicated because no human cultures exist in isolation; cultures influence other cultures and share some attributes. Furthermore, within a culture, a small (micro) culture may exist that possesses unique qualities but shares many features with the larger (macro) culture and, in fact, it may influence the larger culture. As people interact with others from different cultural groups, their cultures do not remain singular or static. Recognizing a singular culture is no simple task.

There are hindrances to our ability to perceive and understand culture, and yet recognition of the existence of culture and the spheres in which cultural teaching take place gives us insight about powerful influences upon our perceptions, behaviors, and values. If we remain clueless—unable to see or understand the predominant patterns and forces that affect our lives—we are without the ability to make substantial changes in the way we conduct our personal lives, live in our society, and—as we hope to explain—educate our young.

## SEEING CURRICULUM AS CULTURE

In recent years, ethnographers have helped us to realize that classrooms and schools (as well as universities and other educational settings) have their own cultures. However, scrutiny of such cultures brings forth many of the same difficulties in studying any culture: There rarely are "pure" cultures that develop without influences from others, people may be unaware of how they learn their culture; and they may find it hard to discern patterns of beliefs and behaviors that seem normal to them. More importantly, although people may share similar understandings of their societies and everyday life and hold shared values, nevertheless, individuals construe their own personal interpretations of events, practices, and symbols; they are not merely docile actors in a scripted cultural play but dynamic creators of meaning.

Thus, when thinking about a school or classroom culture, we must simultaneously imagine not a static entity but a assemblage of individuals who have different family cultures, different understandings and values influenced by race or ethnicity, gender, class, and religion as well as their own creativity and imagination; that in the classroom or school they participate in common activities, understand these activities somewhat similarly, and affirm certain values about knowledge, learning, and conduct—these suggest the existence of a culture, albeit not in a monolithic sense.

We learn to see classrooms and schools as cultures by seeking answers to key questions: In what activities do people participate? What are everyday practices? What rules and laws influence these practices? What behaviors and attitudes are encouraged or discouraged? How are social groups organized? What are the relationships between students and instructors? Who has power to make decisions and who does not and how are these power relationships maintained? How do the surrounding community and other outside stake-holders historically and currently influence the school? What has symbolic meaning in the environment and in what ways are these symbols communicated? What systems of thought are valued and modeled? What is the nature of the course of study? Whose history or literature is considered important or universal? What undertakings and talents are prized and rewarded? What do people believe to be appropriate goals of education? Clearly, all aspects of curriculum reflect culture.

In *The Culture of Education*, Bruner (1996) provides many examples of culture as a mirror to describe and interpret curriculum.

> Schools have always been highly selective with respect to the uses of mind they cultivate—which uses are to be considered "basic," which "frills," which the school's responsibility and which the responsibility of others, which for girls and which for boys, which for working-class children and which for "swells." Some of this selectivity was doubtless based on considered notions about what the society required or what the individual needed to get along. Much of it was a spillover of folk or social class tradition. Even the more recent and seemingly obvious objective of equipping all with "basic literacy" is premised on moral–political grounds, however pragmatically those grounds may be justified. School curricula and classroom "climates" always reflect inarticulate cultural values as well as explicit plans; and these values are never far removed from considerations of social class, gender, and the prerogatives of social power. (p. 27)

Bruner illustrates how curriculum reflects cultural beliefs—folk traditions—as well as social and political values and organization. Using a cultural lens, we can begin to regard curriculum not just as an object (content), but as a series of interwoven dynamics. Curriculum conceptualized as culture educates us to pay attention to belief systems, values, behaviors, language, artistic expression, the environment in which education takes place, power relationships, and most importantly, the norms that affect our sense about what is right or appropriate.

Through the discipline of anthropology or ethnographic inquiry, we can better conceptualize curriculum by evoking authentic representation of schooling, looking for patterns of belief and behavior within classrooms and educational systems. Ethnography permits the study of curriculum not just as explicit aims or plans, but as experiences encountered by teachers and students, the values inherent in the environment of the classroom and school, and connections to the encompassing culture surrounding the school. Ethnography enables a systematic look at the cultures of classrooms and schools—to see beyond planned outcomes, purposes, or instructional strategies to understand how curriculum is manifest as culture through rituals, customs, values, and the implicit beliefs of folk pedagogies.

The ethnographic approach to studying curriculum suggests some ways of overcoming the roadblocks to understanding culture. To begin, ethnographers suggest that those who study classrooms, schools, and communities must temporarily imagine themselves as strangers to get through the roadblocks to perception created by familiarity (Spindler, 1982). Thus, to see the culture of our own school, we should first observe educational systems that are unfamiliar. For example, we might need to discern the beliefs held by other cultures about the benefits of knowledge and who should be educated to come to terms with our often unstated or taken-for-granted assumptions about schooling; or, we would need to identify dominant patterns of how lessons are taught and how students and teachers interact in other cultures to help us to pay attention to our own methods and behaviors.

Even without leaving our homes, we can still gain insight about our own system of education by studying aspects of schooling in different cultures, such as through research, journals, or artifacts. For instance, by reading the history texts of other cultures, we may be better able to see how our own textbooks sanction certain values, such as nationalism. Exposure to the unfamiliar through primary sources helps us to better perceive the familiar.

Experiencing disequilibrium also can occur within one's own neighborhood. A visit to an alternative school in which students choose their own course of study seems fairly "foreign" when one's classroom has a mandated course of study that everyone must teach or learn (and the other way around). We are called upon to examine our own assumptions and structures when we see a classroom or lecture hall with its orderly rows compared to a community-based school or class in which the neighborhood and the resources of the city comprise the learning environment. What we experience as routine is called into question when we have opportunities to see others' situations or hear their stories.

But, without experiencing disequilibrium, how might we understand the goals and lived experiences of curriculum within more familiar settings, such as classrooms in our workplace or schools similar to our own? How can we make the "familiar" strange enough to be insightful about our own classroom cultures?

One possibility for learning about our own practice is to create inquiry along the lines of a qualitative research study. First, we collect data about what we see and hear. We need to capture impressions, engaging in a "pilot study," beginning with several "snapshots" or tape recordings of conversations.

Then, we analyze the record we make of ordinary activities and conversations. What visual and linguistic patterns signal us that a culture of curriculum might exist—what images and metaphors permeate speech, art, mission statements, and public relations materials? Would similar actions and dialogue reappear each time we observed? How do people utilize time and space and create ceremonies? How do they apportion power and authority among people? What seems "normal" to people within that culture and what seems unusual or even taboo? Eventually, we notice patterns—of participants' behaviors and the meanings they give to their experiences. We also must study the less overt expectations and behaviors that undergird curricular cultures—the "hidden" curriculum of unquestioned assumptions and actions.

By looking for prominent aspects—the themes or continual dialogue that point out what members of the culture hold as concerns or aspirations—we start to imagine the existence of a culture of curriculum. We need to ask, is there a core notion or theme that permeates the school and classroom culture tacitly and overtly? What seems to matter most to people? Is there a theme that continues to appear and influence curricular decisions (e.g., the importance of preparing students for jobs or what industry needs from the school)? What commonly held assumptions or beliefs permeate the school culture, for example, assumptions about students, teachers, subjects or parents?

We also learn by the "literature" of theory and practice, sources written by academics, practitioners, or both. These documents articulate the nature of curricular cultures. Discourse contains language special to each culture, for example, "the canon," "meeting the needs of industry," "constructing learning," or "democratic deliberation."

In addition, we need to learn if people who teach or learn in the culture (or advocate for it) identify with ideas expressed decades or centuries ago. Is there a "folk pedagogy"—that is, a collection of deeply embedded notions of learning, schooling, and teaching passed along from generation to generation? By historical investigation we can inquire, is a culture of curriculum linked to long-term commitment to beliefs, actions, or norms? Or do the issues raised and educational activities noticed seem more a response to a recent discovery in psychology, an educational innovation, or a unique social or technological problem reflecting contemporary concerns and aspirations?

Ultimately, analysis of the historical record and contemporary discourse (the continual dialogue)—including conversations among students, teachers, administrators, and the community—and our initial observations of classrooms (impressions) leads us towards identifying the beliefs systems (assumptions) underpinning a culture of curriculum. These sources also reveal the aims of education (implicitly understood or explicitly set forth), beliefs about what individuals might accomplish through education, and visions of what society might become.

## A FRAMEWORK FOR UNDERSTANDING
## CULTURES OF CURRICULUM

We approach the study of curriculum through the development of a systematic framework of analysis that gives us the structure for inquiry used in the following six chapters describing cultures of curriculum. This heuristic provides the means for us both to see and to question explicit practice, underlying beliefs about teaching and learning, implications of curriculum work, and implicit social and political visions.

We begin our depiction of cultures of curriculum (our six content chapters) with a brief crystallization of the culture of curriculum by presenting a telling quote from an advocate. From the start, we wish to make evident a major idea (or ideas) representing each curricular orientation.

We then provide a "snapshot" or impression of the culture by portraying a classroom in which our readers may get a sense of what this culture of curriculum looks like in practice. By interpreting these impressions, our readers will find an introduction to themes, beliefs, and practices that we would find if we observed this culture in a variety of educational settings.

The next steps include a summary of major themes—the continual dialogue or concerns manifest in each culture of curriculum, depiction of the ultimate aims or purposes for education and, ultimately, for society held by individuals whose practices or ideas represent this culture, and the historical background of this curriculum in American schooling including societal events and forces that influenced it.

We then create analyses of the belief systems of the culture, utilizing the concept of "commonplaces of curriculum" (Connelly & Clandinin, 1988) to understand assumptions about students and teachers, content and context, planning and evaluation. We explore explicit beliefs as well as the images and metaphors that implicitly demonstrate them.

We begin examination of the belief system by exploring assumptions about learners held by those who create curriculum. We question, how do those who influence curriculum perceive learners? Expectations of learners and learning (at the crux of folk pedagogy) have dynamic consequences for the development and implementation of curriculum. In a culture of curriculum, do educators believe that students "need" basic skills? enrichment? world-class standards? discipline? or self-esteem? Are students unique learners with their own interests and styles? at-risk? or gifted? Do students learn best by hands-on experiences? drills and repetition? or stories? Answers to such questions have a tremendous impact upon curriculum.

The questions we pose about learners correlate with conceptualizations of the role of teachers. Within the culture of curriculum, what does it mean to be a teacher? Is the teacher's fundamental task to create democratic learning

**TABLE 2.1**

**A Framework for Understanding a Culture of Curriculum**

| Focus | Question |
|---|---|
| Quote | • What statement(s) synthesizes major beliefs within this culture of curriculum? |
| Impressions | • What depiction of education within this culture of curriculum captures many of its important themes and assumptions? |
| Visions | • What are the goals of education or schooling for the individual? |
| | • What is the ultimate benefit for society if all individuals were educated in this culture of curriculum? (May be implicitly stated) |
| History | • How has this culture of curriculum been present in schooling? |
| | • What are the forces, events, and ideas that influenced this culture of curriculum? |
| Students | • What are the beliefs about students' needs, development, competencies, motives, and interests? |
| | • How have these beliefs influenced practice? |
| Teachers | • What are the beliefs about the role of teachers? |
| | • How should they facilitate learning? |
| Content | • What constitutes the subject matter? |
| | • How is the subject matter organized? |
| Context | • What is the environment of the classroom? Of the school? |
| | • How is instruction organized? |
| Planning | • What are the models of curriculum development? |
| | • Who plans the curriculum? Who has the power to make decisions? |
| Evaluation | • How should students be assessed? |
| | • How is the worth or success of the curriculum determined? |
| Dilemmas of Practice | • What problems or challenges do teachers face when they work in or try to implement this culture of curriculum? |
| Critique | • What problems are inherent in the vision of this curriculum for individuals and society? |
| | • What are the blindspots not perceived by advocates of this culture of curriculum? |

communities? To stimulate questioning? To teach habits of discipline? Or, to learn about student's passions for learning and to facilitate their attainment of personal goals?

We then turn to descriptions of content that characterize a culture of curriculum. Are there particular books that exemplify learning in this culture? Do required subjects represent traditional academic disciplines or interdisciplinary topics or fields of study? Furthermore, what content is taught and what is ignored (null curriculum)? And what criteria make the difference between content taught and content excluded? Or, is content de-emphasized with instructional processes or students' own choices predominant?

Also, what educational environment do adherents recommend and create? Do they imagine a class with students responding to the active questioning of the teacher? Students engaged in projects at work stations? Learners interviewing elders within the community? What is the relationship between students and teachers in the learning process and in what ways do teachers interact with colleagues and parents? Is the school day broken into segments according to subjects? Do students study within the classroom walls or make their own choices about utilizing the resources of the entire school?

We also investigate curriculum planning to make sense of the culture. Do teachers employ particular curriculum content stemming from previously developed models? Is the planning based on requirements set by the nation, state, district, or school? Do teachers develop curriculum based on their own professional understanding of students' needs or according to their own expertise and interests? Do students, parents, or the community have voice or power in determining curriculum?

Finally, how does assessment and evaluation of the curriculum occur? Do standardized tests form the basis for continuation or change? Do learners have opportunities for a multiple demonstration of their learning accomplishments? Who evaluates the teachers and on what bases does evaluation occur? What do people deem important for making decisions about resources to support curriculum? Who decides the success of curriculum and on what grounds? And, is there opportunity to consider or reconsider the aims or worth of the curriculum—to ask not only if the curriculum is successful but is it really worth teaching and learning?

This heuristic for understanding cultures of curriculum culminates with two pathways for further examination and reflection. First, we consider dilemmas of practice and secondly, critique of the culture—its essential assumptions, emphases, and visions.

Inquiry into dilemmas of practice enables us to consider what practitioners confront when they teach within the culture of curriculum. Dilemmas include choices in selecting content, the challenges in preparing to teach within this orientation, and the political issues that bring into question community reaction or the beliefs of parents.

Investigation of assumptions and convictions of advocates of each curricular orientation, the critique, leads us to probe advocates' social visions and whether or not there are connections between beliefs and actions—for example, does it make sense to imagine a pedagogical practice bringing about a wider social aim? We question the pedagogical, social, and political consequences of practice and, as well, we revisit the idea of the null curriculum by contemplating what is not taught and the consequences of inattention or disregard, questioning aims and visions in light of moral or social concerns.

## CULTURES OF CURRICULUM AS INQUIRY

In the following six chapters, it is our intention to illustrate archetypes of curricular cultures that are "purer" than most classroom cultures in "real" life. Although we believe it is crucial that our readers see the implicit curriculum of schools and classrooms by learning how to observe the practice, interactions, taboos, values, and beliefs held about learning and bringing children to adulthood, our purpose in writing this book is not to disclose a "slice of life"—despite the intellectual debt we owe to ethnography in revealing patterns of meaning. Rather, our intention is to name, to articulate, and to reveal curricula as visions and belief systems. We analyze these curricular worlds through philosophical inquiry informed by our understanding of various cultural components.

We recognize that it is tremendously difficult to imagine a teacher working only within one culture of curriculum or to find a separate, isolated culture of curriculum. Exceptions can be found in some alternative schools that consciously adhere to a particular philosophy and sustain a distinct culture of curriculum. But even in many alternative schools and certainly in most public school classrooms, a multitude of instructional aims and ultimate goals for students and society exist side-by-side. Even those teachers who have a clear vision of their curriculum work (a solid philosophical core understanding) may not consistently teach according to their own ideals because of a variety of factors. Teachers face pressures to meet the demands of numerous constituencies: individual learners, parents, administrators, community, state, and national influences. Ethnography often shows us that the "real" world is messy; a myriad of experiences, beliefs, aims—often inconsistent and contradictory—coexist in that world.

It would be fair to ask, then, if these cultures border on the hypothetical rather than the real, why attempt to describe them as distinct entities? We answer this question by suggesting that comparing personal practice to coherent models helps educators to gain deeper understanding of their own curriculum work. We believe that an interpretive framework of a culture of curriculum is a starting point for comparison and contrast, for contemplating the goals, visions, and practice within educators' classrooms, schools, and communities, for asking if steps taken as curriculum planners and teachers are congruent with visions as educators and as human beings.

Philosophical inquiry is a powerful means for understanding not only "what's going on here?" but what is the worth of this activity (Scriven, 1988). Conceptual analysis enables us to examine the interrelatedness among various elements of curriculum and to envision ultimate aims of education—the moral visions of education. Such inquiry encourages us to ask: what is the purpose of curriculum? and, how does our curriculum work ultimately contribute to the education of the individual and to a good society? Through conceptual analysis we are able to clarify our beliefs and behaviors, to scrutinize the inconsistencies in our thoughts and actions—to consider when our practices conflict with our goals and to ethically consider the consequences of our actions and aims.

Philosophy, however, does not attend to the disordered nature of individuals teaching and learning in actual schools and classrooms in real communities. Holding a particular philosophical aim of education does not necessarily result in a clearly defined guide for putting ideals into practice; a unified philosophical aim for education may not provide much insight about how to create an environment for day-to-day curriculum making and practice. Still, philosophical inquiry may lead to dialogue about the dilemmas practitioners face pedagogically, politically, and morally as they seek to unify their curriculum work with their vision of education and ultimate purposes they hold for the learner.

Our approach to inquiry in this book, accordingly, is a hybrid of the disciplines of anthropology and philosophy. We do not contend that our study approaches ethnographic research; nevertheless, we learn about curriculum as culture from our own experiences as curriculum workers and from observations of classrooms and conversations with students, teachers, and community members. We have attempted to balance the ideal and the real by not losing sight of how curriculum workers must grapple with dilemmas about planning, teaching, and evaluating curriculum. We ground our understanding of curricular cultures within the context of a of norms and practices, drawing on philosophical inquiry to name, question, and critique visions and practices, to provide a framework for reflection. This book is not just about philosophical aims, but about how educators try to put visions into practice.

## REFERENCES

Bohannon, P. (1995). *How culture works*. New York: Free Press.
Bruner, J. (1996). *The culture of education*. Cambridge, MA: Harvard University Press.

Connelly, F. M., & Clandinin, D. J. (1988). *Teachers as curriculum planners: Narratives of experience*. New York: Teachers College Press.

Foshay, A. W. (1980). Curriculum talk. In A. W. Foshay (Ed.), *Considered action for curriculum improvement*. Alexandria, VA: ASCD, 82–94.

Geertz, C. (1983). *Local knowledge: Further essays in interpretative anthropology*. New York: Basic.

Hall, E. T. (1959/1970). *The silent language. New York: Anchor/Doubleday.*

Hall, E. T. (1977). *Beyond culture*. Garden City, NY: Anchor/Doubleday.

Hannerz, U. (1992). *Cultural complexity: Studies in the social organization of meaning*. New York: Columbia University Press.

Herskovits, M. J. (1967). *Cultural dynamics,* New York: Knopf.

McLaren, P. (1986). *Schooling as a ritual performance: Towards a political economy of educational symbols and gestures*. London: Routledge & Kegan Paul.

Scriven, M. (1988). Philosophical inquiry methods in education. In R. M. Jaeger (Ed.), *Complementary methods for research in education*. (pp. 131–148). Washington, DC: American Educational Research Association.

Spindler, G. D., (Ed.). (1982). *Doing the ethnography of schooling: Educational anthropology in action*. New York: Holt, Rinehart & Winston.

Spindler, G. & Spindler, L. (1987). Ethnography: An anthropological view. In G. D. Spindler (Ed.), *Education and cultural process: Anthropological approaches* (2nd ed., pp. 151–156). Prospect Heights, IL: Waveland.

# 3

# Training for
# Work and Survival

**Nancy Stewart Green**
*Northeastern Illinois University, Emeritus*

*The school is not an agency of social reform. Its responsibility is to
help the growing individual continuously and consistently to hold to
the type of living which is the best practical one....*
—Franklin Bobbitt, 1926, *Twenty-Sixth Yearbook
of the National Society for the Study of Education*

In a large, light, orderly room in the shop wing of a large comprehensive high
school, 15 students are hard at work on their projects. Their teacher, Mr. Willis,
has outlined their work in advance, and they are proceeding, to some degree, independently—some working alone and others coaching each other in small
groups. The atmosphere is serious—neither pressured nor silent. Mr. Willis circu-
lates among the students. "Good," he says to one. "That's a good clean join."
"Hold on a minute," he says to another. "Let me show you how to do that right."

Mr. Willis is himself a skilled technician and finds it satisfying to transmit his
skills to a new generation of workers. He is teaching "something he feels proud
of and values" (Lightfoot, 1983, p. 39). Although he is given a curriculum by

the state office of vocational education, he does not follow it rigidly, preferring to keep it up-to-date by consulting with his colleagues in the industry. At times he feels frustrated by the caliber of students who take his courses, complaining in particular about their weak math skills; he feels that guidance counselors use the vocational courses as a "dumping ground" for unmotivated students, but he finds reward in increasing his students' skills and interest in his field and by helping them become thorough and careful in what they do.

In Mr. Willis's classes almost all the students are male, whereas down the hall in Mrs. Mickelson's home economics classes most of the students are female. Students from minority groups and low-income families are more common in classes like those taught by Mr. Willis and Mrs. Mickelson than in the high school as a whole. Such adolescents participate less in extracurricular activities, except for vocation-oriented clubs, than do other students (Berryman, 1982, p. 181). These students are sometimes defensive about their comparatively low social status in the school, but for the most part they are comfortable with their choice of courses, finding hands-on more rewarding than academic work.

In another wing of the building, which has been designated a school-within-a-school, Mr. Simon is presenting a group of 25 sophomores with assignments in their term-long study of the construction industry. They will visit job sites and listen to presentations by representatives from the industry, the unions, and the local zoning board. "Do we have to write in our journals after the field trip?" asks a student. "Of course," is the reply, "you'll need to keep records to use when you write up your evaluation of the role of each job in the whole industry." Students will learn about ordering and estimating materials while working on math skills at the same time, and will create a joint project using basic design, woodworking, and electrical skills; the project will be displayed at a job fair at the end of the year. "When do we get to job-shadow?" is another question—"I want to see what an architect really does." "That will be next term," replies Mr. Simon, "after you've had a chance to see what all the different job possibilities are. And next year, if you stick with it, you may have the chance to work as an intern."

Though they are enrolled in a vocational program, these students will not learn trade-specific skills to a level of employability; rather, they will gain a broad view of their selected industry. Their teachers, working as a team, have planned their curriculum, but students take considerable initiative in interpreting job roles and in identifying and solving problems.

These teachers are excited to be involved in this new curricular effort, which has given them the opportunity to work closely with a diverse group of colleagues, including specialists in the trades and in academic subjects, as well as with consultants from government, nonprofit companies, and industry. The team concentrates on finding ways to integrate academic and practical knowledge and on challenging students to work productively together to solve open-ended problems.

The students in classes, such as the ones taught by Mr. Simon, enjoy the hands-on aspects of their projects and the opportunity to work as a group and they have the confidence of participating in a new venture and of seeing the importance of their school efforts. Nevertheless, they feel some of the stigma attached to vocational education and there is a higher proportion of minority and low-income youth than in the school as a whole. Males and females are equally represented in such programs which integrate business and academic courses.

On another floor of the high school, Ms. Anyon's advanced math class is in session. Students sit in rows facing the teacher who stands in front of the blackboard. The class begins with a review of homework, which most students have completed, and continues with the teacher's presentation of new material. Ms. Anyon is a well-prepared, no-nonsense teacher, whose explanations are clear and effective. Students pay close attention. When she asks if there are any questions, only one student responds, "Will this be on the test?" Students then quietly return to work, solving story problems while Ms. Anyon grades papers.

Ms. Anyon enjoys this class because the students are bright and well-motivated, but she feels pressured by the amount of material she needs to cover to prepare the students for the SATs. She is aware of other approaches to teaching math, such as group problem-posing and solving, but cannot imagine how she could use these strategies when they would take so much more time from classes that already seems too short.

The students in Ms. Anyon's class are all college-bound and must take this course in order to score well on the SAT and get into the colleges of their choice. A few students genuinely love math and relish the challenge of covering a great deal of material, but more simply see this as another hurdle they must overcome in their journey to college.

These classroom scenarios illustrate different kinds of learning environments, yet all share the goal of preparing for economic success. The first two give us glimpses of traditional and "new" vocational education. In addition to the focus on training leading to job skills and the attempt to engage students from working-class or minority backgrounds, both examples emphasize a setting in which teamwork is emphasized and learning is assessed through demonstration—by products rather than tests.

The third portrayal presents a striking contrast to the first two. The math students' family background and economic future might seem too bright to suggest that their education needs to be "for work and survival." Yet their curriculum, including both the content and the method of presentation, is clearly defined by the need to do well on an exam. This exam acts as a filter, a threshold, for determining whether or not they can attend a prestigious college, which will in turn decides their chances of getting a well-paying job. Moreover, while this third scenario features a particularly well-prepared category of student, the pedagogy modeled in this classroom is typical of what would be found in conventional classrooms generally and for every age group except the very youngest: standardized, test-oriented education intended to prepare students for future economic success.

This chapter will concentrate primarily on forms of curriculum that explicitly prepare students for work, yet the implicit curriculum embedded in virtually all American education—of learning for the purpose of "getting ahead" (or not "falling behind") and of supporting public education because of its role in training workers—will be an fundamental theme throughout. Although there are enormous differences among the classrooms and programs representative of this curricular culture—from vocational skill-training to academic preparation for admittance to competitive universities—they have in common the theme that schooling must have practical and material benefits.

## VISIONS

Underlying the culture of training for work and survival are some of the most basic premises of contemporary American culture: (a) "success," whether personal or societal, manifests itself in material well-being; (b) work has moral significance, and attributes of "good work" such as thoroughness, promptness, neatness, reliability, and punctuality are to be valued; (c) the American version of the free-market system is the most efficient and beneficent economic system; and (d) economic and technological trends are immutable and essentially uncontrollable.

In addition to these basic assumptions, the culture of preparation for work and survival includes widely held beliefs more specific to schooling. First, schools have a vital role in the country's economic future. When state governors meet to address the problem of American education, the issue is framed in economic terms: what will happen to America's economic status in the world if our students cannot perform well in comparison to those of other countries? How can we compete if students can graduate from high school without knowing how to read and write? Second, because the most important goal of schooling is to promote the economic well-being of the country and its citizens, business leaders can assist schools by telling them what future employees will need to know. Third, schools can ameliorate the effects of social and economic inequality created by the free-market system and uncontrollable economic trends. In particular, supporters of vocational education for the immigrant poor and disadvantaged cultural groups have no doubt that education is the crucial means by which members of those groups can become productive members of the larger society. Fourth, there are students who, for reasons of ability, background, or disinclination, do not take to conventional academic schooling. Educators working with alienated youth see vocational education as providing hope for those who have no sense of a future for themselves; these teachers fear that pressure for "higher standards" in the same kind of academic work that already turns off their students is driving them out of school.

It is precisely because the orientation toward training for work and survival is so strong in our national culture that its classroom manifestations may seem hard to recognize. But when the elementary school teacher says, "You must be in your seat with your pencil sharpened by the time the bell rings," or "You must finish your work before you can play in the toy corner," she is preparing her students for jobs just as surely as when the teacher of more advanced students says, "You'll need keyboarding skills no matter what job you get," or "You must learn to work in teams because that's what you'll have to do on the job." Students, teachers, administrators, and parents are often unaware of alternatives to curriculum as direct instruction of a body of skills, practice for the workplace, and readiness for employment.

The culture of curriculum holds a conservative social vision:

> Most conservative plans for education stress the competitive world of markets and the need for young people to develop technical skills that will provide them with jobs in a world that relies ever more urgently on "cutting-edge" proficiencies. The conservative emphasis on "excellence" makes the development of individual talent the most desirable trait of good education. (Kaplan, 1997, p. 427)

Learning, therefore, is for the purpose young people training to "play the game of life." They are educated to know the world as it is, not to improve it or even to deeply understand it.

## HISTORY

Despite the fact that schooling for work and survival is a phenomenon of the industrial age, there were roots of this curricular culture early in American educational history. The pragmatic rationale to teach "what is useful" appeared in a variety of sources including Benjamin Franklin's writing on education and the myriad of informal and formal apprenticeships arranged for young people to learn a trade or craft prior to the industrial age. But as craftsmen and their apprentices were replaced by factories and their armies of workers, and family farms declined in importance while cities grew, educators claimed a place for schools in the production of employees.

There are telling examples of how schools reflected this curricular orientation throughout the history of American schooling. In the 1840s, Horace Mann appealed to employers to support public schools on the basis that educated students (by which he meant students who had completed from three to six years of elementary schooling) would make better workers—more prompt, more responsible, less likely to be led astray by "firebrands." The 19th-century kindergarten established in urban school systems emphasized teaching "moral habits, cleanliness, politeness, obedience, regularity, and self-control" (Spring, 1997, p. 201). The author of a very popular teacher-training text-book in the first several decades of the 20th-century equated classroom man-agement with the building of "good industrial habits of the type needed on the assembly line" (Spring, 1997, p. 216). Inevitably, schooling for work and sur-vival became an established norm in American culture.

Toward the end of the 19th century, as opportunities for employment de-clined for children and youth, the high school was seen as an institution in which idle and potentially dangerous young people might learn productive skills. Keeping young people in school longer than the few years of public ele-mentary education typical of earlier times seemed to require differentiation among students—between the academically inclined and those who rejected or were deemed unsuited for academic work. The earliest program intended for students in the latter category was "industrial education," which was pro-moted as a means for teaching industrial and agricultural skills to African Americans and Native Americans; Hampton Institute and Carlisle Indian School were pioneers in this effort (Spring, 1994).

Later, by the turn of the century, concern with the lack of preparation for employment and the supposed propensity to vice of working-class (especially immigrant) youth in the cities led to a concerted movement for vocational training as part of the public high school. Proponents of "social efficiency," who sought a more rational, functional society organized along the lines of in-dustry, believed in education that would appropriately meet that goal (Kliebard, 1995, p. 24) and, moreover, asserted that schools should sort young people "by their evident or probable destinies" (Eliot in Tozer, Violas, & Senese, 1995, p. 115). This preparation would include agriculture and lower-level industrial work for working-class males, gender-typed, low-skilled industrial work for working-class women, and home economics for females of all classes. Eventually, this sorting of students would begin as earlier as junior high school (Spring, 1997).

Among the groups for whom vocational education was designed, women of all races and classes had perhaps the most rigidly defined "evident and probable destiny," yet preparing young women for homemaking and mother-hood in school never lived up to its supporters' hopes. Although home eco-nomics was fairly popular in the rural south and midwest, it never caught on among working-class women in the industrial cities (Rury, 1991, p. 142).

At the same time that advocates were pushing for home economics, floods of young women (drawn largely from the middle class) were eager to enter commercial education courses to learn skills that they would use in the bur-geoning field of clerical work. Commercial education never counted as a "vo-cational" field, presumably because the main proponents of vocational education focused their attention on training for manual labor, especially of men. Still, it was clearly education for work and was closely tied to the growing demand for clerical workers, most of whom were young women who worked a few years before marriage. Enrollments in commercial courses in public high schools shot up between 1890 and 1920 from less than 15,000 to more than 300,000 students (Rury, 1991, p. 149).

Even though the high school curriculum responded with unusual quickness to the demand for clerical workers needed for the offices of industry, usually the labor market's influence on vocational programs had a delayed effect, as programs struggled to keep pace with technological change. The prejudices of educators, reflecting those of their era, have also often intervened between labor market demands and vocational programs. For example, Booker T. Washington and his northern supporters sought to teach southern African Americans and Native Americans agricultural skills so they would stay on the land instead of moving to cities and looking for work there. And, home economics—reflecting popular attitudes about the destiny of women and fears of social instability—sought to strengthen the family by teaching women home-related skills. In these cases, curricula were defined without reference to the actual experience of young men who already were experienced farmers or the many young women who learned homemaking skills from their mothers.

Besides teaching skills needed for the industrial age, schooling also reflected the need to teach life skills to help students live within the modern industrial world. This theme was dramatically manifest in the curriculum proposed for high schools in the years before and after World War I. Classes in physical education became a standard part of the school curriculum and, eventually, there came other kinds of classes demonstrating how young people could use their leisure time. The ultimate expression of education for life survival was a movement known as "Life Adjustment Education," which included courses on how to get along—making friends and living on one's own (Kliebard, 1995). Remnants of these forms of training for survival exist in such varied curricula today such as drug awareness programs, conflict resolution, parenting classes, and character education. Throughout the 20th century, such courses were designed to give students the education believed to be no longer provided by parents.

Students have not always passively accepted their school's plans for them, as their demand for commercial education and disinterest in home economics illustrate. In a number of cases, institutions that were established for a given "work and survival" purpose were used by students for their own ends, usually to gain the skills to succeed in a higher-status occupation than that intended by the founders. For example, students at Hampton wanted to become teachers; African American students at Lucy Flower Technical High School (a home economics school) wanted to go to college; and students at normal schools (which trained teachers) wanted liberal arts degrees. Within 50 years of their founding, these institutions with their fixed, practical curricula had been transformed into academic institutions.

But so great was the cultural belief in "Training for Work and Survival" that the federal government broke a tradition of noninvolvement in education to provide funds and exact control of precollege education in the United States. The Smith-Hughes Act of 1917, in response to the workforce needs of the newly industrialized nation and fears of the superior technical training and industrial might of Germany, allotted federal funds to the states to establish vocational programs in high schools. The Smith-Hughes Act provided guidelines for curriculum planning requiring that vocational training be separate from academics, that it focus on skills to be used in immediate employment, and that each state provide a curriculum developed by a panel of experts from each industry. For 40 years thereafter, federal funding continued to support vocational programs, though enrollment remained "relatively steady" and resistance on the part of working-class parents to programs preparing students for working-class jobs was high (Grubb, 1989, p. 22). Beginning in the 1960s, vocational education gained in popularity among politicians and educators anxious to address perceived inequities in education and the economy; federal support was expanded, and enrollments increased.

The 1970s saw two new approaches to training for work and survival. One of these, "career education," attempted to orient all students to careers—introducing this idea throughout elementary and high school—but this curricula often was reduced to a series of career orientation courses designed to acquaint students with the labor market (Grubb, 1989, p. 26). Many American schools currently have some elements of career education, such as career days in which there are assemblies, or having students visit industry and "shadow" adults who work in a career of their interests. The other new initiative in the 1970s, which continues in many schools today, was an effort to link schooling with out-of-school work, on the assumption that actual work by students would be the best preparation for adult work. Many high school programs grant credit for part-time work, find jobs for students, and provide some supervision. This represents a reversal of earlier trends, which had gradually removed youth from the labor market and paralleled a growth in the amount of work that high school students were doing on their own, leading some to suggest that "youth policy has in effect turned to the unregulated labor market to socialize adolescents" (Grubb, 1995, p. 33).

During the 1980s, community colleges developed extensive vocational programs that to some extent replaced those in high schools. More recently, efforts have been made to articulate programs at the two levels by means of "tech-prep" programs in which students take integrated vocational coursework extending from the last two years of high school through two years of college. These programs attempt to bridge the formidable gaps between high school and postsecondary education, between academic and vocational training, and between school and work (Bragg, 1995, p. 210).

Prompted by another massive economic transition, to the postindustrial or "information" era, and by renewed fears of foreign competition, Congress passed two federal initiatives supporting the "new" vocational education 73 years after the Smith-Hughes Act. In 1990, the Perkins Act Amendments followed by the School-to-Work Act of 1994 provided a new federal push for vocational education reversing much of the Smith-Hughes Act's curriculum that separated vocational and academic education. This recent legislation stipulated that vocational education should be integrated with academics, that it should expose students to all aspects of an industry rather than focusing on a limited range of skills, and that programs qualifying for funds under the act must be created at the local district level. It provided the impetus for programs that encourage collaboration among teachers, students, and local business and community leaders in the planning and evaluation of curriculum.

But in the quest for a stronger contribution from schools to the economy, not only specifically vocational education has received attention from state and federal governments. In the 1980s, fear that a "rising tide of mediocrity" was reducing our global competitiveness led to a series of reforms that attempted to change curriculum and evaluation in all public schools. Initiated nationally by the 1983 manifesto, *A Nation at Risk,* and followed by President Bush's *Goals 2000* (1991) and President Clinton's renewed *Goals 2000* (1994), these reforms assumed that better education was imperative for the economic future of the nation. But the definition of "better" education was academic rather than practical; the reformers sought to establish standards for academic studies (specifically English, mathematics, science, history, and geography) and to devise tests to evaluate achievement based on academic standards. *Goals 2000,* along with similar state-sponsored reforms, has increased the number of academic courses required of high school students while the number of vocational courses taken has declined (Tozer, Violas, & Senese, 1995, p. 324; Little, 1995, p. 63).

Of the cultures of curriculum discussed in this book, "Training for Work and Survival" is most closely associated with contemporary American society characterized by the "economics of competitiveness" (Kaplan, 1997, p. 441). A combination of factors—including the long tradition of American pragmatism, perceived changes in the current economy prompting anxiety about the future, and the dominance of business interests in politics and education—has created a situation in which preparation for work is simply a given and need not be justified.

## BELIEFS AND PRACTICES: LEARNERS AND TEACHERS

In "Training for Work and Survival," many of the assumptions about students stem from needs or lacks in young people as perceived by educators or spokespeople for the world of work. It is assumed that students *need* to learn the work ethic, or to gain a wider view of their role as workers, as well as to gain the skills and knowledge that will serve them in future employment. Another perceived need is to change students' values about education for those young people who see little value in staying in school and prefer to earn money immediately. In this consumer society, students' need to make money conflicts with what teachers and planners see as in young people's best interest; career awareness programs within academic high schools have aimed at keeping students in school, postponing immediate desires, and working toward a goal.

Assumptions about learners and what they need are based on two different perspectives. The first suggests that education should be differentiated for those learners who are immediately entering the job force and those who will first need academic preparation; the second viewpoint suggests that all students need similar (although not identical) types of educational experiences. These two points of view can be seen in discussions about learning theory and skills.

Two traditions have emerged that reflect distinct ways of learning: one is the traditional academic approach (which critics argued was ineffective with the student clientele of the early 20th century); the other, is the "hands-on" approach (deemed suited to the "manually-minded" students, usually of working-class or minority origin); those pupils were deemed to learn best by doing, and the "doing" referred to narrow practical skills. Founders of the vocational education believed, to a great extent, in manual learning for workng-class students.

Progressive educators, including John Dewey (1916), contested the view that "hands-on" education was meant only for students destined for work in factories and trades; they believed that not just inferior, manually-minded youth, but all students learn best by doing—doing that goes beyond narrow skills to integrated, purposeful activity (Cremin, 1961/1964). But progressive education's views of the importance of hands-on learning were not widely adopted, either in traditional academic classrooms or in vocational education. Until very recently, vocational education remained narrowly focused, and in this curricular culture, the standard view of how students learn academic material continues to be the traditional method of having information delivered to them by adults in a subject-based format.

Lately, education for work has taken a fundamental turn away from direct instruction; many proponents of the new vocational education explicitly return to Dewey's (1916) advocacy of education not *for* occupations but *through* occupations. They maintain that Dewey's approach responds to the ways in which people learn best and therefore leads to more effective preparation for work and life, including a better understanding of traditional academic material than didactic instruction featuring text-based, test-driven teaching (see Grubb, 1995).

Likewise, the new vocational education holds the assumption that all students, not just young people destined for jobs rather than college, need the skills taught in the workplace; this idea pervades contemporary state and national school reform initiatives and school practices. For instance, after spending two weeks observing in high-performance workplaces with a group of colleagues, an English teacher remarked, "All my students are going to need communication skills beyond what I had ever imagined when they enter these workplaces. We can't let anyone off the hook any more—even ordinary jobs today are making enormous demands" (Vickers, 1997, p. 8).

The new vocational education's efforts to break down the barriers between vocational and academic instruction have resulted in new roles both for students and teachers. For example, a teacher in a marine science class (in which students created plans for a fish hatchery), explained:

> I give them the problem and they accept the problem as theirs. In this class ... they're one step beyond that. They not only accept the problem but they design the problem.... I give them the competencies they need to learn from doing the project, and then together we make sure that it matches. (Stern, Stone, Hopkins, McMillion, & Crain, 1994, pp. 51–52)

Thus, in this new paradigm, students are no longer thought of as mere imitators but seen as capable of developing and solving problems within work-related contexts. Correspondingly, teachers' roles are as coaches and exemplar of skills.

In conclusion, assumptions about learners and teachers in "Training for Work and Survival" represent several contrasting perspectives and this curricular culture is in flux from earlier, more traditional models. Nevertheless, educators in this culture seem quite clear that students need what adults determine as necessary for their entry into the world of work and future material and career-oriented success.

## BELIEFS AND PRACTICES: CONTENT AND CONTEXT

The content of curriculum designed for work and survival ranges from highly specific skill training, to efforts at integrating academics with work-related skills, to purely academic studies aimed at successful test-taking. But all manifestations of this culture assume that content will be determined by the needs of society—some of them the needs of the economy, while others the needs of individuals if they are to succeed in the economy. Content therefore changes as needs in the workforce change, or as educators and politicians define social needs—such as those of strengthening the family or finding the right "place" for minority groups. Curriculum also is shaped in response to guidelines decided by centralized funders at the state and national level, although much content depends on local circumstances of the school and district.

It is therefore difficult to compile a list of topics typically included in "Training for Work and Survival," but a few generalizations are possible: Content in existing traditional vocational programs for younger students continues to include woodshop, metalshop, mechanical drawing, drafting, home economics, and typing (now called keyboarding), and for more advanced students, auto shop, computer science, electronics, media communications, marketing, fashion design, and culinary arts. New vocational education programs such as career academies and school-to-work programs contribute additional variety of content, including health science, finance, and environmental science.

More traditional schooling for work curricula emphasized behavioral attributes needed on the job as just as important as specific content knowledge. "Employability skills" included such basics as communication, computation, organizational, and interpersonal skills and more sophisticated attainments such as skills in negotiation, leadership, and problem solving (Gainer, 1988). Additionally, "work maturity skills" contain various habits needed for employment; examples include positive image: good grooming practices, good health habits, appropriate dress, exhibiting self-confidence" and "good work habits": maintain regular attendance, be thorough and diligent, follow safety practices (Lankard, 1987).

New needs have surfaced in recent years and have been reflected as content in all vocational programs. For example, the U.S. Department of Labor's Commission on Achieving Necessary Skills identified five areas of need: working effectively with others; allocating resources; understanding systems—using several specialized tasks to solve complex, interconnected problems; managing and using information; and using technologies (Pauly, Kopp, & Haimson, 1995, p. 3; Grubb, 1995, vol. I, p. 18). Typically, the new vocational education programs attempt to address these five domains.

Within the school and its programs, in both traditional and new vocational education, the context is one in which physical activity is prominent, frequently (though not always) with students working in teams—whether in shops, fields, kitchens, or beauty salons. There is an increasing presence of the active, collaborative atmosphere now being consciously developed in the new vocational education. But it also is apparent that the content of this curricular culture necessarily exists in a context extending beyond the school itself. The marketplace and industry set the scene, influencing content and suggesting the kind of environment for a smooth transition between school and the world of work and competition.

## BELIEFS AND PRACTICES:
## CURRICULUM PLANNING AND EVALUATION

In "Training for Work and Survival," curriculum is strongly influenced by external control. The popular belief that education leads to personal and national economic success guarantees that demands will be placed on schools by national and local political and business leaders as well as by community members. These demands are especially strong during periods of concern about the economic status of particular groups like the inner-city poor, or about the economy as a whole as it adjusts to a new era.

Industry has been involved indirectly with curriculum planning by having its representatives upon commissions that create national and state learning outcomes, and, more directly, by giving specific goals to vocational education programs so that teachers are cognizant of the skills desired by business. Industry also has opened its doors to vocational educators so they would have a clearer picture of current needs and conditions. Researchers have noted instances in which academic teachers' exposure to work settings has given them new insight into their teaching, for example, when teachers visit local "high-tech" workplaces (Pauly et al., 1995).

Curriculum planning also has been influenced by efforts for integrated curriculum. In many new vocational programs, academic teachers are teamed with vocational teachers and are expected to integrate work-related material into their teaching. Besides exposure to business situations, teachers have broadened their ideas about planing through collaboration; for example, when a group of high-school teachers worked to develop curriculum for a technical preparation program, this experience helped them collaborate to adopt new methods and, as one teacher said, it helped her "to break out of the mold" of how she was taught (Pauly et al., 1995, p. 147).

In this curriculum, students' needs are not articulated by students themselves, although many students do influence the curriculum—through dropping out. However, the new vocational education has certainly tried to respond to students' demands for more "relevance" in their required academic work by making academic curriculum more work-oriented.

This curricular culture's approach to evaluation also has been influenced by vocational education's long tradition of authentic assessment in terms of the success of projects completed. Currently, the new vocational education is building on this tradition to include demonstrations, products and services for sale, and student contributions to the community. Evaluation also takes place in that employers provide information to schools about the students who are doing various kinds of apprenticeships or internships; employers also let schools know if their applicants have to be retrained in order to do their jobs.

In fact, evaluation of the curriculum in "Training for Work and Survival" takes a variety of forms and has a breadth of demands placed on it. Large-scale studies have been made of the effectiveness of vocational education in improving the income of vocational education students over those in the general track. International comparisons of students' scores on tests of academic achievement are sometimes used to evaluate American students' ability to contribute to the modern economy, but the connection between scores on academic tests and the prosperity of the nation is not clearly delineated.

The academic, competitive representation of the curricular culture reveals a more rigid paradigm of evaluation. Assessment is primarily based on the premise that "intelligence is sufficiently uniform to permit absolute testing standards as the ultimate arbiters of children's fates" (Kaplan, 1997, p. 426). Standardization of tests promotes standardization of subject matter and instruction; it neither encourages creative, independent, and critical thinking—nor collaboration. Several of the goals and practices of the new vocationalism are in marked contrast to competitive academic education.

Analysis of planning and evaluation suggests this curricular orientation's fragmentation. Clearly, there is a lack of a unified vision as an influence upon curriculum planning and evaluation in "Training for Work and Survival." Attempts to please various "masters" creates contradictions and conflicts.

First, there is a contradiction between the two approaches to curriculum planning and evaluation: one requires local initiative, skills learned in the context of real problems, and evaluation by demonstration; the other opts for state- or nationally-imposed standards, and evaluation by standardized tests. Second, business leaders are assumed to have the answers to what students need to succeed in the work force, but business leaders are not of one mind. Large employers with the resources to give their employees specific training are most concerned to have "trainable" recruits with good basic skills and work habits, but smaller, more local employers are more concerned that schools should provide recruits with directly applicable skills (Grubb, 1995). Third, a further split occurs within the demands of large employers: on one hand, they want workers to be flexible and to continually learn on the job; on the other, they push for standardized instruction more likely to produce inflexibility than confidence. Wirth (1992) asserts that businesses are so used to dealing with the bottom line that they want schools to have "outcome measures," which seemingly can be ascertained by standardized testing. Pushing schools to function in an industrial manner standardizes instruction and undercuts the goal of producing workers who can learn and adapt (p. 75).

## DILEMMAS OF PRACTICE

The prevalence of "Training for Work and Survival" and its promotion as the main legitimate role for schooling in contemporary American culture has led business and government to influence schools through availability of resources, curriculum requirements, and standardized assessments. Pressures from these "outside" sources create dilemmas of practice for educators whose goals and practices are congruent with this culture of curriculum and for teachers whose aims and practice are conflicting.

Traditional vocational education teachers' most troubling dilemma stems from reverberations from somewhat earlier state and national curriculum reform movements. Vocational education programs have been severely curtailed, beginning in the 1980s, because of reforms that increased the number of academic courses required for graduation and concurrently reduced the number of electives (vocational courses are all electives) available to students. It is now unusual to find schools in which extended sequences of vocational courses can bring students to an employable level of proficiency (Little, 1995, p. 63).

Teachers of more academic subjects also are not exempt from dilemmas created by outside pressures for preparation for work and survival. They sometimes feel caught between their own professional goals—to encourage students to investigate subjects in more depth, to work in groups, or to seek original solutions to problems—and the need they feel to prepare students for standardized tests.

A further pressure comes from what influences students' educational values. Young people often do not want to take the time to learn skills or serve apprenticeships when it is easy to find part-time work—work that is a dead-end but allows them to earn what they want for their immediate perceived needs. This is a vivid instance of the widespread problem faced by teachers that adolescents find it difficult to sustain interest in studies that will "pay off" only at some future time.

Another dilemma has been created from the chasm between vocational and traditional academic education. Now that an effort is being made to link the academic and the vocational tracks, to integrate teaching across the divide in order to "teach through occupations," school reformers are confronted with the fact that contact between teachers in the two fields has been almost nonexistent. Academic teachers, unfamiliar with the realities of vocational teachers' work, have welcomed vocational education as a holding place for their less able students and have not taken it seriously, while vocational teachers have resented the lower status of their field and the impression that their programs are "dumping grounds." The well-established hierarchy of subject matters, as well as the strong identification of high school teachers with their disciplines as represented in their departments (Little, 1995, p. 58) meant that even with the best intentions teachers have found it hard to cross subject borders and collaborate. On each side, priorities are firmly entrenched and compromise is difficult.

For vocational teachers who have counted on academic departments to prepare students with the "basics" (though they have often been dissatisfied with the results), taking the time from their own curriculum to teach math or reading is frustrating. At the same time, academic teachers also resist "watering down" their curriculum with practical examples, and rarely have experience that can help them make realistic connections for students. Teachers typically utilize a small body of effective examples, but instructors need a whole repertory if they are to help students make more than a vague, passing connection between work and school.

The new clamor for vocational education also may seem threatening to academic departments. When vocational educators propose that the statistics or applied math they teach be given math credit or "business English" qualifies for language arts credit—the specter of fewer courses (and eventually fewer teachers) for the academic department is raised (Little, 1995, p. 68).

In addition to these pressures on teachers, the new vocational education programs face a number of dilemmas on a programmatic level. One of these is identification of students for vocational education. Concerned with avoiding the stigma of serving only low-achieving students, programs have been careful to recruit a wide range of students. However, some parents are concerned that a vocational education program might result in diluted content and thus reduce their children's chances of getting to college.

A further dilemma for school-to-work programs is how to expand the involvement of business. The existing programs generally are small; because of their manageability, they have had success in finding employers able and willing to collaborate with them to provide career exposure, job shadowing opportunities, and sometimes paid internships for high school students. But in a study of 16 school-to-work programs (Pauly et al., 1995), researchers concluded that

> few employers provide more than three workplace learning positions for students. If school-to-work programs are to serve a substantial number of U.S. high school students, they must recruit additional employers.... This will require energetic work by program staff and intermediary organizations, as well as major efforts to train employers in methods of supervising and training students. (pp. 198–199)

Thus, a major dilemma is simply that there are limits to what employers can, or have been willing to do. Beyond pressures for goal-setting, industry's relationship with schools has been minimal in terms of mentoring and involvement with students. The question of how to sustain authentic school-business partnerships must still be answered.

Lack of connection between schools and employers is also a likely reason for the ineffectiveness of vocational education in helping young people get good jobs. According to a recent study of vocational education teachers, "the United States offers a poorly organized system of labor market entry to work-bound high school graduates," yet, though many teachers informally assist graduates to get jobs, they "are nearly unanimous in saying that work-entry assistance is neither their responsibility nor that of the school, and no incentives encourage them to assist students" (Rosenbaum & Jones, 1995, p. 251). This is a clear problem for vocational education as it is practiced in the United States. It indicates that the schools are not supporting the goal of vocational education—that is, jobs for graduates. In contrast, most high schools assume that it is part of their job to assist students with college choices and to provide recommendations for college-bound students.

The new vocational education attempts to correct many of the alleged failings of traditional vocation education. But, there are those who are concerned that it will just provide students with "add-on" job-finding information rather than really changing either the academic or the vocational curriculum, and others who fear that it will divert high schools from their mission of preparing students for citizenship and for higher education.

## CRITIQUE

Critique of this curricular culture comes form various sources. Some critics heartily approve of its visions, but they are concerned with this curriculum's effectiveness; others are appalled by its visions, fearing their ramifications on individuals and communities. After reviewing positions from supporters and opponents, what is lost with an education for work and survival will be considered.

First, despite its popularity as a curricular culture, critics from business and from education have formed a discordant chorus, attacking schools for failing to prepare young people for future employment. And, as mentioned earlier, even programs that specifically aim at training for employment have not been particularly effective in accomplishing their goals. Further attacks on its effectiveness come from numerous research studies that have indicated that graduates of vocational programs fare no better in the job market than graduates of general programs, with the possible exception of women training for clerical positions (Boyer, 1983, p. 121). As early as the 1920s, employers complained that they preferred generally educated workers whom they wouldn't need to retrain (Grubb, 1989, p. 23), and this refrain is often heard today, most recently with regard to computer work (Oppenheimer, 1997, pp. 54-55).

Researchers who analyze education systematically point out that vocational education is not simply a matter of choice, nor is it a ticket to success in the same way as academic programs. School systems assign students to certain tracks based on the career path that seems appropriate; for example, working-class students go into vocational tracks, whereas students whose families are college-educated are destined for academic courses. They also note that tracking has a significant affect upon how young people visualize their own potentials. This vocational–academic split in the high school originates much earlier—in fact, in the first grade. "Slower" students (disproportionately low-income, minority, and non–English speakers) are placed in slower-moving classroom groups with little to challenge them, no access to higher-level thought and scholarship, and generally low expectations placed upon them. They rarely leave these lower tracks during their school career. As they move through elementary school, the academic gap between them and the more successful students grows ever wider, and their sense of failure and alienation is such that they look forward only to surviving until they can escape school (Oakes, 1994; Sedlak, Wheeler, Pullin, & Cusick, 1986) For these students, vocational education is sometimes a refuge. But despite the apparent comfort of vocational education programs, graduates of college preparatory programs earn more than similar persons who focused their education in vocational or technical areas; an apparent reason for the disparity in earning potential is that nonacademic programs lead to lower literacy skills (Rivera-Batiz, 1995).

The most recent national attempt at school reform, *Goals 2000*, with its emphasis on academic standards including skills needed for industry, would seem to alleviate the problems of tracking, but the record of American schools in teaching academics to lower-class youngsters is not encouraging. Furthermore, the standards proposed by *Goals 2000* (and its state imitators) have been criticized for their omission of any concern for the social realities facing schools, inequality of resources among school districts, as well as for its lack of attention to cultural diversity.

In the face of criticisms such as those detailed above, vocational educators and school systems are attempting to implement changes that they hope will provide better opportunities for all students to prepare effectively for work. These changes include the various manifestations of the new vocational education, such as school-to-work projects, school-based enterprises, and tech-prep agreements; and integration of vocational and academic education, most often seen in career magnet schools but proposed for wider adoption. Much of this culture of curriculum draws on Dewey's notion of "education through occupations." It remains to be seen how the application of this philosophy evolves and whether it will have more success in the 21st century than it had in the 20th.

Also, we question what sort of individuals will emerge from this curricular culture into the world of business. The curriculum appears to have many limitations. For example, there is no attention to occupations in academic courses where work might reasonably be a theme, and where it might provide an impetus for real-life discussion that would be motivating to students. Koziol and Grubb (1995) propose changes in the teaching of literature, history, and civics that would make them more issues-oriented, "emphasizing student interpretation and participation," so that students can "confront the issues of interpersonal work relationships, of private versus public interest, and of individual versus collective responsibility; issues they will continue to face throughout their working lives" (p. 136).

More striking than the absence of notice of work–life issues in the academic curriculum is their absence from the traditional vocational education curriculum. Although students are expected to take their places as employees immediately after high school graduation, they are not exposed to information about workplace interpersonal relationships, the functions of unions, or the role of government and law in conditions of labor. Students are not exposed to the possibility of questioning conditions of the workplace, the economic status quo, or the culture of capitalism and consumerism.

Moreover, a criticism of this curricular culture is that its emphasis on work and the need for future workers contrasts with a wider vision of "the economic, social, and cultural relations that shape their sense of what is possible and desirable" (Simon & Dippo, 1992, p.123). Within this criticism is a rejection of the idea that work experience is educative in and of itself. To define themselves, instead of being defined by others, students need to "address experience as both a process of meaning production and a basis for the educational work of social transformation" (p. 135).

From its inception, vocational education has been subject to vigorous criticism, both from critics who decried its class-based, limiting character and from those who found it merely ineffective. The rationale for vocational education has always been that it serves lower-class and minority students, but some of its critics have argued that its real function is to buttress the established order. The impression vocational education gives of helping the economic underclass deflects attention from the class-based economic system in which poverty is rooted and from the changes necessary in that system for genuine, widespread improvements in the living standards of the less advantaged segments of our society. In this view, vocational education "closes off" young peoples' options for upward mobility. It prepares them for working-class jobs, teaching them narrow, often obsolete skills, and neglects students' academic development. Berryman (1992) points out that "lower skilled youth enroll in the vocational curriculum and the curriculm increases the academic skilll gap between vocational and academic students. Vocational education not only does not contribute to their enrollees' employability on this dimension, but actually impares it" (p. 192).

Education for work and survival clearly represents a curricular system that holds a particular vision of the value of work and success. This kind of education creates a "bound" world in which the status quo is accepted.

> Much of the current discourse about school improvement focuses on the development of measurable and marketable skills. However, admirable the proposed traits or skills may be, the unspoken assumption about character is that students need to acquire what others already know to be significant and appropriate qualities in order to succeed ... training or indoctrination considers the student a passive recipient of doctrine and technique.... (Kaplan, 1997, p. 425)

Moreover, this curriculum's trains individuals for competition and finding worth within a system of rewards.

But the danger of promoting individualism in education is that it accents the natural inequalities among students at the expense of the natural desire that all people have to work for and with others. As Dewey noted almost a hundred years ago, we sacrifice both moral and intellectual growth when we substitute external motivations and rewards for the inherently social spirit that otherwise moves the child through education.... (Kaplan, 1997, p. 427)

Thus, it may be acceptable in this curricular culture to promote collaborative projects and cooperation, but there is no vision of working to create a community in which individuals feel obligation for each other and for the greater society. Furthermore, this limited kind of education has little vision of individual transformation. It suggests that the major worth of an individual lies in economic success and its related power.

In "Training for Work and Survival," the explicit curriculum is preparation for jobs after high school or for college—which will also lead to jobs, although better ones. The implicit curriculum is that different categories of students need and merit different treatment in schools; those students working toward college are more worthy than those who are not. The null curriculum (what is omitted) encompasses all the aims of the other cultures of curriculum we portray in this book—for example, attention to personal fulfillment, learners' intellectual autonomy, learning to live democratically, the attainment of a liberal, humanistic education, critical thinking, and skills for social action. The null curriculum is hardly surprising, and would perhaps not be worthy of notice, were it not that "Training for Work And Survival" is such a pervasive force in American education today. It would be well for those who subscribe to this position to remind themselves of what they abandon when they concentrate exclusively on the economic value of education.

## REFERENCES

Berryman, S. E. (1982). The equity and effectiveness of secondary vocational education. In *Education and work, 81st yearbook of the National Society for the Study of Education, Part II*. Chicago: University of Chicago Press.

Boyer, E. L. (1983). *High school: A report on secondary education in America*. New York: Harper & Row.

Bragg, D. (1995). Linking high schools to postsecondary institutions: The role of tech prep. In W. N. Grubb (Ed.), *Education through occupations in American high schools* (Vol. 2). New York: Teachers College Press.

Cremin, L. A. (1961/1964). *The transformation of the school: Progressivism in American education 1876–1957*. New York: Vintage.

Dewey, J. (1916). *Democracy and education*. New York: Free Press.

Gainer, L. (1988). *ASTD update: Basic skills*. Alexandria, VA: American Society for Training and Development, February. (ERIC Document Reproduction Service No. ED 291 882)

Goodlad, J. (1984). *A place called school: Prospects for the future.* New York: McGraw-Hill.

Grubb, W. N. (1989). Preparing youth for work: The dilemmas of education and training programs. In D. Stern & D. Eichorn (Eds.), *Adolescence and work: Influences of social structure, labor markets, and culture.* Hillsdale, NJ: Lawrence Erlbaum Associates.

Grubb, W. N. (Ed.). (1995). *Education through occupations in American high schools* (Vols. 1–2). New York: Teachers College Press.

Kaplan, A. (1997). Work, leisure, and the tasks of schooling. *Curriculum Inquiry, 27,* 423–451.

Kliebard, H. M. (1995). *The struggle for the American curriculum 1893–1958.* New York: Routledge.

Koziol, K., & Grubb, W. N. (1995). Paths not taken: Curriculum integration and the political and moral purposes of schooling. In W. N. Grubb (Ed.), *Education through occupations in American high schools* (Vol. 2). New York: Teachers College Press.

Lankard, B. (1987). The employer's choice. In *The job search.* Columbus, OH: The National Center for Research in Vocational Education.

Lightfoot, S. L. (1983). *The good high school.* New York: Basic Books.

Little, J. W. (1995). Traditions of high school teaching and the transformation of work education. In W. N. Grubb (Ed.), *Education through occupations* (Vol. 2). New York: Teachers College Press.

Oakes, J. (1994). Tracking, inequality, and the rhetoric of reform: Why schools don't change. In J. Kretovics & E. J. Nussel (Eds.), *Transforming urban education.* Boston: Allyn & Bacon.

Oppenheimer, T. (1997). The computer delusion. *Atlantic Monthly, 280*(7).

Pauly, E., Kopp, H., & Haimson, J. (1995). *Homegrown lessons: Innovative programs linking school and work.* San Francisco: Jossey-Bass.

Rivera-Batiz, F. L. (1995). *The impact of vocational education on racial and ethnic minorities.* (Report No. 108. ED386514). New York: ERIC Clearinghouse on Urban Education.

Rosenbaum, J. E., & Jones, S. A. (1995). Creating linkages in the high school-to-work transition: Vocational teachers' networks. In M. T. Hallinan (Ed.), *Restructuring schools: Promising practices and policies.* New York: Plenum.

Rury, J. L. (1991). *Education and women's work.* Albany: State University of New York Press.

Sedlak, M. W., Wheeler, C. W., Pullin, D. C., & Cusick, P. A. (1986). *Selling students short: Classroom bargains and academic reform in the American high school.* New York: Teachers College Press.

Simon, R. I., & Dippo, D. (1992). What schools can do: Designing programs for work education that challenge the wisdom of experiences. In R. I. Simon, *Teaching against the grain: Texts for a pedagogy of possibility* (pp. 121–136). New York: Bergin & Garvey.

Spring, J. (1994). *Deculturalization and the struggle for equality.* New York: McGraw-Hill.

Spring, J. (1997). *The American school 1642–1996* (4th ed.). New York: McGraw-Hill.

Stern, D., Stone III, J., Hopkins, C., McMillion, M., & Crain, R. (1994). *School-based enterprise: productive learning in American high schools.* San Francisco: Jossey-Bass.

Tozer, S. E., Violas, P. C., & Senese, G. B. (1995). *School and society: Historical and contemporary perspectives* (2nd ed.). New York: McGraw-Hill.

Vickers, M. (1997). Clapping with one hand: Why the school-to-work and standards movements should be linked. *Harvard Education Letter, 13*(2), 8.

Wirth, A. G. (1992). *Education and work for the year 2000: Choices we face.* San Francisco: Jossey-Bass.

# 4

# Connecting to the Canon

**Pamela Bolotin Joseph**
*Antioch University Seattle*

*The prime object of education is to know what is good.... It is to know the good in their order. There is a hierarchy of values. The task of education is to help us understand it, establish it, and live by it.... A liberal education aims to develop the powers of understanding and judgment. It is impossible that too many people can be educated in this sense, because there cannot be too many people with understanding and judgment.*
—Robert M. Hutchins, 1953, *The Conflict in Education*

"I never taught before and you never thought before." So begins new and reluctant teacher Bill Rago's first class in "Basic Comprehension," a class targeted for a small group of boot camp recruits—the Double D's, the "squeakers," "the ones that can't hack it." Bill is not sure what to teach these eight 18-year-olds, seven young men and one young woman, but he was told that he "was it for these guys." If the Double D's couldn't learn to "think a little better on their feet," they would be drummed out of the army and out of their only hope of making a better life for themselves. When he heard what he had to do, Bill asked, "Why not send them home?" and was told, "If we can help them do pushups we can give them a little help in the brain department."

Next class—reading skills. Bill previously assigned students the task of bringing in reading materials of their own choice. But despite Bill's increasingly sincere efforts, the students snipe at each other, ridiculing the choice of an "Archie" comic book as one recruit reads aloud. The next student starts to decipher *Sports Illustrated*, but we know that he is bored and feeling cynical about the class. He stops and looks at Bill.

| | |
|---|---|
| Student: | "What's the book you got Mr. Rago?" |
| Bill: | "This? This is called *Hamlet*." |
| Student: | "What's it about?" |
| Bill: | "It's about sex, murder, incest, insanity." |
| Student: | "Beats the hell out of the garbage I'm reading." |
| Bill: | "It beats the heck out of any book ever written." |
| Student: | "Why don't you tell us more about your book. It sounds more interesting." |
| Bill: | "You guys don't want to hear about *Hamlet*" |
| Another Student: | "I guess we're not smart enough." |
| Bill: | "It's complicated." |
| Another Student: | "We're here, we're listening." |

So Bill begins to explain *Hamlet*'s story. He talks about the character's feelings of grief and anger. The students, even the recruit who sleeps in class, respond. Hamlet wasn't the only one to have such feelings; the Double D's also know about betrayal, grief, and anger.

But the language is hard and they want to know why doesn't Shakespeare just say what he means?

| | |
|---|---|
| Bill: | "Because it's poetry ... it's language ... trying to put things together that evoke a certain ... it sounds better." |
| Student: | "I don't get it. Come on, teacher—teach us." |

So Bill teaches them. He explains similes, metaphors, and oxymorons. As class ends, Bill declares, "Parting is such sweet sorrow." But as the Double D's file out, they thank Bill, give him some "skin," or tell him, "that was neat." We see on their faces their gratitude for his teaching—for kindling their imagination, for giving them the "real stuff."

Eventually the entire curriculum for the Double D's becomes the study of *Hamlet*. The recruits awaken intellectually, learn how to understand Shakespeare, and perceive the existential struggles as well as the nobility in their own lives. The curriculum of *Hamlet* transforms these young people as they gain confidence and wisdom.

The above is a description of scenes from the film *Renaissance Man,* (Marshall, 1994). Although *Renaissance Man* is imaginary, educators who teach in the culture of curriculum we call "Connecting to the Canon" describe similar classrooms as portrayed in this film—classrooms in which their students become engaged with classic works of literature, drama, or philosophy, grapple with complexity of language within these classics, and awaken to the moral and intellectual possibilities within their own lives. There is a fundamental premise stated within the writings of all those who affirmed this curricular orientation hundreds of years ago and those who value it today: a time-honored, stimulating curriculum centered upon the universal truths and persistent quandaries of humankind, aimed at developing understanding of the best way to live one's life, is the ideal education for all students.

Four themes predominate whenever and wherever we find this culture of curriculum. They are the need to transmit knowledge, the wisdom within exemplary intellectual or artistic works, the humanizing potential of study, and learning as power—as mastery and as a commodity that allows individuals access into the dominant society.

## VISIONS

Unique to this culture of curriculum is the significance of a reservoir of cultural consciousness of classic Euro-American knowledge and the necessity for all students to have access to it. Learners become the link between the past and the future, assuring the continuance of the cultural values, beliefs, and behaviors. Advocates have faith in a common core of education—shared experiences, ideas, and values—to allow individuals to live deliberately and humanely within their communities and society. The inherent social vision embodies the expectation that education will provide respectful yet autonomous individuals who behave according to the culture's moral code.

The heart of these visions is the value of continuing cultural heritage from generation to generation based on the tenet that discovered wisdom should not be abandoned; all lives can be enriched by contemplating the questions posed and resolved through the ages. It is believed that young people have a great deal to learn from the experiences and understanding of their elders and ancestors and their ideas that have stood the test of time.

Other intertwining aims include the development of cultural memory and identity. Advocates of "Connecting to the Canon" believe that memory is important and that the teaching of cultural heritage provides knowledge of a common narrative (Bloom, 1994; Thernstrom, 1985). Bruner (1996) aware of the danger of affirming one historical voice, nevertheless explains the worth of historical memory:

But ignore for a moment the pomposity of the self-appointed spokesmen for un-disputable universal truths. For there is a compelling claim on this side too. It in-heres in the deep integrity, for good or evil, with which any larger culture's way of life expresses its historically rooted aspirations for grace, order, well-being, and justice. (p. 69)

However, it is not enough to learn just from the personal experiences of elders or direct advice; there are bodies of knowledge that represent "collective cul-tural activity" (Bruner, 1996, p. 22). Rich historical, literary, artistic, philosophi-cal, and political sources engender the most important inquiries and wisest answers. From generation to generation, classical sources persevere because of their greatness of substance and form.

Yet transmission of cultural values is not a passive phenomena. People do not just read or hear about cultural wisdom and become wise. Rather, each must attain cultural knowledge through individual connections to narratives of conflict, of triumph over adversity, of hope. Humans learn not just from accept-ing the values within the stories from their cultures, but through discovering a personal relationship to these stories, lessons, and dramas.

Supporters of "Connecting to the Canon" have a moral vision for individu-als. W. E. B. Du Bois epitomized this aim in his belief: "the object of all true edu-cation is not to make men carpenters, it is to make carpenters men" (Du Bois, 1903/1965, p. 46). Such vision is conveyed in contemporary times when a ninth-grade English teacher tells parents at an open house, "I will make your children work very hard—but they will learn what it means to be *human*" (au-thor's observation).

Becoming human inevitably involves the development of character (includ-ing self-discipline, spirituality, and compassion) and the cultivation of intellect and rationality. Education becomes "a transformation of a person's mind and character" (Adler, 1977/1988, p. 234) and the fully educated person is one who achieves "the powers of rationality, morality and spirituality" (Hutchins, 1953/1970, p. 352–353). This is curriculum meant for the mind, heart, and soul.

In this tradition, value transmission must include reflection. The idea that people should take ideas and values on faith or accept them without examina-tion is not a part of this worldview. Studying the best that the culture has to offer also means challenging the beliefs and values held dear by the culture, develop-ing the intellectual tools to consider, interpret, and test these values. Autono-mous thinking is an important goal.

But rationality is not the only goal. Proponents of this curriculum believe that rigorous education in the humanities leads to the development of habits of the mind and eventually to habits of the heart, to the strengthening of character or humane feelings. Hence, a university president extols liberal education in a commencement address because it "cultivates the intellect and expands the capacity to reason and to empathize" (Levin, 1995, p. 61). Advocates of home schooling write that "a genuinely classical education developed a particular kind of disciplined heart and mind" (Wilson, Callihan, & Jones, 1995, p. 9).

Access to this education permits the acquisition of cultural capital. Through mastery of appropriate cultural knowledge, students can leave school and go out into the world and relate to others who also know "the right stuff." Students who obtain cultural capital have the "goods"—the assets of having a culturally sanctioned education. Often the belief system of "Connecting to the Canon" includes the creed that students need to feel at home, to negotiate, and to comprehend the prevailing culture. Having the wherewithal to understand classic cultural references (including humor) allows individuals to "fit into" society or to feel "less alienated from the mainstream" (Ross, 1989, pp. 47–48). Hirsch (1987) writes about cultural literacy as a commodity, "common currency for social and economic exchange in our democracy, and the only available ticket to full citizenship" (p. 13) and that lack of cultural literacy excludes learners from full social participation.

Consequently, this culture of curriculum upholds a democratic vision that all young people are *entitled* to have a liberal education (Adler 1977/1988, 1982). As Hutchins declares, "if all men are to be free, all men must have this education. It makes no difference how they are to earn their living or what their special interests or aptitudes may be" (1953/1970, p. 354). Any system of education that tracks students into vocational fields without providing them first with a rich intellectual and spiritual education needed for living and for citizenry would be abhorrent both for learners and for society. Wood (1988), a spokesperson for democratic education, refers to cultural capital as necessary "to better equip students to participate democratically" in his concern that a "political underclass" results from "differentiated knowledge acquisition" (p. 177).

## HISTORY

The goals of enculturation and learning from exemplary traditional sources of knowledge influenced American curriculum in the past and continues to do so. The history of "Connecting to the Canon" is not a one-dimensional story but various congruent as well as misconstrued curricular enactments.

This culture of curriculum for Euro-American colonists first appeared as schooling for religious literacy. The desire for reading and understanding the Bible was the fundamental justification for schooling. Laws requiring support of schooling passed by the Puritans contained the rationale that people themselves must have knowledge of the Bible so that they could ascertain "the true sense and meaning of the original" and that "learning may not be buried in the grave of our fathers" (Massachusetts, Law of 1647). After the religious influence upon this culture of curriculum dissipated in many American schools, the desire for rigorous scholarship—especially the search for meaning of truth and virtue within a religious context—continued in many parochial schools across America (see Efron, 1994; Gutek, 1974) with interest expressed in some secular private and public schools as well (Haynes, 1993).

A second potent influence upon the maintenance of this culture of curriculum was the intellectual tradition of the Enlightenment, emphasizing ancient Greek educational philosophy that virtue and rationality must be taught in order to have an educated citizenry who would see the worth of democracy and work to preserve it. These assumptions stirred Jefferson's argument for liberal education (including the study of Latin, Greek, English, geography, and mathematics) for an educational elite that would furnish leaders—who would thoroughly appreciate and thus safeguard rights and liberties within a democracy. It was a like sentiment for liberal education that Du Bois embraced for developing a "talented tenth" of African Americans. To the present day, support for a classical curriculum (debated as a course of study for all young people—not for just an elite group) centers on the notion that each generation must be exposed to the great ideas of Western civilization to have renewed appreciation and understanding of virtue and freedom (Finn & Ravitch, 1985; Hughes, 1993).

But also, in the 19th and early 20th centuries, a misleading version of this culture of curriculum existed. Classical studies—particularly in Greek and Latin language and later, any course of study that was extremely challenging and involved extensive memorization—gained favor because of the belief that arduous work, especially memorization, strengthens the mind. Education for virtue, critical thinking, or democratic ideals was replaced by curriculum influenced by "faculty psychology"—a psychological rationale emphasizing the mind *as if* it were a muscle. (see Kliebard, 1987, p. 6; Pinar, Reynolds, Slattery, & Taubman, 1995, pp. 75–77). This metaphor captured the imagination of the public, scholars, and teachers. Although the banality of such a curriculum eventually came under attack from various critics and the classical approach became widely discredited, the metaphor of mind as muscle has never completely disappeared from American cultural thinking (e.g., in public debate about lowered academic standards and in films about education such as *Dangerous Minds*).

Another deceptive version of "Connecting to the Canon" was the history of American curriculum exclusively for enculturation—for creating citizens who could identify with a new nation, its customs and institutions. One version of this culture of curriculum we could aptly name "Forging Cultural Identity," the other, "Compelling Enculturation."

The nationalist interpretation of "Connecting to the Canon" began at the birth of the United States as an independent nation. Statesmen and educators passionately believed in "a truly American" education that would not mimic European traditions and that would create a "deliberate fashioning of a new republican character ... committed to the promise of American culture" (Cremin, 1976, pp. 43–44). The widespread use of textbooks by Noah Webster and later,

William McGuffey created the legends of American heroes and leaders. The forging of cultural identity was considered crucial for those who lived under monarchy in America and in Europe; American political values, particularly those of a conservative orientation (as well as sexist and racist stereotypes), permeated the moral and political lessons in textbooks (see Elson, 1964; Fitzgerald, 1979).

In the first several decades of the 20th century in many public schools, teaching cultural heritage meant only cultural transmission and assimilation, especially for poor and working classes, and people of color and non-Anglo ethnicity. In the name of cultural transmission, immigrants and their children were "Americanized" by curriculum taught through rote drill about facts of American history and work habits; also, the United States government continued to take Native American children from their families in order to become "deculturalized" and to learn the traditions of the dominant culture—more often than not, experiencing training in manual labor and the prohibition of native languages (see Spring, 1994). In such manifestations of "Connecting to the Canon," no hints of intellectually stimulating curriculum remained nor did the democratic ideal of providing educational opportunity survive.

Education for enculturation, bereft of an intellectual and moral core, became commonplace in nearly all American schools by the 1920s. Because of anti-intellectualism in American culture (Hofstadter, 1962) and the association of a classical education with elitism (Kliebard, 1987), curricula situated in classic Western civilization works of literature, history, and philosophy dwindled, although instances of liberal studies continued in high schools that prepared students for the more academic universities.

Then, in the mid-20th century and again in the 1980s, stinging critiques of what was considered mind-numbing curriculum—such as courses to help students win friends or "adjust" to life (Kliebard, 1987)—led to a revival of interest in classic studies, first in American universities and a generation later in secondary education. The critics' remedy for vacuous curriculum was a rich education in the humanities. Proposals for curricula with potent intellectual and moral visions and clear ties to classical knowledge eventually entered into public discussion and found some supporters. This curricula had many labels: core curriculum, traditional education, Paideia, general education, humanities, classical education, perennialism, liberal education, liberal studies, the liberal arts tradition, academic rationalism, cultural literacy, great books, and the canon. Some classrooms and schools implemented these curricula, but classical studies in the humanities never predominated in American schooling.

More recently, this culture of curriculum appeared at the center of a national controversy about required curriculum at universities, often referred to as the "Culture Wars." In multicultural America, competing voices in schools and universities argued whether or not the dominant approach to teaching great bodies of knowledge—primarily the tradition of white, male, Western European thought—is appropriate for all students, particularly for women and people from nondominant cultures. The Culture Wars created polarities of thought with little expressed interest in learning from other cultural traditions (Banks, 1993). However, demands for culturally appropriate education sparked heated discussion and sporadically influenced curriculum in public schools and universities; outcomes included required courses in multicultural education for college students and the creation of culturally relevant schools, such as African American academies in public school districts.

The Culture Wars contested as well the accuracy of worldviews and history. Feminist and Afrocentric scholars challenged the idealization of European intellectual tradition, contending that it embodied a history of dominance, oppression, and ethnocentrism. Defenders of the tradition of Western civilization responded by discrediting competing versions of history and insisting that "the victims of oppression have always been able to find a transforming and strengthening vision within the literature and thought of Europe" (Hughes, 1993, p. 150). As the nature of core curriculum widened to include more than what prior generations deemed classical sources, the works of Plato, Dickens, and the Constitution would be joined by Marx and Engels, W. E. B. Du Bois, and Toni Morrison. Currently, required readings in K–12 and higher education do contain more works by women and non-Europeans than they did a generation ago; at some universities, there are required courses so that all students have exposure to something other than the male, Western tradition. Certainly, the notion of canon has not been stagnant.

But despite the gradual additions of works that diversify the male, Euro-American worldview, the transformative vision of multiculturalists does not prevail in this curricular culture; it has not become a norm that there is value in learning and scrutinizing the wisdom and experiences of many cultures and not just one (Banks, 1993; Levine, 1996). As we write this book, the majority of educators who espouse "Connecting to the Canon" write about core knowledge from primarily written European and Euro-American intellectual traditions, albeit with minimal augmentation from nondominant sources. It is that tradition that characterizes the beliefs and norms represented in this chapter.

## BELIEFS AND PRACTICES: LEARNERS AND TEACHERS

Seemingly, curriculum for cultural transmission calls forth images of passive learners—empty vessels or blank slates—into which educators pour cultural literacy and standards of behavior. However, the metaphor of learner as receptacle does not convey how proponents of this curriculum think about students; rather, they insist upon active mental engagement, thinking, questioning, and stimulation of the imagination.

Descriptions of learners imply that cognitive development is an interaction of the student's own knowledge and the stimulation of the environment. Adler (1977/1988), who strongly espoused this curricular culture, refers to "the activity of the student's mind" and fuses learning canon with Piagetian psychology in describing the student: "But because he is a living thing, and not dead clay, the transformation can be effected only through his own activity" (pp. 278, 234).

Despite their dynamic cognitive portrayal, students with natural curiosity, the desire for knowledge, and the ability to learn according their own inclinations are not usually depicted by those who write about this curriculum. Instead, the belief system holds that young people need to be led, stimulated, and coached because learning, the development of intellect, is arduous work.

A reappearing metaphor occurs in the continual dialogue of "Connecting to the Canon"—learners as athletes. Although the belief in the mind as muscle may have vanished as a serious model for learning theory, advocates of this curricular orientation explicitly portray genuine learning as discipline, struggle, strengthening, expanding, and training—replete with pain (Adler, 1977/1988; Pelton, 1985). But, as do athletes, learners often rise to the challenge and find satisfaction in mastery.

Finally, a major corollary in beliefs about students is that this education is not out of the reach of any learner and all can benefit from classic curriculum. Advocates believe that all young people are capable of learning and growing from the powerful ideas within a humanities curriculum and it is their right to have this knowledge; poor children and not just those from affluent families should read the poetry of Robert Frost, Langston Hughes, and Walt Whitman (Kozol, 1991). Furthermore, supporters of the humanities curriculum affirm that students who have experienced the "hard knocks" of life—of poverty and abuse—are even more apt to identify with the conflicts and truths in the powerful stories and metaphors in great works of literature, drama, and philosophy; and they have even more to gain than the elite, not only from acquiring cultural capital but from the liberating knowledge therein (Shorris, 1997).

To believe that all learners can master a classical curriculum—despite their lack of innate interest in it—and to consider the content of the curriculum as impenetrable without struggle, it follows that the teacher must have a crucial role in this culture of curriculum. Students cannot grasp powerful ideas and relate their own moral struggles to lessons from the past without teachers' intervention and creativity. Teachers actively mediate between learners and content.

We see that this culture of curriculum holds two metaphors for teachers: as elders and as masters. Teachers as elders are wise people who have thought deeply and well; they have the knowledge that must be "patiently and imaginatively" conveyed to the current generation (Broudy, 1984, p. 23). Teachers as masters have pedagogical expertise to know how to lead learners to wisdom through inquiry and personal connection.

Educators who work within this culture of curriculum know that they cannot depend on materials to be intrinsically exciting enough to engage learners, so their first task is to interest students in the content. Teachers also must play to their audience as performers or storytellers to spark learners' engagement with classical content. However, teaching does not rest with performance. Educators must have deep understanding of subject matter and tremendous insight about teaching.

Teachers' roles are as questioners, guides, and coaches. Teachers use "discussion, induction, discovery, dialogue, debate, and a variety of procedures [called] heuristic"; teachers help students learn how to learn (Broudy, 1984, p. 26). For example, a teacher in a Catholic high school typifies his practice:

> I teach by the Socratic method—posing questions and not giving answers.... I see myself as a facilitator ... an active questioner.... My metaphor for my role as a teacher is "devil's advocate." For example, when I teach religion, I show the kids the supposition that disproves God exists and then go on from there ... a little knowledge can take you away from God and a lot of knowledge can take you back.... I rely on my study in philosophy to give me empowerment and mastery as a teacher.... I also help kids to become questioners; they learn that it's okay to question and okay to doubt.... (author's interview)

This educator's question posing suggests the Socratic tradition of critical examination of conventional thinking—unsettling questions that lead to disequilibrium, to "intellectual bewilderment, devastation, and even rage" (Purpel, 1989, pp. 78–79). Although teachers themselves may not always have answers to ultimate questions, in this culture of curriculum teachers encourage doubt, guide learners through their bewilderment, but ultimately lead students toward meaningful answers and affirmation of values. In this culture of curriculum, students are not left in confusion.

## BELIEFS AND PRACTICES: CONTENT AND CONTEXT

The content of "Connecting to the Canon" depends upon a platform of subject matter, so that learners will have an essential background in language arts, mathematics, science, history, and geography. Through teachers' guidance and coaching, students develop skills for critical reading, writing, speaking, and problem solving. Advocates believe that this learning eventually gives students the ability to comprehend and apply to their own lives the ideas and values within exemplary works of cultural wisdom (Adler, 1982; Broudy, 1984; Frazee, 1993). Content, as the repository of wisdom, receives the greatest emphasis within this culture of curriculum.

Advocates discuss several features that indicate a classical source of wisdom (Barzun, 1991; Broudy, 1984): *thickness,* so that "every sentence contains an idea ... the whole work covers acres of thought and feeling" and these thoughts and feelings may convey to us new ways of thinking about ourselves and the world around us; *adaptability,* our learning about the situations of others long ago must cast light on our present predicaments or about existence itself (Barzun, 1991, pp. 124–135); *endurance,* so that "a work has withstood long and intense criticism"; *creativity,* in that "it is a seminal work that anticipated the future or bridged two phrases of development of disciplines"; *artistry"* a superb elegance or lucidity of form"; and finally, *pedagogic value,* "with good returns for the time invested in study" (Broudy, 1984, p. 23).

The study of history, philosophy, drama, art, and religion—as well as myths and heroic stories in which forces of good and evil do battle—becomes the content that leads to the acquisition of wisdom (Barzun, 1991). The content is chosen not because it is immediately accessible or clear, but because it stretches learners intellectually, artistically, and morally. The curricular content also should convey social and political knowledge. Cultural wisdom is found within complex and sometimes enigmatic stories, speeches, art, plays, or in the logic of mathematics and the ethical dimensions of the sciences. Content helps students "exercise their imaginations" (Banas, 1987) and allows them to have a glimpse of "creative genius" (Wilhelm & Wilhelm, 1991).

Humanistic study is characterized by the idea that human beings have choices, that they may be tested and have opportunities to demonstrate courage and persistence, even when confronting the power of nature and God (or gods). It is assumed that great storytellers—Homer, Brontë, Wiesel, Angelou—thus tell us something important about living as human beings and about perseverance. Neither direct moral indoctrination nor mastery of bodies of factual knowledge (despite the popularity of E. D. Hirsch's lists for cultural literacy) are considered appropriate curricula for the humanities.

Of special importance is the study of history. We acquire wisdom and knowledge of culture through historic memory. Advocates of this culture of curriculum stress the need to learn the discipline of history so we can see the interconnectedness of events and ideas so we can better learn what shaped our cultural heritage—"to understand fully who we are today and how we came to be that way" (Thernstrom, 1985, p. 78). Narrative is important for "framing accounts of our cultural origins" and for the "cohesion of a culture" (Bruner, 1996, p. 40). Educators also believe that content must be taught so that learners have deep understanding of the cultural and historical significance of literature to fully appreciate its meaning (Graff, 1979/1995, p. 123).

Many canon-based programs purposely choose integrated curriculum so that learning becomes multidimensional, deeper, and richer; for example, integrating literature, art, and drama into the study of history to learn about personal perception and experience. A Humanitas program taught in high schools organized interdisciplinary curriculum within conceptual topics as courses—for example, "Women, Race, and Social Protest and The Protestant Ethic and the Sprit of Capitalism" (Aschbacher, 1991, p. 16). The core curriculum at Central Park East Secondary School was utilized to develop themes through organizing questions such as "How do people achieve power?" and "How do people respond to being deprived of power?" in cross-disciplinary classes such as humanities–social studies (Wood, 1992/1993, pp. 47–48).

The environment for learning commonly consists of small seminars in which students are actively engaged in questioning and answering questions. A Chicago high school that enacted Adler's Paideia Program created a learning environment of a "Socratic seminar, a question-and-answer study group where students learned to articulate thoughts in a reasoned form, group lectures, and one-on-one coaching" (DeBartolo, 1985).

Educators writing about the context of learning refer to the image of "a community of scholars" (Adler, 1977/1988; Aschbacher, 1991). Classrooms with a core curriculum are depicted as scenes of "back-and-forth interaction among groups of students and between students and the teacher" (Hirsch, 1993, p. 25). Teachers sit with the students at a table or in a circle. Although teachers may be masters in subject-matter depth, they also are seeking answers to quandaries; they pose "genuine questions" that lead to "interpretive discussion" with an exchange of ideas (Haroutunian-Gordon, 1991).

Most likely, we would recognize this culture of curriculum by its classroom milieu: that of a forum, ideally with few enough students to facilitate active discussion among all the participants and frequent feedback from the teacher. In addition, there are resources such as encyclopedias in the classroom so that students can find some answers to their questions during discussion or in preparation for debate, although students might also engage in activities that enact famous experiments in science or dramatic scenes.

## BELIEFS AND PRACTICES:
## CURRICULUM PLANNING AND EVALUATION

The predominant influence upon curriculum development is the norms about content—the beliefs held by educators and parents about what knowledge and traditions that children should receive. Such norms often are deeply imbedded and resistant to change; inclusion of contemporary and multicultural sources happens very slowly. This conservative approach to content was revealed in the consistency of literature curricula in American high schools (Applebee, 1990). Creators of explicit published lists of authorized works in the humanities, for example from The Great Books Foundation, also have been reluctant to vary from their deeply rooted traditions (Lev, 1994). A good many decisions about curricular content stem from the knowing or tacit acceptance of sources believed to connect young people to cultural wisdom.

In this culture of curriculum, teachers appear in the circumscribed center of curriculum planning. The multitude of decisions about what ideas, themes, and questions to emphasize comes from educators' academic strengths and interests, their professional goals, and their understanding of what is meaningful to young people. The pivotal role of teachers in orchestrating the curriculum is supported by the presumption of their expertise in subject matter and pedagogy. Those schools adopting thematic integrated curriculum encourage collaboration in which teachers themselves become a community of scholars as they work in interdisciplinary committees to decide on concepts and questions as they plan the curriculum for the year (Aschbacher, 1991).

Teachers also are at the heart of the assessment process. Despite some call for standardized testing of knowledge standards (Hirsch, 1993), most of the advocates of "Connecting to the Canon" place faith in teachers as masters to assess what their students have learned. Demonstration of learning occurs through individual writing of essays through papers and examination; such essays often require students to take a position and argue using evidence to support their positions. Teachers also evaluate students' knowledge through the Socratic questioning approach or as students engage in debate. In some classes, students illustrate they have learned important ideas and quandaries through the creation of art and drama. Instructors also may utilize portfolio assessment, as students collect their essays and art illustrating their intellectual and perhaps moral growth.

However, assessment practices do not appear to include evaluation of the curricular content itself. The ardent belief in the accumulated wisdom within presumably great moral, intellectual, and artistic sources thwarts the re-evaluation of the universality of a classic or whether or not it should endure. Rather, it is suspect that individuals or even a generation of individuals should make serious changes to choices of content that may have evolved over decades, hundreds, and even thousands of years. The basic premise about curriculum evaluation simply is this: the content is good (for learners) because it is good (because it has endured). Critical examination of the worth of the curriculum usually does not take place in this culture of curriculum.

## DILEMMAS OF PRACTICE

Teachers choosing to initiate "Connecting to the Canon" as the culture of curriculum in their classrooms face several dilemmas. These predicaments relate to the crucial knowledge and skills needed to become a superlative practitioner, the controversial nature of subject matter, and the unpopularity of this curricula in contemporary America.

The first dilemma is whether or not practitioners will invest in the remarkable depth of content and pedagogical knowledge needed to successfully assume their roles as teachers in this culture of curriculum. The richness of their knowledge of the humanities, their talent as a superb questioners, and their capacity to engage students in content would require an extensive and continual liberal arts education and instructional preparation.

To achieve excellence in this curricular approach, teachers need deep knowledge of a variety of areas. They should have strong grounding in the humanities, of narrative and historical context, knowledge of symbols, dramatic devices, and themes. Integrated curriculum would require teachers to work collaboratively across academic fields. Furthermore, teachers' own education would be deficient without keeping abreast of scholarship reflecting an expanded notion of human experience that is increasingly becoming more inclusive; for example, ethnicity and gender must be considered if curricular content is chosen because of its potential for universality. Even when curricular choices emphasize the Eurocentric tradition, teachers are called on to include some works by women (see Whaley, 1993) and people from nondominant cultures (Forrest, 1990; Graff, 1992) in order to teach what it means to be human to a diverse student body.

In conceptualizing this curriculum so that it reflects contemporary scholarship, teachers also must have knowledge of political perspectives within great cultural works and help their students to see through such lenses. Obliteration of political issues not only creates one-dimensional interpretations from the dominant culture's worldview, it robs students of opportunities for critical thinking and perspective-taking. For example, Graff (1992) explains how teaching the politics of *Heart of Darkness* takes students beyond existential themes to include a focus on cultural dominance and racism. Such scrutiny of art, literature, sciences, and social sciences might call for enriched education of teachers if they themselves had received an apolitical education in the humanities.

Besides needing tremendous subject-matter depth, teachers in this culture of curriculum must know how to engage students with content. Great works of literature, history, and philosophy may initially be inaccessible to many students. Popular culture's fleeting visual imagery requires little intellectual stamina (see Finn, Ravitch, & Fancher, 1984); the great books do not automatically reflect the immediacy of contemporary children's or adolescent's lives. So, to "know their audience," teachers must stay savvy, current, and responsive to their students' interests and lives and be conversant with the popular culture enjoyed by their students. More importantly, practitioners need to be sensitive to their students' personal struggles to better guide them toward discovering meaning in their studies. Such a task means that educators must make a deep commitment to their own learning—from Shakespeare to rock music—in order to connect learners to the classics.

Another difficulty facing practitioners is dealing with explosive controversies over the content of this curriculum. Educators choosing to teach within this culture of curriculum could encounter opposition from the political conservatives who fear both teachers' autonomy in choosing content and children's learning of critical thinking skills (Elliott, 1994). Or, caught in the crossfire of the canon wars, educators would have to articulate their visions and account for their decisions to teach primarily from the cultural wisdom from the Euro-American tradition or to defend their efforts to broaden the canon and make it more multicultural.

Finally, we heed the dilemma that educators who desire to connect students to cultural wisdom encounter adverse public perception about the nature of this culture of curriculum. Popular culture and media often portray "Connecting to the Canon" as caricature, as an elite curriculum full of "dead" allusions and information. Its sources are not considered worthwhile by teachers or the public (Public Agenda Survey, 1996) within the current climate of schooling with its emphasis on computer literacy and skills for employment; such curricula certainly get little support from national or state school reform efforts. That this culture of curriculum has not persisted as a dominant culture of education in the United States resides in its dissonance with American culture's anti-intellectualism, preference for the new to the old and novelty to tradition, fascination with scientific methods and technology above humanities and narratives of human experiences, and preference for the practical over the theoretical. Finding support for this culture of curriculum surely is an uphill battle.

## CRITIQUE

There are three interrelated areas in which we offer critique of "Connecting to the Canon." The first involves inherent contradictions that call into question whether its goals are attainable, the second refers to the nature of knowledge or wisdom, and the third dimension concerns the issue of power related to the decisions made as to what engenders wisdom.

Critical inquiry begins with examining the fundamental vision. If the main goal of this culture of curriculum is to learn what it means to be human, can we recognize this outcome? How can we know about qualities of character that are "within a person"? Will we find out if learners become adults who have acquired wisdom? Clearly, it is difficult to appraise intangible consequences.

Calls by advocates to educate both the hearts and minds of learners also call for scrutiny. Can this curriculum teach learners to lead moral lives through knowledge acquisition? Advocates only discuss affect when they discuss how students connect emotionally to content—such as having empathy with young Hamlet's dilemma. Moreover, teachers' roles are essentially cognitive—to stimulate, provoke, and broaden—and to make learners work hard; such teachers command the respect of students but compassion and friendship are not mentioned. Although teachers may demonstrate that they care about students by helping them reach their intellectual potentials, there is no focus here on students engaging with their hearts with the community, other learners, or in a caring relationships with teachers. Noddings (1994) defines moral dialogue as a relationship of "deep concern for the other" (p. 5); thus, we can say that this culture of curriculum has dialogue about moral dilemmas, but it does not generate "moral dialogue."

We also must reflect on the nature of knowledge in "Connecting to the Canon" and the ramifications for learners. Curricular content is traditional and resistant to change; proponents judge contemporary cultural sources as unworthy, except as a catalysts for students' engagement. The conservative nature of the curriculum raises several concerns about choices of content and visions for the learner and society.

First, we need to be circumspect about upholding classics as the only appropriate study. Conservatism resists the new, exciting, different, and challenging—closing off sources that may also tell us about what it means to be human. Garber (1995) warns:

> What is disturbing is the risk that the back-to-basics emphasis of self-appointed guardians of literary and critical values will render respectable a dismissiveness about new ideas that amounts to a doctrine of anti-intellectualism. Just as the now classical was once "popular," the now "high" was once "low" and threatening—Impressionist painting, film noir, jazz, Mozart, Wagner. But art, as writers from Sophocles to Marlowe to Baudelaire to Joyce to Woolf to Morrison have always known and shown, is threatening. It is about transgression, and daring, and engagement.... (p. 55)

We might rightfully fear that the substance of content becomes static as a particular set of values and ideas is taught from generation to generation with little modification.

However, one might soften this criticism that classicists fear the new by remembering the difficulty in recognizing a potential classic among contemporary sources. Bruner (1996) suggests that interpretation of narrative construal is "deeply affected by cultural and historical circumstances." Thus, literature can be misconstrued by contemporary readers responding to the immediacy of the context but who may not yet have an appreciation for the richly insightful and potentially enduring themes it may contain. We simply may not be able to see the existential themes in drama, art, literature, or history that portray events in our immediate world.

We must also ask, can this curriculum educate people to be responsive to current social conditions and the dynamics of cultural change? If students are not encouraged to construct their own understanding of the world, is their vision not shaped and limited by the perceptions of previous generations? As Moretti (1993) concludes, "Any pedagogy not focused on the intellectual empowerment of the young is ultimately dysfunctional. We don't want to teach the young the right history. We want to teach them to create histories of their own" (p. 124).

Even though the underpinning belief of this curricular culture is a vision of liberating intellect, "Connecting to the Canon" also holds a conservative ideal of enculturation and cultural identification. Advocates for this culture of curriculum strongly suggest that young people not only embrace the guidelines for conduct deemed exemplary throughout the generations, but that they learn to see themselves as part of the culture's common narrative. Can teachers connect learners to cultural wisdom but also have them become autonomous—to critique their culture and its values? Ultimately, it is far more likely that learners, as they become insiders within the cultural tradition, will defend rather than challenge or reject traditional values.

Moreover, besides resisting innovation, this curricular culture ordinarily rejects insight from sources outside the mainstream cultural heritage. Critics of this curricular orientation attack the narrowness of the themes and materials deemed worthwhile or classic; they argue that knowledge becomes extremely limited when educators only value a particular worldview; in this case, the predominantly male Eurocentric canon. A monocultural educational system "closes us off to all other possibilities of human experience" (Asante, 1992, pp. 22–23). Thus, the classic educational position in particular ignores non-Western intellectual, spiritual, and moral contributions. The result is the omission of oral traditions, holistic education (with its emphasis on harmony of spirit, mind, and body), connectedness, the relationship between humans and the environment, and the concept of multiple realities (Allen, 1998; Collins, 1991; Okur, 1993; Reagan, 1996; Saucerman, 1988).

Finally, advocates of the canon must confront the sanctioning of one culture's intellectual and artistic dominance over another. This is not a benign or unbiased occurrence, despite their insistence upon neutrality. Critics of Eurocentric, male-dominated curriculum point out that "traditional" curricula "ignored most of the groups that compose the American population whether they were from Africa, Europe, Asia, Central and South America, or from indigenous North American peoples" (Levine, 1996, p. 20). African American authors are "invisible" on Adler's list of classic literature (Forrest, 1990) and "the culture and experience of [African Americans] have been virtually excluded from treatment in the textbooks and curricula of the educational system" (Anderson, 1990, p. 3). Furthermore, "women were excluded from the lives of scholarship, as from 'significant' subject matter, as from positions of authority and power, when the basic ideas, definitions, principles, and facts of the dominant tradition were being formulated" (Minnich, 1990). Although Adler (1977/1988) writes that "the list of the great books results from the most democratic or popular method of selection" (p. 320), he does not take heed of the work of those from nondominant cultures ignored or rejected by classicists.

In American schools and universities, the Western civilization tradition not only was taught to students of all cultural backgrounds, it was taught as the superior wellspring of wisdom—presented as "civilization itself," as universal, as the "norm and the idea" (Levine, 1996, p. 20; Minnich, 1990, pp. 37–38; Okur, 1993. p. 92). Although learners may benefit from having the "cultural capital" of "wisdom" from the dominant culture, what effect does denial of cultural heritage have upon learners who have to negate or remain ignorant of their own? Allen (1988) explains that "contemporary Indian communities ... believe that the roots of oppression are to be found in the loss of tradition and memory because the loss is always accompanied by a loss of a positive sense of self" (pp. 14–15). The relegation of other cultural traditions to a realm of not-human and not-civilized not only manifests arrogance, it leads to cultural annihilation. It is no wonder that Asante (1991) describes an education in the European traditional culture as death for learners from others cultural backgrounds.

Notwithstanding, it stands to reason that deep knowledge of more than the dominant Western tradition could be taught in schools and still we would have curriculum congruent with "Connecting to the Canon." Swing (1995) observes that besides the traditional Eurocentric humanities curriculum in which all students—regardless of their cultural backgrounds—receive the cultural capital of the dominant culture, or a displacement curriculum in which the worldview of the minority culture displaces the dominant (traditional, Eurocentric) cultural focus, other models exist: a bicultural configuration that recognizes both the dominant culture and the most significant minority culture with the aim to help students live within both their worlds; an interactive bicultural model that shows the influence of both dominant and minority cultures on each other. It is clear, however, that incorporation of a multitude of cultural traditions into a curriculum would not be feasible because a potpourri of cultural knowledge is inconsistent with the deep understanding called for in this culture of curriculum.

In conclusion, there are several reasons why this culture of curriculum is deficient as a monocultural model. If students connect to a single intellectual and moral tradition and do not attain a deep and rich knowledge of at least another culture's wisdom and experience, it is unlikely that they can have a standpoint to critically examine dominant beliefs and values; accordingly, they cannot vigorously appreciate the wisdom of the canon because they have not genuinely challenged it. Also, lack of scrutiny may mean that they have difficulty modifying their beliefs and actions in light of real and changing social conditions. Moreover, it is "tunnel vision" and "racial chauvinism" (Moses, 1991, p. 87) to assume that one culture has the best answers, the one true story, the only keys to civilization. To give students the "goods" to navigate in a diverse and interconnected world, this culture of curriculum must acquire wisdom from sources beyond a dominant worldview and cultural narrative.

## REFERENCES

Adler, M. J. (1977/1988). *Reforming education: The opening of the American mind.* New York: Macmillan.

Adler, M. J. (1982). *The Paideia Proposal: An Educational Manifesto.* New York: Macmillan.

Allen, P. G. (1988). Who is your mother? Red roots of white feminism. In R. Simonson, & S. Walker (Eds.), *The Graywolf annual five: Multicultural literacy,* 13–27. Saint Paul, MN: Graywolf Press.

Allen, P. G. (1998, April). *Native American construction of knowledge.* Paper presented at the American Educational Research Association, San Diego, CA.

Anderson, T. (1990). *Black studies: Theory, method, & cultural perspectives.* Pullman: Washington State University Press.

Applebee, A. N. (1990). Book-length works taught in high school English courses. (ERIC Clearinghouse on Reading and Communication Skills. ED318035)

Asante, M. K. (1991). Afrocentric curriculum. *Educational Leadership 49,* 28–31.

Asante, M. K. (1992). Learning about Africa. *The Executive Educator 14,* 21–23.

Aschbacher, P. R. (1991). Humanitas: A thematic curriculum. *Educational Leadership 49,* 16–19.

Banas, C. (1987). Study: Schools lax on content. *Chicago Tribune,* August 21.

Banks, J. A. (1993). The canon debate, knowledge construction, & multicultural education. *Educational Researcher 22,* 4–14.

Barzun, J. (1991). *Begin here: The forgotten conditions of teaching & learning.* Chicago: University of Chicago Press.

Bloom, H. (1994). *The Western canon: The book and school of the ages.* New York: Harcourt Brace.

Broudy, H. W. (1984). The uses of humanistic schooling. In C. E. Finn, Jr., D. Ravitch, & R. T. Fancher (Eds.), *Against mediocrity: The humanities in America's high schools.* New York: Holmes & Meier.

Bruner, J. (1996). *The culture of education.* Cambridge, MA: Harvard University Press.

Collins, P. H. (1991). *Black feminist thought.* New York: Routledge.

Cremin, L. (1976). *Traditions of American education.* New York: Basic Books.

DeBartolo, A. (1985). Sullivan High program: A lesson in questioning. *Chicago Tribune,* April 3.

Du Bois, W. E. B. (1903/1965). The talented tenth. In F. L. Broderick, & A. Meier, *Negro protest thought in the twentieth century,* 40–48. Indianapolis, IN: Bobbs-Merrill.

Efron, S. G. (1994). Old wine, new bottles: Traditional moral education in the contemporary Jewish classroom. *Religious Education, 89,* 52–65.

Elliott, B. (1994). Education, modernity and neo-conservative school reform in Canada, Britain, and the US. *British Journal of Sociology of Education, 15,* 165–185.

Elson, R. (1964). *Guardians of tradition: American schoolbooks in the nineteenth century.* Lincoln: University of Nebraska Press.

Finn, C. E., Jr., & Ravitch, D. (1985). The humanities: A truly challenging course of study. In B. Gross & R. Gross (Eds.), *The great school debate: Which way for American education?.* New York: Simon & Schuster.

Finn, C. E., Jr., Ravitch, D. & Fancher, R. T. (1984). *Against mediocrity: The humanities in America's high schools.* New York: Holmes & Meier.

FitzGerald, F. (1979) *America revised: History schoolbooks in the twentieth century.* New York: Vintage.

Forrest, L. (1990). Mortimer Adler's invisible writers. *Chicago Tribune,* December 3.

Frazee, B. (1993). Core knowledge: How to get started. *Educational Leadership, 50,* 28–29.

Garber, M. (1995) Back to whose basics? *The New York Times Book Review.* October 29, 55.

Graff, G. (1979/1995). *Literature against itself: Literary ideas in modern society.* Chicago: Elephant.

Graff, G. (1992). *Beyond the culture wars: How teaching the conflicts can revitalize American education*. New York: Norton.

Gutek, G. L. (1974). *Philosophical alternatives in education*. Columbus, OH: Merrill.

Haroutunian-Gordon, S. (1991). *Turning the soul: Teaching through conversation in the high school*. Chicago: University of Chicago Press.

Haynes, C. C. (1993). Beyond the culture wars. *Educational Leadership, 51*, 30–34.

Hirsch, E. D., Jr., (1987). *Cultural literacy: What every American needs to know*. Boston: Houghton Mifflin.

Hirsch, E. D., Jr., (1993). The core knowledge curriculum—What's behind its success? *Educational Leadership, 50*, 23–30.

Hofstadter, R. (1962). *Anti-intellectualism in American life*. New York: Vintage.

Hughes, R. (1993). *Culture of complaint: The fraying of America*. New York: Oxford University Press.

Hutchins, R. M. (1953/1970). The conflict in education. In J. W. Noll, & S. P. Kelly, *Foundations of education in America: An anthology of major thoughts and significant actions* (pp. 351–356). New York: Harper & Row.

Kliebard, H. (1987). *The struggle for the American curriculum 1893–1958*. New York: Routledge & Kegan Paul.

Kozol, J. (1991). *Savage inequalities: Children in America's schools*. New York: Crown.

Lev, M. A. (1994). Beyond Plato: Great books to include living authors. *Chicago Tribune*, October 14.

Levin, R. C. (1995). Liberal education and the Western tradition. *Yale Alumni Magazine, 58*, 61–63.

Levine, L. W. (1996). *The opening of the American mind: Canons, culture & history*. Boston: Beacon.

Marshall, P., (Producer), Touchstone Pictures. (1994). *Renaissance Man* [Film]. (Available from Buena Vista Home Video, Burbank, CA.).

Minnich, E. K. (1990). *Transforming knowledge*. Philadelphia: Temple University Press.

Moretti, F. A. (1993). Who controls the canon? A classicist in conversation with cultural conservatives. *Teachers College Record, 95*, 113–126.

Moses, W. J. (1991). Eurocentrism, Afrocentrism, & William H. Ferris' *The African Abroad. Journal of Education, 173*, 76–90.

Noddings, N. (1994). Learning to engage in moral dialogue. *Holistic Education Review*, 5–11.

Okur, N. A. (1993). Afrocentricity as a generative idea in the study of African American drama. *Journal of Black Studies, 24*, 88–108.

Pelton, C. L.(1985). Education reform: A teacher responds. In C. E.Finn, Jr., D. Ravitch, & P. H. Roberts (Eds.), *Challenges to the humanities*. New York: Holmes & Meier.

Pinar, W. F., Reynolds, W. M., Slattery, P., & Taubman, P. M. (1995). *Understanding curriculum: An introduction to the study of historical and contemporary curriculum discourses*. New York: Peter Lang.

Public Agenda Survey. (1996). *Seattle Times*. February 14.

Purpel, D. E. (1989). *The moral & spiritual crisis in education: A curriculum for justice and compassion in education*. New York: Bergin & Garvey.

Reagan, T. (1996). *Non-Western educational traditions: Alternative approaches to educational thought and practice*. Mahwah, NJ: Lawrence Erlbaum Associates.

Ross, K. (1989). Bringing the humanities to the lower achiever. *English Journal, 78*(7), 47–48.

Saucerman, J. R. (1988). Teaching Native American literature. In J. Reyhner (Ed.), *Teaching the Indian child: A bilingual/multicultural approach*. Billings, MT: Eastern Montana College.

Shorris, E. (1997). *New American blues: A journey through poverty to democracy*. New York: Norton.

Spring, J. (1994). *The American school 1642–1993,* (3rd ed.). New York: McGraw-Hill.

Swing, E. S. (1995). Humanism in multicultureland: A comparative looking glass. *Educational Foundations, 9,* 73–94.

Thernstrom, S. (1985). The humanities and our cultural heritage. In C. E. Finn, Jr., D. Ravitch, & R. T. Fancher, *Against mediocrity: The humanities in America's high schools* (66–79). New York: Holmes & Meier.

Whaley, L. (1993). *Weaving in the women: Transforming the high school English curriculum.* Portsmouth, NH: Boynton/Cook.

Wilhelm, M. P., & Wilhelm, R. M. (1991). Bringing the classics to life. *Humanities, 12,* 13–16.

Wilson, D., Callihan, W., & Jones, D. (1995). *Classical education & the home school.* Moscow, ID: Canon.

Wood, G. H. (1988). Democracy and the curriculum. In L. E. Beyer, & M. W. Apple. *The curriculum: problems, politics & possibilities.* Albany: State University of New York Press.

Wood, G. H. (1992/1993). *Schools that work: America's most innovative public education programs.* New York: Penguin.

# 5

# Developing
# Self and Spirit

**Stephanie Luster Bravmann**
*Seattle University*

*[We] do endorse, by common consent, the obvious hypothesis that the child rather than what he studies should be the centre of all educational effort.*
—Burton Fowler, 1930, *Progressive Education VII*

**M**onday through Thursday at 3:30 P.M., just after classes were dismissed and before leaving for the day, students usually dropped by the eleventh-grade classroom where Meyer would have posted a note on the bulletin board right inside the door. Just to check. Scrawled on a bit of yellow paper, usually ripped from someplace else, would be a word or a phrase: "*On Liberty,*" "$C_2H_5$-O-H; $C_2H_5$-O-$C_2H_5$; $C_2H_3$O-H; $C_2H_3$O-O-$C_2H_3$O," "Mondrian," "Ontogeny recapitulates phylogeny," "Simone de Beauvoir," "Hunger." This was the subject. In the morning there would be a question that had something to do with the displayed words.

Anyone who was interested could come to school 30 minutes early the following day, perhaps having done some preliminary investigation on the topic, and try to answer the teaser that Meyer had appended on a second piece of yellow paper. "Where might there be a relationship between John Stuart Mill's writing and a school principal?" "What do $C_2H_5$-O-H, $C_2H_5$-O-$C_2H_5$, $C_2H_3$O-H and $C_2H_3$O-O-$C_2H_3$O have to do with modern chemistry?" "What is considered revolutionary about Mondrian's painting?" "How is the theory that ontogeny recapitulates phylogeny reflected in the study of history?" Responses were to be written and handed to Meyer, personally, no later than 10 minutes before class began at eight.

Did everyone take part in this activity? Of course not, it was not required. Did the same students always participate? No, individuals and groups changed daily. Were these questions related to anything in the general science and biology classes which Meyer was hired to teach? Not often; they were chosen by Meyer from a deeply rooted knowledge of his students, their current and past interests, and what might complement them. Were there grades or "extra-credit" points for getting the correct answer to the questions? Never. Were there correct answers? Rarely.

Very occasionally, a well-considered response produced a pass to leave the school grounds for lunch. Even more occasionally, students who had created particularly thoughtful or intriguing replies were invited to select a subject, devise a question themselves, and post it for whomever might wish to take it on. Was this some kind of strange alternative activity trying to pass for schooling or was it education proceeding from a sound, articulated set of principles? Why did adolescents, so often self-absorbed and blasé, bother?

Alfred North Whitehead speaks often of the "romance" of learning—the fascination that initially wells up when a student is fully engaged, intellectually and emotionally, in the process of learning. Teachers such as Meyer knew their students, their students' interests and directions of thought, and their own subjects to so great an extent that they could create curriculum that emanated from the learner him or herself.

This short scenario represents an enactment of aspects of the culture of curriculum we refer to as "Developing Self and Spirit," an orientation that maintains that if the educational process begins with the student at the center—and engages the intellect, the emotions, the body, and the spirit—then all learners will proceed freely and naturally to greater knowledge of themselves and of their world. Proponents of this believe that we must learn according to self-directed interests, with the goal of nurturing each individual's potential, creativity, spirituality, and self-knowledge. Beginning with the conviction that good emerges from each of us as we grow and develop, this curricular culture proposes that affirmation of self is the basis for the greater good.

## VISIONS

The aims of those who advocate for "Developing Self and Spirit" sound remarkably similar in spite of the differences in time and attitude between those promoting them. They all speak to the well-rounded development of the heart, the body, the mind, and the spirit to the end of lifelong learning; the desire to develop (or retain) the goodness, morality, and ethical foundations for leading a righteous life; and the betterment of the immediate community, society and the world. Fostering both independence and dependability as full participants in society is an auxiliary but not subordinate goal. It is a given that those committed to "Developing Self and Spirit" conceive of such affirmation without regard to gender, ethnicity, ability, or need. Sometimes markedly similar declarations are evident in historical portrayals (from Plato to Pestalozzi, Herbart and Froebel, Parker, Dewey, Montessori, Neill, and Steiner), those that are more contemporary (Samples, Pearce, and Greene), and works decidedly modern and postmodern (Moffett, Noddings, Miller).

As comparable as the central goals may in fact be, the major ideas embedded in "Developing Self and Spirit" are, by the very nature of their grounding in the uniqueness of each learner, often disparate. They do, however, share some basic tenets, beginning with the contention that there is an inseparable unity of mind, body, and spirit in all humankind. They agree, as well, that students who are allowed to learn independently and at their own pace willingly channel their energy into learning. Motivation and reward are, to the greatest possible degree, intrinsic.

Another shared idea is that mutual trust and respect form the foundation of a true learning community. It is only in such an atmosphere that students are empowered and encouraged to take risks, and to succeed or fail in a setting that honors all of their attempts to learn. Most also believe that students helping one another, in community, facilitates both learning and wholesome social interactions, whether under the guise of peer tutoring, cooperative education, or some other rubric.

Whether stated in terms of spirituality or developmental psychology, the most ancient to the most modern thinkers in this mode share two notions: that the human organism seeks continued growth throughout its lifetime and that there is a natural, self-regulating order to human growth and learning that must be observed if we are to honor the needs of each individual. They share, as well, the conviction that nature itself is a powerful educator and must be represented fully in the educational process. The importance of a loving, accepting environment, and of respect for children as human beings are seen as the cornerstones of self-discipline, as well as communal discipline. Finally, all seem to agree that happiness and joy are critical components of a full and contributing life whether as a child in school or as an adult in the larger society.

Notions of spirituality, which theorists agree is a common and critical element of humanness, are perhaps the most divergent components in this curricular culture. Believers in learner-centered education come from every variety of religious and secular background; the schools they support are, variously, parochial, independent, and public. John Amos Comenius (a 17th-century Moravian clergyman), Rudolf Steiner (an Anthroposophist and founder of Waldorf education), and Felix Adler (the founder of the Ethical Culture Society) combined their religious convictions with educational theories that were concerned with the whole child and natural learning. Schools that run on these models do so from a solidly religious base. Theorists such as Edith Cobb (*The Ecology of Imagination in Childhood*), Bob Samples (*The Metaphoric Mind*), and Joseph Chilton Pearce (*The Magical Child*), on the other hand, acclaim the fundamental spirituality of nature itself as the basis of their beliefs. Maria Montessori, Francis Parker, John Dewey, and Helen Parkhurst (The Dalton Plan), whatever their personal religious convictions and feelings about the importance of nature, used the secular world as their point of departure.

While every social group seeks to transmit its dominant or most cherished values to succeeding generations, political, economic, and social visions change, sometimes radically, with the times in which one is living, working, and theorizing. The distinction between values and visions, therefore, is particularly important in this context. Typically there is at least some complementarity of values from age to age and culture to culture—humans generally esteem good before evil, plenty before need, fairness before injustice. The visions that are held to attain these values, however, are often discrepant and dependent upon particulars of time, place, political structure, and personal proclivity; in other words, visions are more mutable commodities. "Developing Self and Spirit" as a curricular culture must by its nature be open to broad degrees of difference in vision, relying on its belief in human goodness to mediate disparities in individual thought, feeling, and sense. This being said, there is a strong and abiding assumption that this curricular culture is most consistent with the furthering of democratic, nonsexist, and multicultural political, economic, and social institutions.

"Developing Self and Spirit," as a school culture, strives to impact the social vision of our world in a number of ways. It acknowledges and accepts the manifestations of human diversity evident in the larger culture and attempts to achieve equality in terms of the power relationships inherent in any human interactions. Additionally, it promotes individual and social tolerance—not in the sense of forbearance but in the sense of acceptance—of all people without regard to ethnicity, gender, or other so-called defining characteristics. As an educational culture, it is grounded in the belief that people are fundamentally decent and well-meaning, that education through experience and interaction is liberating, and that schooling is not, as Dewey would have said, preparation for life but life itself. "Developing Self and Spirit" enables us to use the past and the present to both inform and create a morally defensible future.

## HISTORY

Ideas promoting the importance of "child-centered learning," of educating the "whole child," of "natural learning," of "freedom to learn," of "learning by doing," and of "practical application" are actually as old as Plato. The importance, even the primacy, of the place of the individual in religious, spiritual, social, economic, and political constellations of thought—and thus in the thought of educational theorists—has changed throughout history with the only surety being that whatever theory is currently in ascendance, it will change again.

While "child-centered" or "progressive education" first became popular in the United States during the late 19th century, its roots were solidly European. Although the ideas brought from overseas were shaped, by time and individual thinkers, to reflect a uniquely American consciousness it is important to look, at least briefly, at the foundations from which they arose.

The Platonic ideal of education outlined a theory concerned with the well-rounded development of the mental, physical, and spiritual aspects of individuals; it focused on the whole person. While early schooling was based in large part on imitation and memorization, as the child grew he or she was expected to self-teach through activities—training the mind, the body, and the spirit through practical interaction with the surrounding society. John Amos Comenius (1592–1670) firmly believed that all human development was governed by certain indisputable laws of nature that formed the constituent base for all educational theory and practice. He maintained that it was only possible to learn by doing: "Artisans learn to forge by forging, to carve by carving, to paint by painting, ... let children learn to write by writing, to sing by singing, and to reason by reasoning" (Comenius, 1907, pp. 100 and 152).

Jean-Jacques Rousseau (1712–1778) is generally named as the source of the ideas that are the framework of modern child-centered progressive education. Believing, contrary to traditional Calvinist teaching, that the individual was pure in nature, Rousseau suggested that the only way to rid society of corruption and evil was to return to adults the virtue and innocence of children. Based on his assumptions that every child was born unsullied and with inherent natural powers, Rousseau wrote *Emile* in 1762, a work designed to articulate the components of a "real" education. Leaving behind the notion of children as miniature adults, Rousseau saw childhood as a unique time of life, as an unfolding. Children, he felt, were to be educated in nature until they were at least five years old, free to play and explore and learn unencumbered by the artifice of society; sensory experience in concrete situations was the next focus and abstract learning came later, developed naturally, from the ages of 12 to 15. While many of the precepts proffered in *Emile* are today considered impractical, such as the concept of the child being educated for many years in isolation from others, Rousseau's ideas made the child the central figure in the educational process.

Holistic theories of children were the touchstone of many who followed Rousseau. Lest one think that such ideas were confined to the education of an elite, one need only to look at the work of Johann Heinrich Pestalozzi (1746–1827) who, following the devastation of the Napoleanic Wars, established a school at Yverdon, Switzerland for children whom today we would call disadvantaged and at risk. Working from a philosophical base that believed in the innate powers of children and contending that the only way to improve society was through the development of each individual's moral and intellectual capabilities, Pestalozzi prescribed, in addition to students' regular lessons, the tasks of farming, cooking, and sewing and, (to help support the school financially), the activities of spinning and weaving. Advocating the need for balanced development of the head, the heart, and the hand, Pestalozzi supported the use of sensory experience to develop powers of perception, a study of science and nature, and discipline based on love and respect for children as human beings.

Friedrich Froebel (1782–1852), who worked for Pestalozzi at Yverdon, was particularly interested in young children. In his belief that childhood was part of the greater unity of human life, he started the world's first formal kindergarten in Blankenberg, Germany in 1836. A religious mystic, he believed that children were born free of evil but were tainted by it through "arbitrary and willful interference with the original orderly and logical course of human development" (Froebel, 1887, p. 119). Froebel's aim was to help the child's mind grow naturally and spontaneously but, unlike Rousseau, he felt that social activity and participation were the keys to growth and learning in young children Additionally, he saw the world of play as the single most important developmental component of childhood, an arena for purposeful and creative activity. This, Froebel felt, provided the ideal setting for uniting the spiritual, intellectual, emotional, and physical aspects of the individual as he grew and matured.

Although John Dewey is hailed as bringing "progressivism" to American education almost singlehandedly, he was, of course, influenced by others. Chief among those educators who advocated the development of self as an educational doctrine in this country was Colonel Francis Wayland Parker. Parker's philosophy of teaching and learning were singular for his time, and were shaped in large part by his travels and studies in Europe after the Civil War. Speaking of his first official words as a Carrollton, Illinois, school principal in 1858, Parker recalled telling the students "that my idea of a good school was to have a first class time, and that in order to have a good time they must all take hold and work together" (Griffin, 1906, p. 121). Later, as superintendent of the Quincy, Massachusetts public schools, the system Parker developed was characterized by its intense concentration on individual students, a belief that the ultimate goal of humankind was freedom, and an abiding faith that only under democracy could such freedom be fostered. Moving from the east coast to the principalship of the Cook County (Illinois) Normal School, Parker was able to expand his views on freedom for children to the realm of adult education and teacher training and to include in his growing philosophy the concept of freedom for teachers themselves.

Parker saw public schools as the footing upon which a free nation rested and as the only arena in which prejudice could be erased and various peoples knit into a new and better society.

> Here in America we are bringing together all peoples from all parts of the known world, with all their prejudices born of centuries.... Here they come into our broad continent and we propose to have them live together.... The social factor in school is the greatest factor of all; it stands higher than subjects of learning. (Parker, 1894/1937, p. 420)

Parker believed that children working together in the environment of the school "before prejudice has entered their childish souls, before hate has become fixed, before mistrust has become a habit, ... make the public school a tremendous force for the upbuilding of democracy" (Parker, 1894/1937, p. 420).

John Dewey (whose son and daughter attended Parker's school during the years that the Dewey family lived in Chicago and before the opening of Dewey's Laboratory School) was strongly influenced by Parker's ideas. Dewey, as an intellectual and academic, was able to "translate" and explain the practice-based work of Parker into language that was more suited to the university. Dewey's work as a philosopher, a psychologist, and an educator enabled him to append the "why" and the "how" to Parker's "what"; he could articulate explanations and rationales for the practices that Parker instinctively felt were best for children.

Although Dewey was opposed to the sentimentality of those who proposed a child-centered philosophy so narrow that it all but denied the teacher any role in helping to guide students' experiences (Dewey, 1938/1963), his work clearly mirrored many of the visions and historical antecedents of this curricular culture. Dewey declared that "the educational process has two sides—one psychological and one sociological—and neither can be subordinated to the other.... Of these two sides, the psychological is the basis. The child's own instincts and powers furnish the material and give the starting point for all education" (Dewey, 1897/1981, pp. 443–444).

There are a number of educational principles based on individual development that come directly from those of the Laboratory School that Dewey began at the University of Chicago in 1899. The school itself is seen as a community where all members have responsibilities and obligations to the whole rather than merely a place where lessons are learned. It is a place where the child's own curiosity leads to active engagement with learning problems and to the challenge to solve them him or herself. Finally, the teachers need to believe that the learner, not the subject matter, is the center of all teaching and that the child's total growth is the primary objective of teaching. The teachers' job, therefore, is to select worthy experiences for each child that will be both engaging and challenging. In addition, Dewey contended that while schools were a function of society, so society was a function of education. The school was considered by Dewey, as by Parker before him, to be a micro-society (Dewey, 1897/1981). Despite the fact that a century has passed since the creation of the Laboratory School, the "Dewey model" is currently experiencing renewed popularity (Fishman & McCarthy, 1998, Semel & Sadovnik, 1998).

Numerous schools representing varied curriculum models have developed over time that support the culture "Developing Self and Spirit." These models differ from one another, sometimes radically, depending on the ideas—not the goals—that underlie the particular situational reality. They are not, as it were, "pure" in any sense as perhaps the only truly comparable characteristic of the various iterations of this culture is that they emanate from the needs of the learners.

Helen Parkhurst founded the Dalton School and developed the three-part Dalton Plan in 1919 (the House, the Assignment, and the Laboratory) grounded, in part, on her work with Maria Montessori. The objectives of the Dalton concept are simple: to adapt the school program to each student's individual needs and interests; to encourage independence; to build students' social skills and feelings of responsibility for others; and affiliation with the broader community. Private schools established on the Dalton formula exist today in Europe, Asia, and South America. Public schools are beginning to explore the possibilities of regularly and systematically providing students with opportunities to make choices about their own learning, to find meaningful ways to discover their own interests, and to take personal responsibility for pursuing those interests in the educational setting.

The Dalton Plan, the Winnetka (Illinois) Plan, the Morrison Plan (Henry C. Morrison, University of Chicago, School of Education) , and others like them favor the creation of a contract between the student and the teacher that forms the basis of each individual's educational program. The use of contracts is experiencing renewed popularity in today's schools and the concept yields a double benefit for students—they are allowed to learn in "natural progression" and, of equal import, are often able to structure their school day in ways that allow for maximum concentration on the topic at hand rather than having the hours broken up into unrelated activities.

Maria Montessori left a widespread legacy of schools throughout the world that are based, totally or in part, on her model. Her writing of *The Montessori Method* (1909) and other works influenced many teachers and parents in America. Although Montessori advocated activities selected by teachers as well as students, and designed materials intended to further her philosophy of sensory, manipulative-based learning, she is still considered part of the group of educators promoting development the individual. Montessori practice emerges from the interests and desires of the child at any given point in time and education proceeds only from that starting point. Often cited as the "creator" of developmentally appropriate educational practice, Montessori advocated multi-aged classrooms where children could learn by doing, both individually and with older and younger classmates, in a carefully prepared environment. While Montessori's work focused on schooling three, four, and five year-old children, modern iterations of her ideas continue through the 12th grade. Besides the numerous Montessori private (and parochial) schools throughout the United States, of particular interest is the growth of public Montessori schools in the United States; there are currently almost 100 school districts that have some form of elementary program that is grounded in Montessori principles, employ teachers trained in the Montessori method, and use materials specifically designed for such settings.

Rudolf Steiner, a German educator who in the early part of the 20th century developed the Waldorf School system of education, is another whose ideas are reproduced, often less in whole than in part, in many schools today. There exists an established and growing worldwide network of Waldorf Schools, "the great aim [of which] is to bring up free human beings who know how to direct their own lives" (Steiner, 1973, p. 201). The Waldorf model advocates preparation for the child's future life as a member of the broader society. Operating from a strongly spiritual base, Steiner's philosophy advocates, among other things, the integration of stories, art, and movement into the curriculum at ages "appropriate" for students. It also advises that teachers should remain with their students through a number of years (sometimes for all eight elementary grades), in order to enhance the replication of family and community within the school and create optimal conditions for developing feelings of safety and nurture. Forms of the latter idea are present, in varying degrees, in an expanding number of American public and private schools today. Less likely to be adopted is Steiner's admonition to delay the teaching of reading until the individual child signals developmental readiness by the loss of the first baby tooth.

Another model of schooling, the Summerhill School, was begun in England, but its founder, A. S. Neill, is credited by many as having discovered "alternative education" and pioneered the concept of the "open classroom," both of which were extremely popular in the United States the late 1960s and 1970s. Summerhill is, and was, an international boarding school based on the concept of absolute freedom tempered only by a concern for health and safety; children can do as they wish as long as they do not physically endanger themselves or others. It is a doctrine, in Neill's words, of "freedom not license," with freedom being defined as the right of all, children and adults, to personal choice. The Summerhill School is operated by a one-person, one-vote government that meets on a weekly basis to establish community "laws" and norms, handle student and staff concerns, and deal with infractions of rules. All classes are optional for students and required for staff. Elements of Summerhill can be seen in the prevalence of class meetings or community meetings of various types found in today's schools and in principles that encourage children's natural cognitive and emotional growth in settings devoid of fear or coercion and where they, not adults, have control over their lives in school.

An important historical influence derived from psychotherapy and humanistic psychology is the learning theory of Carl Rogers, which continues to influence those writing about holistic education. While his ideas apply primarily to work with adult learners, they must also be contemplated as an extension of earlier theories about children's learning. Rogers believed that meaningful learning must be experience-based and always address the needs and desires of the student; experiential learning, in his framework, is equivalent to personal change and growth. Learning is optimal when the student initiates and has control over the nature and the direction of the process, when it directly confronts practical, social, or personal problems, and when self-evaluation is the primary method of assessment (Rogers, 1969). These principles are applied in numerous high school and adult education settings; Rogers' view complements adult self-directed learning theory (androgogy).

Most commonly encountered in schools of today are those models that explicitly or implicitly enact the developmental unity of "head, heart, and hands." Examples of such models include the ubiquitous "country day schools" located throughout the United States; a variety of small, nontraditional parochial schools, and institutions like the Piney Woods Country Life School in Piney Woods, Mississippi. The first are generally private, nonsectarian schools, the second too varied to really categorize in any way. The latter, Piney Woods, is a private, mostly scholarship-supported school that has worked for almost a century to enhance the development of at-risk, primarily African American, young people. All of the schools subscribing to this particular model share a devotion to the development of the intellectual, physical, and spiritual in each student. Many, in addition, have manual work components (maintenance requirements, animal keeping, farming, grounds work, etc.) as an integral part of their programs. In the past five years, with the growing popularity of "alternative" public schools, many charter schools are being formed that are based (loosely or strictly), on interpretations of these beliefs.

## BELIEF AND PRACTICES: LEARNERS AND TEACHERS

"Developing Self and Spirit" as a curricular culture focuses first and most intently on the learners in all of their complexities as physical, intellectual, social, and spiritual beings that naturally seek growth. Perhaps the most basic assumption that sustains this culture is that students need love, safety, freedom, and guidance to be able to learn. Stated another way, it is presumed that students need all of those things that combine to make anyone an active, participating human being. They need, like any sentient being, to find meaning in what they do through purposeful activity and reflection, to feel valued and valuable, and to be provided access to the skills and knowledge with which to fulfill their goals.

When educators who subscribe to this orientation are questioned about how students learn, their responses are remarkably similar. Children are described as learning "through experience," "by engagement," "when material is meaningful," "when they are empowered," "by doing and experiencing, and everything is an experience," "actively," "through all of their senses," and "when they love what they're doing; not every minute of the time, but when they basically love to learn." One middle school teacher summarized her assumptions about how students learn in this curricular culture as:

> Proceeding as if they were on a trip, not a vacation but a long, loosely planned journey. On a journey you don't necessarily know what you're going to encounter in your travels, you have a general plan and then you interact with the your physical environment, the people around you, the things you already know, your own assumptions and feelings and all of these things have an effect on what turns you make, where you stop, what you concentrate on. The fact that you're going on the journey is a given; where and how it progresses, what stalls it, when it ends, and if it will ever end, are all unknowns. (class journal)

It is not surprising, given the holistic foundations of this curricular culture, that many of the metaphors used by educators to describe the learner cluster around conceptualizations from the natural world—for example, of the "many plants and flowers in a garden, each needing basic nutrients but each growing in its own unique way," of "bees gathering honey," or "butterflies flying from place to place." Another commonly used metaphor of how students learn is a variation on "an artist's palette, made up of various colors, a dab of this, a dab of that, all combining in a broad spectrum that needs to be utilized, explored, blended, re-blended, and sometimes turpentined away … and then started again" (class journals).

The teacher's role is crucial when the child is considered at the center of the process of education. Teachers, as older and more experienced, protect and nourish students' growth; they are guides in, rather than directors of, the process of education. They are active participants in their students' learning and in their own learning as well. Words that teachers in this culture generally use to refer to their roles include "gardener," "facilitator," "authentic co-learner," "role model," "resource," "nurturer," "personal and intellectual support system," "objective guide," "coach," and "mentor." One high school teacher regularly describes himself as "a river guide, accompanying [students] on a waterway which challenges, excites, and teaches them. I may steer the boat but I am as challenged and excited as they are" (class journal).

Advocates of this curricular culture believe that student motivation is self-sustaining and self-reinforcing; teachers' work largely consists of allowing each learner's motivation to continuously energize itself. By applying this principle, teachers can respond to each student's inner world and act as a bridge between it and the external world. It is this ability to provide students with access between the realms of internal and external reality that is the source of meaningful, creative learning.

The role of the teacher, according to Murphy (1961), "will not be fulfilled by turning over a thousand stones, but by enabling the child or youth to see in the stone which arouses his interest the history of this world, the evolution of its waters, atmospheres, soils, and rocks, prying into deeper meanings 'just because they are there'" (p. 27).

Teachers who follow this orientation are characterized as passionate about students, the pursuit of knowledge, and knowledge itself—they encourage the potential in every child and are responsive to all areas of need. They are exquisitely aware that learning depends principally on the relationships between themselves and their students, students and other students, students and content, and students and the context of the learning process. Moreover, teachers themselves must have a high tolerance for ambiguity and for the active (and sometimes messy) pursuit of learning; they must also have the love and patience to await the natural evolution of each individual's participation in the process.

## BELIEFS AND PRACTICES: CONTENT AND CONTEXT

One of the greatest areas of misunderstanding surrounding the culture of "Developing Self and Spirit" arises from discussions of curriculum content. Content generated by student interest does not, as many believe, typically mean that students only study what they want and when they want. While proponents of A. S. Neill's Summerhill model and similar "alternative" schools believe that students don't need to study anything until they are ready to—each in his own way, each in her own time—this is not in any way the norm.

The culture, in practice, provides a broad array of content that is presented and processed in ways that encourage maximum student participation and creativity. Teaching is designed to allow and encourage students to question, to express themselves, to formulate and reformulate their ideas, and to make connections between the personal and the objective. What makes the topic of content particularly difficult to deal with in this curricular culture is the almost impossible task of separating how and in what environment the content is offered from the content itself.

The content offered falls into one of four specific categories: academics, athletics, arts and aesthetics, and service. Psychological, emotional, spiritual, and social growth are presumed to be a part of each content category.

The academic content gives students almost limitless opportunities for shaping and interpreting material to address their own interests and inclinations. In this way, curriculum integration is commonly practiced. Study explores themes across subject areas. Literature, philosophy, psychology, anthropology, sociology, theology, mathematics, and the sciences are all compatible with this mode of thought; there is, in fact, no academic subject matter that would be deemed unsuitable for exploration.

This curricular culture's holistic approach provides for the physical growth of all students no matter the extent of their specific athletic abilities. Proceeding from the premise of the unity of all aspects of the individual, children are encouraged to physically participate in one or many activities; in line with the desire to operate from a base of student interest, the opportunities are plentiful and varied. It is not unusual for even the smallest school to offer a broad choice of activities ranging from the popular team sports like basketball, football, soccer, and baseball, to the less-played lacrosse and field hockey. Individual sports activities are also available, again often in a variety that does not seem warranted by the number of potential participants. These can include swimming, bowling, golf, tennis, and horseback riding among others. There is a strong commitment to physical health and activity as an essential and pleasurable lifetime habit; while skill development and excellence are stressed in all student endeavors, ability is secondary to participation.

The arts are another basic component of content. Mirroring Plato's contention that aesthetic development was basic to the wholeness of the individual, opportunities in the visual, performing, and literary arts are many. Students are presented with ongoing opportunities to paint, draw, build, sing, act, write, and otherwise enliven their participatory and appreciative aesthetic sensibilities. Such activities, moreover, are considered neither peripheral to the "regular curriculum" nor "extracurricular," but are esteemed as an integral part of the general curricular offerings.

Service, within and outside of the classroom and school setting, is the fourth content area emphasized. Students are expected, as they mature, to take increasing responsibility for their own well-being and that of others. This content area takes many forms. Student governance is always a part of the content in a learner-centered orientation. In situations where schools serve all age or grade levels (pre-kindergarten to grade 12) cross-age tutoring, big and little sister programs, adopt-a-class programs, and peer tutoring are all common. Environmental responsibilities within the school community, such as gardening and recycling, are typical. Additionally, students often choose to contribute to their communities outside of school through the avenues of group or individual service projects. Long before service learning was a trend in education circles, it was an actuality in classrooms and schools that focused on individual growth and development.

The goal for curriculum content provided in a holistic environment is to develop mind, heart, the body, and spirit. By modeling these curricular goals in the content provided to learners, the education in this culture of curriculum strives for a totality of purpose and method.

The physical–social environment in the classroom is probably the most "prescribed" component of a learner-centered orientation to curriculum. The classroom itself—at the preschool, elementary, high school, and university levels—is characterized by activity, motion, and conversation.

It is expected that learners will approach content through animated, practical engagement with subject matter, teachers, and peers. Educators in this curricular culture often abandon traditional textbooks in favor of primary source materials, and both human and technological resources. The internal and external matériel brought to bear on learning is almost limitless; it is not uncommon, or regarded as "special," for students to regularly interview members of the school or the larger community to gain information needed to solve a dilemma presented by classroom content. Nor is it unusual for the learner-centered classroom to have a number of "non-teachers" in attendance at any given time including parent volunteers, community members, staff colleagues, or older or younger students. Trips and excursions outside the school or classroom are a regular part of the learning environment; a park is used for science study, a community center to shed light on a project dealing with adult day care, and a grocery store the setting for counting, measuring, and mathematics. Libraries, computer technology, and other resource avenues are accessed more often and with greater regularity than is customary in either elementary or high schools. These realities are consistent with the idea that the classroom is a part of the world and that students can and should partake of all the various stimuli and resources, human and material, available within it.

The classroom itself looks busy, as if many things are going on at one time; this is a fair representation of what is actually occurring. One teacher, for instance, describes his fourth-grade classroom as one in which "the structure and content are flexible and varied, the expectations and focus are high, and the students are purposeful and engaged" (class journal). Cooperation is the norm, there is a balance of individual and group work, and interaction is based on dialogue and discussion, listening and sharing. How students *feel* about the material they are studying and learning is considered to be of great importance.

The physical context in which learning occurs must be comfortable—not grand, but comfortable—with adequate light, sufficient room in which to move about, and different areas where students can work alone or with others. Emotionally the environment must, above all, be safe, caring, respectful and, thereby, conducive to experimentation and risk-taking. There is an assumption that the classroom "belongs" to the students, as a family and a community, and that it is their desire and responsibility to keep it usable and inviting. Parker (1894/1937) describes a school in three ways, as a "model home, a complete community, an embryonic democracy"; this curricular culture reflects Parker's vision through the physical and psychological environment found in the classroom and the school.

## BELIEFS AND PRACTICES: PLANNING AND EVALUATION

The question of who "makes" the curriculum in such a setting is in one way simple to answer, for everyone affected—and everything imaginable—is involved in curriculum making. The curriculum plan itself is determined by the goals, ideals, visions, and values of the curricular culture. Specific programs of study, course work, developmental sequence and scope (in part) are a combined effort of professional educators (teachers and administrators), and subject-matter specialists. They are also informed by the desires and needs of students, especially in terms of topics emphasized, depth and breadth of treatment, and the tangents and sequences of study. The specific activities of the offered curriculum are often "negotiated" by teachers, teachers and students, students and students, and sometimes other parties integral to the successful realization of study and learning goals. Outside of the foundational premises of the culture, curriculum is planned and developed with as broad a brush as possible, allowing for maximum input and participation.

Curriculum making in this context, moreover, is never considered complete; it is under constant modification and revision to meet the developing needs of students through the discoveries and realities of society. Curriculum design is envisioned and enacted as a process, not as an end, for the ultimate goal is to continue the inquiry to ever greater lengths and depths. Because of the ongoing use of multiple resources to animate learning, for example, so-called progressive schools are often the first to incorporate "new knowledge" into their programs. But, because the philosophical base of this curricular culture is so strongly bound to the incorporation of all possible avenues of learning, it is less likely than other orientations to fall prey to educational fads.

Methods of assessment and evaluation are of ongoing concern in "Developing Self and Spirit." Standardized measurements designed to assess externally prescribed curriculum and outcomes, however, are notably inappropriate when dealing with schooling that takes the student as its central focus. It is felt by many educators who work in this curricular culture that the zealous urge to quantify learning creates an environment where the measures used become of greater import and interest than the goals that inform the schooling itself.

Over time, beginning during the era of progressive education, different kinds of evaluation tools and instrumentation were designed to measure the broader concepts embraced by a student-centered curriculum. These alternatives were expected to measure not only student growth, but also growth among teachers and within the school itself, and changes in curriculum processes. Because teachers, students, parents, and administrators are all involved in creating the curriculum in this culture, it is considered essential that all be somehow involved in assessing and evaluating it.

Long before portfolio assessment and authentic evaluation strategies became popular in the 1980s and 1990s, their precursors were found in schools designated as "experimental." Students were involved in self-assessment from a very young age; and teachers and administrators were likewise expected to evaluate their own progress and growth. Reports to parents were anecdotal and extensive, focusing specifically on the development of the individual child. Academic grades were, to a large degree, done away with and classwork was evaluated less by testing and more by portfolio, performance, production, or presentation. What was clear in all evaluative activities was that the process of enacting the curriculum took precedence over the content, for it was by way of the process that real learning occurred.

In schools that represent this curricular culture today, students are typically assessed in multiple ways, the majority of them nonstandardized and more "subjective" than "objective." Tests, when they are used, are most often teacher or teacher/student constructed and based on the specific problems upon which students are working. The concern, when it comes to students' academic achievement, focuses more on complex forms of problem solving than on performance on standardized multiple-choice tests. Equally as important to teachers, administrators, parents, and students is the development of a positive attitude toward learning and school. Standardized, normed, objective tests such as the Iowa Test of Basic Skills, the California Test of Basic Skills, and others are given when necessary for purposes of external evaluation by funding and/or accrediting agencies; the College Boards, SATs, and like instruments are administered when needed for admission to institutions of higher education.

Can students educated in such an environment, and assessed by "nontraditional" means, pass muster in the competitive world of jobs and university admissions? Experimental schools received scrutiny in a classic research study, known as the Eight-Year Study, that was conceived and conducted by the Progressive Education Association in the late 1930s. Secondary school students from 30 experimental schools who entered college in 1936–1939 were paired and matched with students from more conventional institutions and evaluated on the basis of a variety of traits, including academic achievement. Arrangements had been made with the colleges, over 300 in number, to admit students from the nontraditional schools based solely on teacher recommendations and without regard to specific course credits or test results.

Regardless of the measures used to evaluate these students after college entrance however, or of the attributes measured, the graduates of the student-centered schools "outscored" their counterparts in every area, including academics (Chamberlin, Chamberlin, Drought, & Scott, 1942; Smith & Tyler, 1942). But perhaps more importantly, the Eight-Year Study highlighted that students from innovative schools seemed to "possess a higher degree of intellectual curiosity and drive, often demonstrated a high degree of resourcefulness in meeting new situations, and showed a more active concern with national and world affairs." An evaluator of the study concluded that schools from the less conventional approach send on to college "better human materials" (Cremin, 1961, pp. 255–256). Advocates believe that students are similarly successful in this curricular culture today.

## DILEMMAS OF PRACTICE

Teaching within the culture "Developing Self and Spirit" has exceptional requirements for dedication to students, to learning, and to process. Teachers are obliged to be artists rather than efficiency experts, to be devoted to the act and acquisition of learning and desirous of increasing their own reserves of knowledge, and to be responsive to individual educational needs rather than prescribed, standardized goals and outcomes.

Those who work in such an environment must be dedicated to dealing with the "whole child" in all of his or her complexity as a social, emotional, academic, intellectual, spiritual, and practical being. Because students do not leave their "other lives" at the schoolhouse door, the realities of their personal existence outside of school must be recognized, appreciated, and dealt with on a daily basis. Additionally, the broader social and political challenges of the society in which students reside must be acknowledged and contended with. This demands both commitment and skill on the part of teachers.

Teaching successfully in this culture implies the ability to create and shape environments in which children are motivated to question, act, react, assess, evaluate, and question again. Teachers must be able to derive conundrums and problems from everyday activities and situations and, in order to do this well, they must have an understanding of both the child him or herself and of the intellectual possibilities of ideas and bodies of knowledge. Artistry emerges from the teacher's ability to match each child's experience with opportunities to grow cognitively, emotionally, socially, and spiritually through tasks that are challenging but not impossible. The school and schoolroom should be rich in resources, or in access to resources, and this becomes exceedingly difficult when the financial state of educational systems is in disarray. Also linked to larger issues of school finance is the question of class size—it is not easy to enact student-centered practice when classes are overly large and teachers work without support.

Although the individual school district (or even the state or federal government) might provide the framework for curriculum development, the primary responsibility for program design resides with the teacher. Therefore, teachers must be skilled at, and enjoy, developing curriculum within the context dictated by the combined realities of the student and the classroom. This means that teachers must be able to grasp and utilize "teachable moments" as they occur in within the every day moments of schooling.

Perhaps what is most important and demanding of all is for teachers to accept and embrace the vision and principles of the culture in which they work, for "Developing Self and Spirit" is more than a philosophy of pedagogy. This culture is intended to encompass the school in its entirety, not just in terms of curriculum content, teaching techniques, and assessment strategies but also in terms of its social life and organization. It is meant to extend beyond the walls of the school as well, and see itself in relation to the realities its students encounter at home and in the world outside of the educational institution. One cannot foster individual development only during school hours; this is a culture that presumes a shared and reflected conception of life itself.

## CRITIQUE

The strength of "Developing Self and Spirit" as a curricular culture lies in its holistic, fluid approach to learning, an approach that creates no unnatural barriers between the individual and the community, work and play, art and science. Education becomes an unfolding process that itself serves to stimulate learners' natural curiosity and encourages ongoing and increasing involvement in life. A weakness in this curricular culture may be its lack of agreed-on cognitive (or academic) end-products: there are no "goals" in the sense that we use the word other than the desire for well-educated, good people. It is taken for granted that learners have innate good sense and that, presuming they are guided by skilled teachers, they will choose wisely of the knowledge important for them to participate fully in society and to live well as individuals. We must ask, however, can the learning process fall prey to idiosyncratic interests of teachers and learners, directed by nothing more than vaguely articulated learning goals? Without articulation of goals, what will inspire deep knowledge of subject matter, proficient skills, or the ability to engage in critical reflection?

Notwithstanding, a good many criticisms of "Developing Self and Spirit" stem from stereotypical notions about its beliefs and practices rather than from serious analysis. These misconceptions compel us to answer criticisms that would only have credibility if their premises were sound.

One frequently voiced concern is based on the mistaken notion that "Developing Self and Spirit" all but repudiates the importance of subject matter in the curriculum, relying instead on individual interest and desire to shape learning. This misunderstanding has done more to discredit the culture than any other as it commonly leads to the assumption that students study what they want when they want with benefit of neither supervision nor guidance. More accurately, in this curricular culture, teachers are charged with the responsibility for finding material suitable for learning through experience and then, after it is discovered, with utilizing it to build on students' earlier experiences so that their encounters will be as rich and full as is possible. What is at issue is an attempt to assure that student learning is not dependent on the conventional academic disciplines but that it grows from connecting and transcending the disciplines in creative and cognitively defensible ways. Rather than dealing with separateness, the goal is to deal with wholes; instead of discrete bits of knowledge, the focus is on interaction and continuity.

A second stereotype of this curricular culture is that it rejects of all authority and simply celebrates untrammeled freedom. Undoubtedly, educators in "Developing Self and Spirit" do oppose authority that is externally imposed, the kind that impels through fear or compulsion engendered by an inequality of power. Their rejection of external authority, however, does not suggest that all authority be repudiated, but simply that it must come from a more effective source; it should be earned rather than assumed. Freedom, then, becomes not unfettered but dependent on the exercise of intelligent judgment and responsibility in the assignment of authority to oneself or to others. Greene notes that only by way of education can people be

> provoked to reach beyond themselves in their intersubjective space. It is through and by means of education that they may be empowered to think about what they are doing, to become mindful, to share meanings, to conceptualize, to make varied sense of their lived worlds. (Greene, 1988, p. 12)

A third common misapprehension about this curricular culture focuses on individual learners, suggesting that this culture's characteristic nature is a representation of American society's effort to educate individualists able to function in a society based on competitive capitalism. Yet such charges of blatant individualism fly in the face of a strong focus of "Developing Self and Spirit"—the cooperative, problem-centered work within the process of schooling and the concomitant necessity of extending this work into the community itself. We might instead fear that this curriculum so downplays competition that young people educated in this culture have not experienced the realities of competitive life.

Related to the criticism of excessive individuality is the contention that this culture makes learners self-indulgent—that they are encouraged to care only for their own wants and needs. Advocates instead believe that the holistic process of education helps to develop individuals who are strong physically, spiritually, and intellectually (and have a wide range of academic skills) to become energetic, self-governing participants within the larger society.

In conclusion, the dominant paradigm influencing schools today is one of imposition of goals and aims on school communities that value products more than people, that promote factory (or Information Age) imageries rather than human ones. We see valuing of measurement and accountability, constraint, regimentation, sameness, and the construed—and indifference to freedom and the natural. These paradigms and values reflect a shift from a philosophy that presumes the innate, genuine goodness of humankind to one that sees a need to somehow "make" people good in the face of evil. It may not be so much that the methods of "Developing Self and Spirit" are in such dispute, but rather, that current societal beliefs about the nature of children and humankind are so overwhelming out of step with the premises on which this culture of curriculum rests.

## REFERENCES

Chamberlin, D., Chamberlin, E., Drought, N., & Scott, W. (1942). *Adventure in American education, Vol. 4: Did they succeed in college?* New York: Harper & Brothers.

Cobb, E. (1977). *The ecology of imagination in childhood.* New York: Columbia University Press.

Comenius, J. A. (1907). *The great didactic.* M. W. Keatinge (Trans. and Ed.). London: Adam & Charles Black.

Cremin, L. A. (1961/1964). *The transformation of the school: Progressivism in American education, 1870–1957.* New York: Vintage.

Cremin, L. A. (1988). *American education: The metropolitan experience, 1876–1980.* New York: Harper & Row.

Dewey, J. (1897/1981). "My pedagogic creed." In J. J. McDermott (Ed.), *The philosophy of John Dewey.* Chicago: University of Chicago Press.

Dewey, J. (1916/1923). *Democracy and education.* New York: Free Press.

Dewey, J. (1938/1963). *Experience and education.* New York: Collier.

Fishman, S. M., & McCarthy, L. (1998). *John Dewey and the challenge of classroom practice.* New York: Teachers College Press.

Froebel, F. (1887). *The education of man.* W. N. Hailman (Trans.). New York: Appleton.

Greene, M. (1988). *The dialectic of freedom.* New York: Teachers College Press.

Griffin, W. M. (1906). *School days in the fifties: A true story with some untrue names of persons and places, with an appendix, containing and an autobiographical sketch of Francis Wayland Parker.* Chicago: A. Flanagan.

Kliebard, H. M. (1992). *Forging the American curriculum: Essays in curriculum history and theory.* New York: Routledge.

Martin, J. R. (1992). *The schoolhome.* Cambridge, MA: Harvard University Press.

Miller, R. (1990). *What are schools for? A history of holistic education in America.* Brandon, VT: Holistic Education Press.

Moffett, J. (1994). *The universal schoolhouse.* San Francisco: Jossey-Bass.

Montessori, M. (1909/1964). *The Montessori method.* New York: Schocken.

Murphy, G. (1961). *Freeing intelligence through teaching.* New York: Harper & Brothers.

Neill, A. S. (1960). *Summerhill.* New York: Hart.

Parker, F. W. (1894/1937). *Talks on pedagogics: An outline of the theory of concentration.* New York: John Day.

Pearce, J. C. (1976). *The magical child.* New York: Dutton.

Rogers, C. R. (1969). *Freedom to learn.* Columbus, OH: Merrill.

Rousseau, J. J. (1762/1911). *Emile.* London: J. M. Dent and Sons.

Semel, S. F., & Sadovnik, A. R. (Eds.) (1998). *Schools of tomorrow, schools of today: What happened to progressive education.* New York: Lang.

Smith, E., & Tyler, R. W. (1942). *Adventure in American education, Vol. 3: Appraising and recording student progress.* New York: Harper & Brothers.

Steiner, R. (1973). *A modern art of education.* London: Rudolf Steiner Press.

Whitehead, A. N. (1929). *The aims of education.* New York: Macmillan.

# 6

# Constructing
# Understanding

**Mark A. Windschitl**
*University of Washington*

*If we cannot make these new connections for ourselves, we do not really grasp what we have been told.... If a child is told that water runs downhill, he is much more likely to be able to repeat those same words than he is to be able to rephrase them with all the meaning that they represent. He is very unlikely ... to be able to draw significant connections—as, for instance, that the outlet from the Great Lakes must be uphill from Quebec City. Piaget's emphasis is that we have to do the work ourselves making the connections, even if others take pains to point out the connections they have been able to make.*
—Eleanor Duckworth, 1996, *The Having of Wonderful Ideas*

Ms. Garcia's sixth-grade classroom is a noisy place, and if you come to visit, she is often hard to find. Today, students are clustered in small groups, bent over note cards and diagrams they have assembled in order to determine whether Australian dingoes can cohabitate with the marmosets—and just how much it will cost to feature Australian mammals rather than North American mammals. Ms. Garcia conferences with a group of student in a corner of the room, encouraging them to consider what would happen if they include carnivores in their plans.

It is mid-year and the students have just participated in three days of discussion and readings about interrelationships among mammals. Ms. Garcia has negotiated with each of four student groups (as she has done several times earlier in the year) about their work with a complex problem reflecting the students interests and abilities. One group chose a design problem: create a habitat for a local zoo that will support at least three kinds of mammals naturally found in the same geographic area. After the students decided on this problem, Ms. Garcia led the group in two brief brainstorming sessions. The first session concerned the possibilities and constraints of building such habitats and the second session was to come to consensus on what the criteria should be for a successfully designed habitat. Among other conditions, students decided that the habitats should be economical to maintain, should not be cruel to animals, and should be as self-sustaining as possible.

The students are now engaged for the next two weeks on this project. They find and share dozens of resources, many of which are spread out on tables and on the floor around the room. Allen brings to class a video he shot at the zoo last week so everyone can see what different habitats look like. Michelle loads up a CD-ROM on mammals that she brought from home, and James donates one of his mother's landscape architecture books for ideas on how to diagram spaces and buildings.

Watching the students work, it seems that solving small problems generates new insights, and the insights provide opportunities to pose new problems.

| | |
|---|---|
| *Allan:* | We can have coyote, deer, and opossum together because the opossum can just climb a tree to get away from the coyote, and the deer can just run away. |
| *Michelle*: | Trees? How big do trees have to be to hold a opossum? |
| *James*: | We can't have any trees 'cause deer come into our back yard at home and eat the bark off the trees and kill them. |
| *Allan*: | That's just because in the winter they don't have enough food, and we are going to supply their food so they won't eat the tree bark. |
| *James*: | We still can't have deer because the coyote will eat their young unless we can find a way to separate them. |
| *Michelle*: | We can build a wall! |

| *James:* | No, we can do it naturally. We'll make a low spot in the habitat and flood it during the season when the deer are young. That will work if the coyotes can't swim. |

Ms. Garcia has been listening to this dialogue and senses that good ideas are developing, but worries about her students' assumptions.

| *Ms. Garcia:* | I guess if I were solving these kinds of problems I'd try to find out more information first. You may be basing some of your decisions on an idea that isn't accurate. Are you sure that coyotes prey on young deer? Is there a way to divide up some of this work and check these kinds of facts? |

During the next two weeks, these students will develop an understanding of how animals interact with one another, how they exhibit purposeful behavior, possess evolved form and function to aid survival, and are subject to the natural cycles of reproduction, the seasons, feast and famine, and so on. These complex ideas begin with kernels of the students' own personal experiences, and they mature with guided exposure to resource materials and with goal-oriented collaboration with others. Concepts such as "competition for resources" and "reproductive capacity"—whose definitions could have been memorized—are instead, made sense of within a problem-solving context. These concepts are built upon the experiences of the students and are essential, interconnected considerations in the success of these students' habitat design. In the end, the students have created a physical model for the habitat that embodies their collective understanding of these ideas and represents their ability to work together.

During the final presentation of their model to the class, the students describe the rationale for its design, offering statements about what they have learned from this project. Michelle concludes with a surprising remark:

> When we were almost finished with our habitat, we thought, "Isn't this pretty artificial?" I mean, we were making this plan work for us, *for our benefit*, but animals don't really live like this. They eat each other, they migrate, they go off by themselves if they want to, they do all kinds of behaviors they can't do in a zoo. So … maybe that's the best thing that we learned.

This is one of many faces of the constructivist classroom.

The culture of curriculum "Constructing Understanding" is characterized by three themes. Although there are wide variations as to how this curricular culture manifests itself, these themes permeate the goals and activities of all constructivist classrooms.

The first theme is the centrality of the learner. The students' lived experience acts as a powerful referencing framework that allows them to compare new concepts with what they already know and to give these concepts meaning within the students' world. Also, learners are recognized as capable agents of knowledge production, rather than passive consumers of information; as such, they have the periodic freedom to identify intellectual problems and approaches to tasks that are relevant to their own lives as well as to curricular content.

The second theme is complexity. Teachers employ problem-based learning as a way for students to participate in the kind of complex inquiry that characterizes most human endeavors outside the classroom. Students also investigate ideas from various perspectives including the practical, aesthetic, historical, and scientific dimensions. In doing so, they strive for a richer, more integrated view of the world. Complexity also refers to the ways in which teachers incorporate diverse learner abilities such as musical, physical, interpersonal, linguistic and mathematical, into the life of the classroom. The unique distribution of such abilities in individuals mediates how they make sense of their world and how they are empowered to express their understandings to others.

The final theme is engagement. Students begin units of study by experiencing the content they are studying, rather than having abstract explanations provided to them ahead of time. For example, students manipulate computer-generated graphs in math class before they discuss what "slope" is, they breed fruit flies in science class and analyze the results before formulas for inheritance are suggested by teachers, and, in social studies, they contemplate Martin Luther King's "Letter from a Birmingham Jail" before explanations of nonviolent protest are introduced.

Also, learners are engaged in class projects because they work closely with the teacher to negotiate the specifics of problems that they will address, as well as the kinds of evidence of learning they will provide. Students select problems that are important to them, and these problems stimulate an authentic curiosity that connects experiences in their own lives with the themes under study. In addition to being engaged with their own projects and interacting with teachers, students collaborate with each other on tasks of inquiry and design, engaging in discussion and challenging each other's ideas.

These themes suggest that students learn best by first interacting with phenomena and ideas, and by having opportunities to reorganize their view of the world. This curricular culture encourages learners to utilize their lived experiences, intellectual strengths, and interactions with others to bridge the domains of formal knowledge with the rich, continually evolving world of the individual mind.

## VISIONS

Constructivism, as a theory and philosophy about the nature of knowledge and how learners come to know their world, underpins this curricular culture.

Constructivism is appreciated more fully when it is framed against the antithetical but historically dominant position of objectivism and its influence on education. Objectivism suggests that there is an external world, independent of human consciousness, which serves as a foundation for claims of truth (Willis, 1995). Related to this view is the belief that language can be used as a precise, neutral tool to describe the real world and to effectively map knowledge from the minds of instructors to the minds of learners. These two philosophical views have supported the persistent presence of transmission models of instruction (also known as direct instruction, didacticism) in which lecture and demonstration are the preferred modes of "delivering knowledge" to learners. Psychological theories, most notably behaviorism, have been consistent with objectivist philosophies and have attempted to make learning processes more efficient (with success in many contexts). Behaviorist instructional principles suggest, in part, that knowledge and skills may be decomposed, the components removed from context, acquired separately by learners through systematic reinforcement of incremental target learning behaviors, and then concatenated by the learner to form a coherent whole (Reynolds, Sinatra, & Jetton, 1996).

In contrast to objectivism, constructivism is premised on the belief that learners actively create and restructure knowledge, constantly comparing ideas introduced in formal instruction to their existing knowledge, which has been assembled from personal experiences, the intellectual, cultural, and social contexts in which these ideas occur, and a host of other influences that serve to mediate understanding.

When learners make sense of the world, they are in fact creating knowledge. A central aim of the constructivist culture is cultivating learners who believe that they can create knowledge themselves, and that knowledge does not exist outside them as some objective, universal entity. All students hold epistemological beliefs about whether or not they can learn how to learn, if there are alternatives to knowledge being accepted from unquestioned "authoritative" sources, and whether or not knowledge has contextual limitations (Schommer, 1993). Children who are immersed in the constructivist culture tend not only to have a greater capacity for generating their own knowledge through problem solving but also for identifying problems, and perhaps most importantly, for persisting in problem-solving efforts (Duckworth, 1978). Constructivist teachers believe that students, when provided with intellectual opportunities, can be motivated to explore subject matter, create understandings at various levels of sophistication, and effectively solve problems.

Constructivists believe that one of traditional education's hallmarks is the monolithic presence of an external, authoritarian body of knowledge immediately represented in the teacher and the textbook. Learning, in that tradition, is roughly equivalent to accepting a set of irrevocable truths that older and more able others have acquired through processes that are inaccessible to students.

To discover something significant for oneself, to come to a unique understanding or to have your own "way of knowing" is not a norm of traditional education.

By contrast, in a constructivist culture, a premium is placed on creating unique rather than uniform understandings and developing a powerful sense of agency in learners. This sense of agency relates directly to Piaget's larger view of the purpose of education: to develop intellectual and even moral autonomy in learners. Kamii (1984) elaborates on this moral aspect of Piagetian constructivism:

> The idea that children acquire moral values and knowledge by construction from within—by putting things into relationships—still stands, as does the idea that social interactions are essential for this construction to take place. Moreover, according to Piaget, honest exchanges of points of view are bound to lead, in the long run, to autonomy. (p. 415)

Piaget (1963) argued that children refine their existing notions of personal ethics as well as their use of logic when, during social interaction, they view the ideas of others in critical comparison with their own. It is clear that developing autonomy, both intellectual and moral, involves more than the common-sense view of internalizing the observed behaviors of others—it involves exchanging viewpoints with others, to immerse oneself in intersubjectivity.

Beyond autonomy, however, constructivism does not offer a coherent vision of a society that transcends the notion of a collective of capable, independent thinkers. From the roots of constructivism—learning psychology, anthropology, and linguistics—come a system of values that have been difficult to locate within the sphere of human concern. Some scholars, however, have described a type of critical constructivism (Loving, 1997) that endorses "questioning the value of individualism, objectivity, rationality and efficiency as well as the resulting forms of pedagogy and curriculum" (Matthews, 1994). This version of constructivism suggests that teachers should convey to learners that all knowledge is provisional and make explicit the political and social context of this knowledge. Knowledge itself, then, becomes an object of study.

In addition to fostering a critical attitude toward knowledge, constructivist cultures also encourage learners to expand on the ideas of other—to explore the possibilities not only of how to solve authentic problems, but to consider alternative ways of seeing what problems "exist" in a given situation. These are the ways of thinking that are so valuable to many disciplines and to the 21st-century image of the capable worker. Even outside the work environment, as citizens who shape the social and political landscape, individuals who have participated in the constructivist culture should be able to stimulate dialogue in fellow community members by asking questions that probe, prompt reflection, and organize thought—What is the purpose for … ? Can we reframe the problem by… ? or, How can we work together to … ?

What, then, is the larger vision of a society of individuals educated within the constructivist culture? Citizens are able to collaborate effectively with one another in addressing challenges facing the community. They have the ability to understand and appreciate the points of view of others, as well as incorporate diverse ideas into problem solutions. Negotiations are tempered by open-mindedness with regard to intellectual and moral differences. These citizens are also life-long learners who understand the value and limitations of knowledge; they appreciate the different forms that "knowing" can take and accept that knowledge is only one dimension of human experience. Furthermore, there is a prevailing respect for children's ways of seeing the world, which avoids paternalism and embraces the complexity of the young intellect.

## HISTORY

Historically, elements of constructivist thought have appeared in the philosophical framework of several educational institutions. Notable schools founded over the past 100 years have based their curriculum on the intellectual curiosity and social experiences of the learner rather than on the development of prescribed skills or the transmission of subject matter. Although institutions such as John Dewey's Laboratory School, the Montessori schools, or the Reggio Emilia schools of Italy were not founded explicitly on constructivist philosophy, they serve as models for reframing the design of formal schooling around the experiential, culturally mediated world of the child.

The image of modern constructivist instruction has been shaped in no small way by.John Dewey and the historical record of his progressive schools established earlier this century. He opened his laboratory school in Chicago in 1896, and with it he set out to "test, verify, and criticize" educational theory as well as to contribute new ideas to education (Dewey, 1972). Dewey's successes with the laboratory school led him to argue eloquently that: a) the curriculum should spring from the "genuine" experiences of children, b) authentic problems should be identified within these experiences to serve as stimuli for thought, c) students should be allowed the freedom to gather the information necessary to deal with these problems, d) students should accept responsibility to develop solutions in an orderly way, and, e) students should be given opportunities to test these ideas through application to make their meaning clear and test their validity (Dewey, 1916).

Dewey effectively took a stand against the inculcation of learners into a culture of compliance and rote learning in which subject matter had little connection with the life of the child. He suggested that the child, if presented with situations of interest and relevance, would be capable of independent exploration, experimentation, and reflection. Dewey did not, however, advocate an extreme version of child-centered education. He contended that education was a process of the continuous reconstruction of a child's present experience by means of adult experiences that were organized into "bodies of truth we call studies" (Hendley, 1986, p. 23). These bodies of truth contained a valuable intellectual and cultural heritage and represented a set of preconfigured knowledge bases. Although Dewey could not be identified as a practitioner of the more radical forms of constructivist instruction, which do not recognize the existence of objective "truths" nor advocate instructional convergence on prescribed concepts (Von Glaserfeld, 1993), his focus on children's experiences and respect for their ways of knowing did foreshadow the extensive documentation during the latter 20th century that children strive to construct meaning from social and scientific phenomena, and that their mental models of these phenomena do indeed serve to organize and explain the world around them (Driver, 1981).

Other schools have emerged in this century that emphasize the natural powers of children to fashion elaborate understandings of the world around them, with little influence from direct instruction. Montessori schools, particularly popular for early childhood education, utilize highly trained teachers who act as facilitators for children who are free to pursue learning experiences out of innate interest and curiosity, albeit within a controlled setting of materials supplied by the teacher. The children are envisioned as busily reconstructing themselves as adults as they try to understand the world around them. The curriculum accommodates rather than dictates a developmental path for the child to become a participant in society, as well as to gain the basic knowledge and skills necessary to deal with the world (Montessori, 1967). The teacher acts as the architect of the environment, the resource person who plans the array of materials and activities from which the child ultimately chooses. A fundamental belief of Montessori advocates is that children are natural learners and are in a better position to make appropriate learning choices than their adult mentors. Other than periodic didactic presentations to the children, the adults play a supportive rather than a directive role in the learners' environment (Loeffler, 1992).

Other schools that exemplify the constructivist philosophy are those of Reggio Emilia in northern Italy. Founded in 1946, the primary educational activities in these schools are long-term, intrinsically interesting projects carried out in a rich variety of physical settings both in the school and throughout the community. The activities include not only teachers but family and community members as participants. Proponents assert that the objective of the schools is to increase the possibilities for the child to invent and discover, and furthermore, that schemes or structures should not be presented directly to children nor should words should be used as shortcuts to knowledge. Children are viewed as capable of making meaning from their daily life experiences through mental acts involving planning, coordination of ideas, and abstraction (Edwards, Gandini, & Forman, 1996).

In one Reggio Emilia project, four young children were asked to design the school's upcoming long-jump competition (Forman, 1996). They were asked not only to conduct the event, but to construct the long-jump area, decide on a method for measuring the jumps, and devise a set of rules for competition. With minimal adult help the students engaged in repeated cycles of dialogue with each other, analyzing photographs of Olympic jumpers, modeling the jumping motion using wooden dolls and drawings, and developing a system of measuring distance that involved transforming marks on a measuring tape to tally marks and finally to a number system with place values. In short, the students learned how to use models and symbol systems in a meaningful context, employing a persistent attitude toward invention in order to successfully complete a complex task. Perhaps the most amazing aspect of the activity was that each of the children was only five and a half years old!

The history of constructivism is not restricted to its various incarnations in school settings. The metaphor of "construction" is perhaps most closely associated with the work of Piaget. Piaget viewed learning as a way of constantly reorganizing one's world, reconciling new information with past experience. Knowledge, according to Piaget, is not an internalized representation of the real world, but rather a collection of conceptual structures that are sensible only within the knowing subject's range of experience (Von Glaserfeld, 1989). To know something, said Piaget, is to act upon it, and transform it. The work of Piaget has been foundational to theories associated with *cognitive constructivism*—that is, the system of explanations for how learners, as individuals, impose structure on their worlds. Some of the major ideas connected with cognitive constructivism are: that meaning is rooted in and indexed by personal experiences (Brown, Collins, & Duguid, 1989), that young learners possess complex but inaccurate conceptions of how the world works, and that these conceptions influence how they respond to formal instruction (Driver & Easley, 1978).

Related to cognitive constructivism are the theories of *social constructivism* and *sociocultural learning* that describe how knowledge has social and cultural as well as individual components, and how these components cannot be viewed as separate in any meaningful way (Cobb, 1994; Rogoff, 1990). More specifically, individuals construct knowledge in the presence of others who both constrain and enrich the environment through the use of tools such as language, conventions (such as pre-established concepts), and accepted practices for creating and judging knowledge (Vygotsky, 1979). An illustration of how accepted classroom practices can mediate learning is found in a study by Cobb and Yackel (1996). They observed a group of first graders who took it for granted that, when conversing with the teacher during mathematics class, they were to infer the answer that the teacher had in mind rather than articulate their own understandings. The teacher found that she had to renegotiate classroom social norms with students in order to liberate them from previous expectations, to allow them to relate to her as young inquirers, and to encourage them to interact in a more exploratory way with the subject matter.

Both the classroom culture and the larger culture influence how people interpret the world, and without acknowledging this basis for "common understanding," an individual's personal constructions would be meaningless. Indeed, "it is the cultural situatedness of meanings that assures their negotiability and their communicability" (Bruner, 1996, p. 3). Within the sociocultural perspective, knowledge is not an individual possession but is socially shared and emerges from participation in cultural activities (Cole, 1991). Scholars have synthesized the cognitive and sociocultural constructivist perspectives, claiming that knowledge is personally constructed and socially mediated (Tobin & Tippins, 1993).

## BELIEFS AND PRACTICES: LEARNERS AND TEACHERS

One of this curricular culture's central tenets is that learners are continually involved in reorganizing their world, actively imposing order and meaning on their experiences and "creating" the world in which they live. The ideas in their world are linked to a constellation of life episodes, images, models, and metaphors that give shape to their conceptions and provide references against which they interpret new ideas. Students' personal knowledge about the world is often elaborate although lacking in depth and consistency. Students' ways of explaining phenomena are often quite satisfactory to them, even though these explanations may contain inconsistencies and may not be applicable across different contexts. Their perceptions are not dismissed as flawed or insignificant, but used as an intellectual and motivational standpoints from which they will build more coherent ideas. As learners are confronted with new information they often can organize and integrate it unproblematically into their existing understanding of the world.

There are, however, some confounding aspects to the learners' world of experiences, such as the influence of alternative conceptions. Students develop naive or alternative conceptions about such ideas as how electricity flows through circuits, how a polygon's perimeter is related to its area, or how the branches of the American government operate. These can be more than simply mistaken ideas or lack of knowledge. Many alternative conceptions, particularly about topics central to a discipline (e.g., photosynthesis, supply and demand, ratios) are remarkably persistent, even in the face of well-sequenced, logical instruction.

A central belief in this culture of curriculum is that students' extant ideas about the world are not always remediated in some straightforward fashion by direct instruction, but that these alternative conceptions form the foundation upon which more intellectually persuasive approaches to the curriculum must be built. Activities such as independent student experimentation in science class or extended research using a variety of original sources in social studies class often serve to confront students with evidence that runs counter to their alternative conceptions. Students, with teacher guidance, experience firsthand the processes as well as the products of knowledge-building, and these situations provide opportunities for students to carefully reconsider the way in which they explain key aspects of the world.

In concert with this view of learning, teaching becomes less the sequencing of events and more the application of principles responding to the needs of a situation (Lebow, 1993). Teachers put learners in direct contact with the phenomena being studied and then ask students to explain the sense they are making. So, instead of explaining things to students, the teacher joins with them in making sense out of their developing conceptions (Duckworth, 1986).

To complement the active role of the learner, this curricular culture redefines the teacher as a learning facilitator and a codeveloper of understanding with the student rather than a dispenser of knowledge. The teacher often begins instruction by eliciting student ideas about a topic so learning experiences can be fashioned from learners' current understandings. Special techniques such as probing discussions, interviews, having students draw concept maps or other representations of ideas are some of the ways teachers put themselves in touch with where the learner is coming from. Teachers may then engage in judicious direct instruction (presentations, demonstrations), but they also design semi-structured activities that allow students flexibility in incorporating their own experiences and background knowledge. Teachers periodically negotiate with students the inquiry questions, activities, and methods that will stimulate knowledge-building and promote students' regulation of their own learning. When students are engaged in learning activities, teachers select from a range of strategies that guide students and prevent them from encountering frustrating deadends (even though mistakes are generally treated as learning opportunities). These strategies include: scaffolding, in which teachers reduce the difficulty of learning tasks by helping students with more complex aspects of problems and gradually give more responsibility to learners as time passes; modeling, in which teachers either think aloud or act out how they would approach a problem; or, providing hints to learners by asking probing questions or redirecting their attention.

There is an additional demand on the teacher beyond that of developing facilitative skills. Constructivist instruction based on design tasks or problem-solving requires that the teacher have a substantial understanding of the subject matter. The teacher must not only be familiar with the topic of study, but must also be prepared for the variety of ways in which the topic may be addressed by students. For example, if students in science class are studying density, the teacher may need to support the understanding of students who want to approach it from a purely abstract, mathematical perspective as they construct tables, equations and graphs. In this case, the teacher must understand how tabular data, equations, and graphs are translatable from one to another, interpret how student understandings are developing, and select appropriate interventions if students encounter difficulty. Another group of students may recount the story of the *Titanic*, emphasizing how density played a role in the visibility of the iceberg, the ballast of the ship, and the sinking itself. In this case the teacher must be able to apply his or her "clean," abstract mathematical understanding of density to a real-life, inevitably more complex situation.

## BELIEFS AND PRACTICES: CONTENT AND CONTEXT

There is no consistent pattern of content selection that effectively characterizes the constructivist culture. However, several norms about content are apparent: the way in which learners approach the subject matter is as important as the topics themselves; the long, critical engagements with the subject matter favored in the constructivist culture suggest that less is more—that is, understanding is fostered by prolonged engagements with a few key topics and encyclopedic coverage of content is avoided; and, the organization of content lends itself to the integrated curriculum (studying, for example, the historical perspectives of art, the mathematics of geography, literature in science).

Certainly the ways in which content is approached has some bearing on what is studied. "Big ideas" such as symmetry in mathematics, voice in language arts, laws and justice in social studies, or conservation of energy in science, which can be investigated in various ways, may be identified as required central themes by the teacher. Students may then elect to study a topic like symmetry by comparing examples of symmetry in nature, by examining the relationship between temporal symmetry in music and spatial symmetry in other art forms, or, by identifying ratios in symmetrical patterns. In this way, students have content structured only to a moderate degree and they are allowed to contextualize that content in a way that stimulates them, thereby creating the powerful "collateral" or incidental learning that often serves to give personal meaning to the original theme selected by the teacher.

Concerning the context of instruction, the focus is the learner rather than the subject matter. The classroom, however, may occasionally appear like the traditional classroom, with the teacher offering structured, didactic lessons. During these didactic lessons teachers adhere to familiar tenets of good instruction (beginning with engaging questions, starting with references to concrete experiences and moving to the abstract, offering analogies and examples to bolster ideas), but even within this didactic framework the teacher uses techniques informed by constructivism such as situating examples and analogies within contexts meaningful to students, eliciting alternative conceptions that students hold, and confronting existing ideas through classroom dialogue. Teachers are careful, however, not to introduce students to topics by providing exhaustive detail, "authoritative" explanations or descriptions of the topic that would leave the students in the position of engaging in their own activities simply to verify canonical knowledge.

Following an orientation to the subject matter area or theme of study, students then engage in those activities most closely associated with the constructivist culture. Teachers provide opportunities for students to witness and participate in each other's thinking by assigning work in small groups. Learners in this environment are exposed to examples of the clear, cogent thinking of some peers as well as the meandering, unreflective thought of others. They express to one another not only opinions, but how they see loosely associated bits of information coalescing into an idea, interpretation, or explanation.

In addition to working in groups, students learn to collect evidence and generate interpretations consistent with such evidence. A group of students in a social studies class, for example, might investigate the Civil War by examining its effects on several families living in the border states. Students would have access to copies of letters, diaries, newspapers, and other relevant primary documents. Their understanding would not be circumscribed by the previous historical interpretations of others. Students, together with teachers, also examine questions about this learning process. What is problematic about interpreting history this way? How will this help us understand the Civil War in a novel way? How will we be able to synthesize our ideas and demonstrate what we know? These types of questions foster a "thinking about thinking" environment in which students become critically conscious of their own intellectual activity.

Constructivist learning involves long-term engagements with projects and problems. The 50-minute class period is ill-suited for these purposes; block scheduling and interdisciplinary curricula, then, are natural outgrowths of this culture's approach to learning. Teachers team with partners in other subject areas and capitalize on the longer class periods by developing more integrated themes for study that bridge the world of science, social studies, math, and the arts. These themes are "big ideas" that span disciplines, such as the responsibility that humans have for the environment, and the influence of art on scientific discovery.

Although there are endless possibilities for how curriculum can be shaped in this culture, there are some common characteristics included in the design of most learning experiences:

- Teachers find out "where students are" intellectually before instruction and then monitor how students gradually make sense of the subject matter

- Teachers provide students with early investigative experiences relevant to the subject matter rather than start with explanations
- Students are given frequent opportunities to engage in problem or inquiry-based activities
- Such problems are meaningful to the student and not oversimplified or decontextualized
- Students work collaboratively and are encouraged to engage in dialogue
- Students have various avenues to express what they know to their peers and to the teacher
- Teachers encourage students' reflective and autonomous thinking in conjunction with the conditions listed above

## BELIEFS AND PRACTICES: PLANNING AND EVALUATION

In "Constructing Understanding" it is considered normal and proper for teachers to shape day-to-day curricular experiences. Although educators may be may be influenced by the demands of the community and state to set standards for curricular goals, only teachers could have enough knowledge of learners' interests and abilities to be the actual curriculum planners. Teachers shape the curricular process, determine standards for the students' work, and create the structure of classroom activity. Students can, however, have some latitude in choosing problems or designing projects that relate to curricular themes. Students negotiate with the teacher what the criteria are for selecting problems to study, and what kinds of evidence must be provided to demonstrate their learning.

Criteria for curricular planning become articulated in the classroom, and teachers and students refer to a framework of questions that—although not standardized—embody constructivist principles for learning: Is the chosen problem meaningful, important to the discipline and complex enough? Does it deal with the theme of the unit under study? Does it require original thinking and interpretation or is it simply fact-finding? Can this problem help you think about related problems? Will engaging with this problem result in the acquisition of contextualized facts, concepts, and principles that are fundamental to the theme under study?

Evaluation is based on the processes as well as the products of intellectual activity. Teachers note features of students' learning processes for the purposes of providing feedback but not necessarily for assignment of grades. Teachers also pay attention to how students regulate their own learning, the quality of collaboration with peers, and how well learners use available resources. This curricular culture does not dismiss the learning of certain relatively unambiguous facts, concepts, and skills that may be taught and assessed objectively, nor does constructivist philosophy absolutely preclude objective testing as one source of evidence of understanding. If used exclusively, however, objective testing provides only a limited picture of the scope of learner's knowledge.

Evaluation in the constructivist culture is based primarily on student performances or artifacts generated as a result of substantial effort. These performances or artifacts are rigorously judged against criteria that the students jointly develop with the teacher. The works are publicly displayed/performed so that all class members see a range of both quality and creativity in the projects. Students not only explain but also defend their work; they connect their presentations with the agreed-upon criteria for excellence and describe how their work reflects these criteria.

Over the course of the school year, students maintain portfolios that contain both typical and exemplary works. These works may be videotapes of performances, physical models, research reports, artistic renderings, or any other type of evidentiary "text." The portfolio can also contain objective tests, reflections by the students on their own progress, teacher observations and completed rubrics. Evaluation in the constructivist culture is rigorous and multidimensional. It is focused on the quality of the learner's understanding, its depth, and its flexible application to other relevant contexts. In short, it is congruent with other aspects of the culture such as the kinds of learning objectives promoted, the nature of the learning activities, the role of the student as autonomous learner, and role of the teacher as a facilitator of learning.

## DILEMMAS OF PRACTICE

One of the most difficult challenges in maintaining a culture of constructivism is the need for many teachers to reconceptualize their view of instruction. Models of how we were taught shape our behavior in powerful ways. Just as we use images and metaphors to make sense of concepts associated with subject matter and the teaching of subjects, practicing teachers use images to envision lessons in their classrooms, develop innovations, and plan for learning (Kennison, 1990). Even though teachers are exposed to instructional theory from teacher educators, when they finally enter the classroom they are more likely to be guided not by theory, but by the familiar images of what is "proper and possible" in this setting (Russell, 1993).

Teachers who choose to create a constructivist classroom culture reject many of the images linked to traditional education. However, they can be seduced by an oversimplified version of constructivism if they consider only the reactionary admonitions against the imagined evils of traditional instruction: "Don't tell students *anything*, let them construct their own knowledge!" Attached to this simplistic view is an attraction to an idealistic, approach to teaching that, on the surface, counters traditional authoritarian methods but nevertheless fails to translate into systematic, effective practice (Airasian & Walsh, 1997). If attempts at constructivism remain at such an uncritical level and are left unelaborated, resultant instruction can be chaotic as well as indefensible to peers, parents, and administrators. Constructivist instruction, then, is reduced to "anything goes." In its most sophisticated and effective forms, constructivism actually integrates both teacher-centered and student-centered models of instruction, has systematic and purposeful structure, and values rigorous evaluations of learning progress.

Constructivism redefines the roles of learners and teachers. It offers a new look at how we gather evidence of understanding and what it means to understand. Much of the responsibility for this framework of instruction resides with teachers, and unfortunately, the constructivist culture requires that they have an almost unrealistic degree of subject matter knowledge and pedagogical skill. Cremin (1961/1964) suggested that progressive pedagogies required "infinitely skilled teachers" who, historically, had never been prepared in sufficient numbers to effect change nationwide. Today's constructivist models of instruction appear to require just such high levels of skills in teachers. These skills include negotiating subject matter and evaluation criteria with students, maintaining a pro-social atmosphere in student groups, and coordinating the timetables of the various student projects. When we view the constructivist culture not as an idealized setting, but as people with real limitations trying to work together, we see the demands placed on the teacher as more than a dilemma—for many teachers they are a practical impossibility.

Providing a constructivist learning environment taxes the intellectual resources of even the most experienced teachers because they must question what types of instructional approaches, problems, and problem-solving environments will lead to a deep, albeit highly individualized, understanding of the subject matter. Teachers must also understand what a "problem" is, and how to help students select nontrivial problems that have some promise of guiding them to an understanding of the subject matter. And, if autonomy and personal relevance are important, teachers need to decide how far to go in letting students select their own problems.

Also, if students are to work collaboratively, teachers must have some understanding of cooperative learning theory and how productive, pro-social interactions can be fostered. Constructivism places great emphasis on students taking advantage of each others' knowledge and constructing shared meaning in collaboration with peers. The tentative nature of collaborative work among schoolchildren is a grave concern in this regard. Group work, collaborative or cooperative, is no instructional panacea. Students require training to function effectively in these groups. Even with training, many of the more capable students may be patently disinterested in helping their peers and unintended consequences of group work such as bickering, exclusion, and academic freeloading frequently affect learning (Slavin, 1995).

Features that make constructivist instruction effective also serve to unnerve teachers, especially new teachers who are concerned about their ability to manage the classroom. There is a common perception that the more quiet and orderly classrooms are, the more likely it is that learning is taking place. Constructivist classrooms, by contrast, are busy places—students generally work in groups and are engaged in activities of their own design. Students may need to move in and out of the classroom to access different resources such as computers, telephones, and materials found in media centers. Teachers are often uncomfortable with their apparent lack of control over students and they may be quite unwilling to allow these learning activities when guests, who may or may not be supporters of the constructivist culture, plan to visit the classroom.

Another dilemma is addressed by the simple question: What exactly do we want students to construct? In the world of ideas there are facts, concepts, principles, and the like. There are also skills ranging from single-digit multiplication to building consensus among peers or conducting inquiry. Further, there are habits of mind such as inquisitiveness and persistence in the face of adversity.

The issues around construction are the stuff from which critics of constructivism set up the straw man: "We don't want our children to construct that two plus two equals five," or "We don't want a poem or work of literature to mean just anything!" Admittedly, ideas fall along a continuum of openness or restriction with regard to "re-construction" by learners. However, in the constructivist culture, if a student asserts that the shortest distance between two points is not a straight line, it is an opportunity for the teacher to listen rather than to offer a knee-jerk response—does this student have a rationale for this? Perhaps the student is referring to two points that lie on a sphere rather than in two-dimensional space—in which case, the student is correct. Would students who believe that water freezes at five degrees Fahrenheit have some experiences that would lead them to believe this? Are they right under certain circumstances? If a student suggests that dictatorships are beneficent forms of governance, they must provide evidence and a framework of interpretation that supports these views; this testimony then would be held up to group scrutiny, allowing the teachers and other students to generate challenging evidence and arguments.

Finally, ideas in the academic disciplines will differ in the extent to which they can be taught through constructivist instruction. Mathematics has rule-based propositions that may be open to discovery via many experiential pathways. And it is equally important that students engage in sense-making experiences about why three times two equals six as well as engage in rote learning so that they can master the skills of speedy, accurate single-digit multiplication. Science and social studies learning also have characteristic skills, some of which are axiomatic and others that are open to more degrees of discovery and interpretation. Dealing with the "correctness" of constructions is an ongoing concern and the arguments have barely been introduced here, but reflection upon these epistemological and curricular issues helps educators develop a critical awareness of the relationships between disciplinary "truths" and learning, between knowledge and ways of knowing.

## CRITIQUE

This curricular culture offers a view of learners as capable agents of knowledge construction and emphasizes individual as well as socially constructed understandings of subject matter. These perspectives provide a set of values that shape decisions about the roles of teachers and learners. These values are derived, in part, from constructivist theories about learning, and elements of these learning theories are used as references for designing instruction. Curiously, these descriptive constructivist ideas about how students learn have not translated well into complementary designs for instruction. Although constructivism can be viewed as a philosophy that provides guidelines for learning such as promoting student autonomy, collaboration, and sense making, it remains difficult to represent constructivism as a single, coherent set of pedagogical methods. There is little consensus about whether any of the classroom conditions cited in this chapter are necessary or sufficient to help learners construct meaningful understandings, and critics may fairly characterize constructivism as little more than thematic, project-based learning.

Additionally, we must be concerned that the goals of education, articulated in national, state, and local standards, do not always seem compatible with the rich and diverse understandings of individual students. Students engaged in projects on photosynthesis, for example, may take radically different approaches to developing their knowledge of this phenomenon. One group of students may choose to focus on chemical reactions at the molecular level, while another group may examine how oxygen and carbon dioxide are exchanged between animals and plants on a global scale. These two groups will take disconcertingly divergent paths to understanding but the skilled teacher will ensure that each of the groups approaches its problems from multiple perspectives. That is, the group examining chemical reactions should be prompted to consider the effects of photosynthesis on the larger environment, and the students examining the implications of the global effects should be familiar with the biochemical bases for these macrophenomena. Artful guidance by the teacher notwithstanding, it can be unsettling to attempt to reconcile the language of "standards, benchmarks, and objectives" with the diversity of understandings that develop in a constructivist classroom.

The strongest criticism that can be leveled at constructivism as a culture is the assertion that it represents merely a set of guidelines for instruction and does not have import with regard to the larger issues of curriculum. There is, for example, no social vision promoted by this culture—therefore there is no concern for caring about others or for the environment, for combating oppression, or for making the world a better place. There are no incentives for learners in this culture to participate in the community or in the larger culture outside of school. Learners are given the intellectual tools to think effectively and autonomously, but there are no sustaining moral or social visions that members carry with them from this classroom culture. Constructivism also pays little attention to how politics and privilege affect meaning-making by learners; its pedagogy would clearly be richer and more transformative if students were compelled to consider the influences of race, class, and gender as they "construct" their own images of history, science, and literature (Rivera & Poplin, 1995).

Developing autonomous learners—who believe in their own powers as creators of knowledge—is a start for creating a society in which authority is never blindly followed and individuals' worldviews are not controlled by miseducative influences of peers and popular culture. Autonomy, however, does not automatically translate into community or a shared vision of a better society. In truth, the constructivist culture may be a means, but not an end.

## REFERENCES

Airasian, P., & Walsh, M. (1997). Constructivist cautions. *Phi Delta Kappan, 78*(6), 444–449.

Brown, J. S., Collins, A., & Duguid, P. (1989). Situated cognition and the culture of learning. *Educational Researcher, 18*, 32–42.

Bruner, J. (1996). *The culture of education.* Cambridge, MA: Harvard University Press.

Cobb, P. (1994). Where is the mind? Constructivist and sociocultural perspectives on mathematical development. *Educational Researcher, 23*(7), 13–20.

Cobb, P., & Yackel, E. (1996). Constructivist, emergent, and sociocultural perspectives in the context of developmental research. *Educational Psychologist 31* (3–4).

Cole, M. (1991). Conclusion. In L. B. Resnick, J. M. Levine, & S. D. Teasley (Eds.), *Perspectives on socially shared cognition* (pp. 398–417). Washington, DC: American Psychological Association.

Cremin, L. A. (1961/1964). *The transformation of the school: Progressivism in American education.* New York: Vintage.

Dewey, J. (1916). *Democracy and education.* New York: Macmillan.

Dewey, J. (1972). *The university school.* In J. A. Boydston (Ed.), *The Early Works of John Dewey* (p. 437). Carbondale, IL: Southern Illinois University Press.

Driver, R. (1981). Pupils' alternative frameworks in science. *European Journal of Science Education, 3*(1), 93–101.

Driver, R., & Easley, J. (1978). Pupils and paradigms: A review of literature related to concept development in adolescent science students. *Studies in Science Education, 5*, 61–84.

Duckworth, E. (1978). *The African primary science program: An evaluation and extended thoughts.* Grand Forks: North Dakota Study Group on Evaluation.

Duckworth, E. (1986). *Inventing density.* Grand Forks: North Dakota Study Group on Evaluation.

Duckworth, E. (1996). *The having of wonderful ideas and other essays on teaching and learning.* New York: Teachers College Press.

Edwards, C., Gandini, L., & Forman, G. (1996). Introduction. In C. Edwards, L. Gandini, & G. Forman (Eds.), *The hundred languages of children: The Reggio Emilia approach to early childhood education* (pp. 3218). Norwood, NJ: Ablex.

Forman, G. (1996). Multiple symbolization in the long jump project. In C. Edwards, L. Gandini, & G. Forman (Eds.), *The hundred languages of children: The Reggio Emilia approach to early childhood education* (pp. 171–188). Norwood, NJ: Ablex.

Hendley, B. (1986). *Dewey, Russell, Whitehead: Philosophers as educators*. Carbondale, IL: Southern Illinois University Press.

Kamii, C. (1984). Autonomy: The aim of education envisioned by Piaget. *Phi Delta Kappan, 65*(6), 410–415.

Kennison, C. (1990). *Enhancing teachers' professional learning: Relationships between school culture and elementary school teachers' beliefs, images and ways of knowing*. Unpublished specialist thesis, Florida State University, 1990.

Lebow, D. (1993). Constructivist values for instructional systems design: Five principles toward a new mindset. *Educational Research, Technology, and Development, 41*(3), 4–16.

Loeffler, M. H. (1992). Montessori and constructivism. In M. H. Loeffler (Ed.) *Montessori in contemporary culture* (pp. 101–113). Portsmouth, NH: Heinemann.

Loving, C. (1997). From the summit of truth to its slippery slopes: Science education's journey through positivist-postmodern territory. *American Educational Research Journal, 34*(3), 421–452.

Matthews, M. R. (1994). *Science teaching: The role of history and philosophy of science*. London: Routledge.

Montessori, M. (1967). *The absorbent mind*. New York: Holt, Rinehart & Winston.

Piaget, J. (1963). Cognitive development in children: Piaget. *Journal of Research in Science Teaching, 2*, 176–186.

Reynolds, R. E., Sinatra, G. M., & Jetton, T. L. (1996). Views of knowledge acquisition and representation: A continuum from experience centered to mind centered. *Educational Psychologist, 31*(2), 93–104.

Rivera, J., & Poplin, M. (1995). Multicultural, critical, feminine and constructive pedagogies seen through the lives of youth: A call for the revisioning of these and beyond: Toward a pedagogy for the next century. In C. E. Sleeter & P. L. McLaren (Eds.), *Multicultural education, critical pedagogy, and the politics of difference* (pp. 221–244). Albany: State University of New York Press.

Rogoff, B. (1990). *Apprenticeship in thinking*. New York: Oxford University Press.

Russell, T. (1993). Learning to teach science: Constructivism, reflection, and learning from experience. In K. Tobin (Ed.), *The practice of constructivism* (pp. 247–258). Hillsdale, NJ: Lawrence Erlbaum Associates.

Schommer, M. (1993). Comparisons of beliefs about the nature of knowledge and learning among postsecondary students. *Research in Higher Education, 34*(3), 355–369.

Slavin, R. E. (1995). *Cooperative learning*. Boston: Allyn & Bacon.

Tobin, K., & Tippins, D. (1993). Constructivism as a referent for teaching and learning. In K. Tobin (Ed.), *The practice of constructivism in science education* (pp. 3–21). Hillsdale, NJ: Lawrence Erlbaum Associates.

Von Glaserfeld, E. (1989). Cognition, construction of knowledge and teaching. *Synthese, 80*, 121–140.

Von Glaserfeld, E. (1993). Questions and answers about radical constructivism. In K. Tobin (Ed.), *The practice of constructivism in science education* (pp. 23–38). Hillsdale, NJ: Lawrence Erlbaum Associates.

Vygotsky, L. S. (1979). Consciousness as a problem in the psychology of behavior. *Soviet Psychology, 17*(4), 3–35.

Willis, J. (1995, November-December). A recursive, reflective instructional design model based on constructivist-interpretivist theory. *Educational Technology, 5*–22.

# 7

# Deliberating Democracy

**Edward R. Mikel**
*Antioch University Seattle*

*A democracy is more than a form of government; it is primarily a mode of associated living, of conjoint communicated experience.... Since a democratic society repudiates the principle of external authority, it must find a substitute in voluntary disposition and interest; these can be created only by education.*
— John Dewey, 1916, *Democracy and Education*

It is the second day of the new school year at Lookout Middle School, located in a working-class area of a midwestern city of nearly 200,000 people. An ethnically and racially mixed group of 58 sixth graders file into a double classroom, where they are greeted by their two teachers, Ms. Bryant and Ms. Reed. Both teachers are assigned to their respective departments: one is in language arts–social studies and the other in math–science. The students will be in this class for five four-hour block periods each week.

This is the first of four consecutive days of curriculum planning and organizing for the block. After attendance is taken and the usual random banter of early adolescents has subsided, Ms. Reed announces the next day's agenda and explains: "This year we will be doing something quite different with your—with our—curriculum in this language arts and social studies block. We won't start by trying to figure out what's language arts and what's social studies, we're going to concentrate on only what you are concerned about, what you think is important, and what everyone together thinks is important, too."

The organizing process is hardly spontaneous or ad hoc. It comprises a set of structured activities over four days intended to carve out and set in place the building blocks of a term-long curriculum, including a set of thematic areas of study and the substance of the first area of study: key learning activities, designated knowledge and skill outcomes, potential resources, and procedures for assessing the progress of students' learning and evaluating the curriculum.

The design and planning process starts with students individually and privately answering three organizing levels of questions in sequence: a) Who are you? What are you like? What are your interests, problems, needs? b) What questions or concerns do you have about yourself? and c) What questions or concerns do you have about the world you live in?

The sixth-graders' questions about their own lives are: "When will I die?" "Will I 'make it' in life?" "Will I achieve my goals?" "Would I be scared if I had to go to war?" "Am I really like what other people say I am?" Then, they have these questions about the world: "What will happen to the world (greenhouse effect, ozone, air pollution, rain forests, etc.)?" "Will there ever be world peace?" "Why do insane people have rights?" "Why do people hate blacks?" "Will prejudice ever end?" "Why do we use money?" "Why do we need a president?"

A central activity begins on the first day and lasts well into the second. Small groups record and compile individual responses to self and world questions; no one was compelled to share self questions or concerns. Ms. Reed and Ms. Bryant go from group to group, helping to facilitate the activity. Students chart the frequently asked questions, but note rare or unique ones as well. The activity continues with groups noting the convergence of self and world questions. Through deliberation and consensus, each group then names two or three "organizing centers" such as "Jobs, Money, Careers," "Death and Dying," "Living in the Future," "Environment and Health," "Conflict," and "Sex, Life, Genetics."

On day three, deliberations move from small groups to the whole class. With chart-paper listings of small groups' work posted around the double classroom, students need to decide upon one organizing center to use for the first unit and make suggestions for subsequent units. Students vote by raising their hands for as many ideas that they like. After the votes are cast, Ms. Reed excitedly announces, "We have our first unit—'Living in the Future!'"

Day three of planning ends and day four begins with another small-group activity: selecting initial self and world questions to be addressed that coincide with the first organizing center and developing a description of learning activities. Teachers and students also identify outcomes of knowledge and skills that should result from learning activities. They decide that it is important to have knowledge about current events and history, cultures, anatomy, health, statistics on population growth, and technology. They also choose to develop skills of critical thinking, research, writing, graphing, map reading, communication, and using computers.

Finally, students and teachers begin to establish a process to daily check on students' grasp of key ideas and understandings across the several activities of study. They further work to devise a means by which students can have a significant role in evaluating unfolding curriculum as well as their own learning goals and achievements.

These four days in the sixth-grade classroom illustrate defining elements of the democratic culture of curriculum: deliberation of curriculum design and democratic process in learning activities. This is a recreated account of what its originators call "integrative curriculum." Beyond the resolve to create interesting and significant learning experiences, the overriding intent of this curriculum is to "design the core of democratic education" (Beane, 1997; Brodhagen, 1995; Brodhagen, Weilbacher, & Beane, 1992). Education that allows students to understand and to experience the process of democratic decision making is at the core of this culture of curriculum.

## VISIONS

The culture "Deliberating Democracy" holds three principal visions that capture the form and spirit essential to what has been called strong or participatory democracy, a tradition that has struggled over time against the conventional, more restrictive, less inclusive, and more narrowly political–electoral versions: (a) democracy as animated by idealized values that together seek the well-being of all individuals within a vital and healthy community; (b) democracy as organized on shared authority and mutual responsibility; and (c) democracy as reliant upon knowledge that is open to alternative sources and ends.

Democracy is about decision-making in groups and the conditions of relationships, values, and activity structures that enable decision-making to be democratic. Democratic decision-making requires that all members of the group be significantly (ideally, equally) engaged in both the making of and abiding by decisions on matters affecting the group as a whole. Furthermore, decisions are to be made with full regard for the suitability and good effect of decisions on the lives and futures of all members.

Democracy invokes a moral imperative that permeates all our social arrangements and interactions—including life in schools, as Dewey argued in the words opening this chapter. It is experience directed toward a set of "idealized" values that "we must live and that must guide our life as a people" (Apple & Beane, 1995). The core values and principles of democracy together make up what may be seen as a complex of social, political, and moral "goods" for individuals and the community as a whole: freedom, autonomy, and pluralism, as well as equality, caring, and justice. Likewise,

> Democracy connotes wide-ranging liberty, including the freedom to decide one's own destiny. Democracy means social and civil equality and a rejection of discrimination and prejudice. Democracy embraces the notion of pluralism and cultural diversity. It welcomes a wide range of perspectives and lifestyles, moving different social groups toward peaceful coexistence or respectful integration. Democracy represents the ideal of a cohesive community of people living and working together and finding fair, nonviolent ways to reconcile conflicts. (Gastil, 1993, p. 5)

Underneath all layers of democratic participation, from routine daily life through society's momentous events, is what Dewey and others have called the "democratic faith." This is an unshakable faith in democracy as the best mode of social life, one that captures the full allegiance and dedication of all those who experience it. To hold this faith is also to believe in the inherent capacity and good will of all members to make their "experiment" in democracy work in best way humanly possible. Faith in fellow members of a democratic community keeps alive the critical vision of mutual responsibility and shared authority.

A democratic society may be seen as a "commonwealth" of "little publics," including even schools and classrooms (Dewey, 1916; Parker, 1996a). Little publics of several types—schools, churches, neighborhood associations, civic groups, recreational and sports clubs, business and political organizations—are nested within the larger realms of little publics of the same type, of related and distant types, and ultimately of larger national and global societies. Members of little publics can learn and practice the democratic arts of participation intensively within that primary community. But to ensure that society becomes and sustains itself as a commonwealth of democracy, members of all small publics must participate as fully as possible in the affairs of the larger society.

Within the democratic culture of curriculum, as Beyer (1994) claims, the continuing question is "how we foster more widely shared decision-making which diminishes inequalities of power and influence." Collaboration, in turn, cannot abide the naked exercise of power as standard practice, but depends on participants feeling and exercising responsibility toward one another.

Formal knowledge can serve as a cornerstone of this wider participation and, thus, of the commonwealth of democracy. Knowledge becomes at once a vital private and public holding. The pertinent vision is one of knowledge that is open to alternative sources and ends, just as any fully democratic project would be. Many writers have underscored the open and generative nature of learning and knowledge in the democratic culture of curriculum. Apple and Beane (1995), Beyer (1996), and Sehr (1997) point to such requisites as the "free flow of ideas," forums for public discussion to "create, clarify, and reevaluate positions and perspectives," opportunity and abilities to "locate relevant information, and to uncover multiple interpretations," habits of "critical reflection and analysis" by which to examine assumed reality conveyed in written, spoken, and image texts, and awareness of the complexities and interconnections of major public issues to each other past and present.

Knowledge provides a common ground, assuming neither a uniform nor monolithic shape that enforces a single "regime of truth." Indeed, it may encompass parts that are quite divergent, from origins quite diverse. Its unifying force lies in the evolving conversation it provokes and sustains, and the contingent and transitory moments of shared understanding it expresses.

In *Democracy and Education,* Dewey (1916) referred to three vital process of democracy: association, communication, and deliberation. Democratic association entails the conscious seeking out of the "numerous and varied interests" that lie behind actions—undertaken or contemplated. Democratic communication is, in Dewey's words, "vitally social or vitally shared" and allows each person—or primary affiliation group or local community—to experience the perspectives of others in their public spheres and, by that connection, to develop understanding and appreciation for that other's experience and understanding of the world. Democratic deliberation is the hallmark of democratic life. Just as full and free association imparts awareness of alternative paths and communication, deliberation ultimately charts the course mutually taken together. Deliberation may form the nucleus of decision-making, but democratic deliberation cannot exist apart from the daily practices, continuing relationships, and persisting values that inhere in communication and association as the warp and woof of democratic society.

## HISTORY

The notion that schools should become completely democratic cultures has made a very limited appearance in the history of American schooling. The traditional culture of schooling places the source of knowledge and authority within texts and teachers; there are few examples of children and adolescents fully participating in determining the course of their education as a deliberative body. The democratic concept of freedom is even somewhat dissimilar to the philosophy of many child-centered schools. What distinguishes this curricular culture is its sociopolitical emphasis upon the group process of deliberating the curriculum rather than individuals making choices that mainly affect their own course of study.

Although it is natural to assume that this curricular culture would adopt as its model the American political system, its history is rooted in a far more expansive form. The philosophical and political origins are in a broader, fuller concept of democracy and democratic experience, one far more reminiscent of the New England town meeting than representative government. Democratic educators reject the limited, representative form of democracy because it is "weak"—not strongly participatory.

Historically, there have been discourses about inequality (a primary fact of society throughout human history) that have informed the understandings within this curricular culture. All ventures in democracy have necessarily faced questions of the moral rightness of social and economic inequality, not to mention the unmistakable practical effects on public participation of substantial inequality among groups and individuals.

This has been an American problem as well. Various writers have questioned the norms and traditions of the American system of democracy, characterizing them as "weak" rather than "strong" (Barber, 1984), "protectionist" rather than "participatory" (Pateman, 1970), and "limited" instead of "inclusive" (Mansbridge, 1983).

As well, throughout history, there have existed fears of "pure" democracy. As Tarcov (1996) points out, the ancient Greek root of the term, rule by the *demos* does not translate as "rule by all" but, rather, "rule by the many"—the many being the poor or common people. To the extent that the *demos*, the many poor or common folk, may exercise rule in their narrow class self-interest, their rule becomes a very real threat to the unequal wealth, social privilege, and political influence held by aristocratic or other elite groups.

American political history also has been influenced by this fear. Sehr (1997) traces the origins of this "weak" and "nonparticipatory" system to the Federalist constitutional design and, further, to the preeminence of Hobbes and Locke in the heritage of Anglo-American political thought. The Federalist constitutional design was primarily intended to embody an "antipathy toward direct democracy." This design also provided for the formal guarantee of many fundamental freedoms such as those of religion, speech, and the press, and security against unrestricted government incursion into citizen's private lives. But the freedom of direct popular participation in government was also feared as a looming threat to individual liberties, particularly that liberty to acquire property and wealth. The exercise of this liberty in colonial times had led to quite dramatic inequalities in wealth and privilege and a system buttressed by a popular social ideology of unlimited opportunity for success as well as assumed "natural differences" in ability giving rise to the evident imbalances (Sehr, 1997).

This curricular culture owes much to the writings of John Dewey, who made conscious the relationship between schooling and democracy. Dewey's own theoretical formulation of democracy and education was intended to overcome what he termed the "either-or dualisms" formed out of oppositions between the ideas of ends and means, of individual and society, of child and curriculum—assumed to be fixed and absolute. What was critical for Dewey

(1938) was how present experience can engender the realization of "growth" in future experience. Where present experience does so, future experience becomes "deeper and more expansive" in quality. The developmental effects of present experience do not happen accidentally, of course, but through a deliberate "reconstruction" of the primary meaning of present experience.

The reconstruction of experience for true individual and collective growth can happen, in Dewey's view, only under certain social arrangements—those characteristic of what has been previously described as "strong" democracy. To be sure, the reconstruction of experience for growth does, and indeed must, occur in all social spheres, including schools, but democratic arrangements must be sufficient to permit an authentic personal and collective reconstruction of experience for further growth and heightened democracy.

In spite of common values and beliefs, democratic progressivism as an educational movement—over its historical course and in its contemporary expressions—itself exhibits a clear tension between alternatives taken to realize the hope of education for democracy. Carlson (1997) characterizes this tension as existing between "two overlapping but distinct" currents of thought and practice: "democratic pragmatism" and "social reconstructionism" (that we, in this book, consider as separate but related curricular cultures). Carlson notes that, while offering decidedly alternative approaches to the democratic project in public education, the two find common roots in Dewey's writings and practice.

Democratic pragmatism and social reconstructionism have adopted independent, though intersecting paths (Carlson, 1997). In the former, participation primarily means active engagement and anticipates emerging forms of community that may become quite novel. In the latter, participation primarily means commitment to expected new forms of community that are radical departures from what is presently known. In short, there are opposing perspectives in the two projects that have led to quite substantial differences in their actual implementation. Both promote the freedom to participate directly and fully in public life. But the pragmatists presume that ends will be determined in the course of examining positions and circumstances; the reconstructionists presume that positions will be determined in the course of examining ends and circumstances.

Despite schooling's often stated goal to teach about American democracy, it is difficult to find any clear historical examples of schools and teachers that have attempted education aimed at strong democracy and using the means of full, direct participation of all involved. For these examples, it is necessary to look at a loosely connected array of initiatives within the democratic wings of the educational progressivism movement, from approximately 1880 to 1940 (Carlson, 1997; Cremin, 1961; Reese, 1986). However, a number of important advocacy projects, school and classroom based efforts at change, and theoretical writings did press for an education governed by such principles as freedom for public participation, direct self-governance, social and political mutuality, and just and caring community (Beane & Apple, 1995; Carlson, 1997; Darling-Hammond, 1996; Parker, 1996a).

The progressive commitment to democratic education and curriculum stretched into the 1960s, a time when the federal role in promoting new directions in schooling blossomed. Admittedly, it has stayed a minority concern among change projects over the last three decades—when federal and state monies and mandates have supplied the highest octane fuel for school change and reform. Yet democratic curriculum and schooling remain the aim of a dedicated number of school people, activist parents and community members, professors, consultants, and developers. Democratic education also flourishes in classrooms and schools influenced by the curriculum models developed by Beane and Brodhagen and in alternative private and public schools that endorse the democratic process as the most important aspect of learning.

The idea of democratic education also has been encouraged through sharing ideas and support through journals, newspapers, and networks. These resources have been very helpful to democratic educators: Public Education Information Network, the urban education journal *ReThinking Schools,* the magazine *Democracy and Education* (published by the Institute for Democracy in Education), and the newsletter *Action for Better Schools* (published by the National Coalition of Education Activists). Such exchange of ideas and support have nurtured and sustained those who have kept the democratic vision alive.

## BELIEFS AND PRACTICES: LEARNERS AND TEACHERS

As a Deweyan "laboratory of democracy," the classroom can approach the model of an ideal democratic small group (Gastil, 1993). Such groups are relatively sovereign over the conduct of their own affairs and work to distribute authority equally among all members. Even in the best of circumstances, of course, classrooms can only approximate democratic small groups in this sense. They are highly subject to the direction of legally authorized boards and officials. Teachers have superordinate standing as "citizens" of the classroom community, and rightly so, by virtue of their being adults, their professional qualifications, and their status as the agents of the overseeing school authority. Yet even within this circumscribed democracy, authority and relationships can be significantly altered from the norm. Students can take on the active role of "citizen" of the classroom community, exercising explicit determination over the substance and processes of learning for their benefit and that of their fellows at the same time.

Power to determine what constitutes meaningful learning is redistributed to be more equal among teacher and learners, and the roles of teacher and learner are not so rigidly distinguished. This assumption of shared authority reflects a primary "democratic faith" in the individual and collective capacity of all people to create possibilities for resolving problems and achieving commitments affecting the community as a whole.

How is this shared authority exercised? The short answer is, *in everything*. Whereas it can be said that even in classrooms that would not be considered democratic, teachers will negotiate some learning procedures (e.g., choices of activities), in the democratic curricular culture the most crucial issues of learning is the determination of content; it is not assumed that the teacher or an external authority has the right to make this decision.

As is evident in the earlier example of integrative curriculum, determination of the substance of learning takes a strongly democratic character beginning with the primary experience of the learner and moving out toward the "funded knowledge" and other expected outcomes of the official curriculum. From the original questions and concerns put forth by learners come the constituents of learning: the overarching themes and component questions, topics and particulars of study, and the vocabulary and methods for inquiry. These are "negotiated" against official mandates from school, district, and state authorities, but hold first importance.

Openness in knowledge and learning are vital to the democratic curriculum culture. Not all the constituents of an area of knowledge and skill that may be learned must be fully open to collective determination, but a substantial number of them must be open to determination—in respect to major units of study and on a continuing basis—for the culture of curriculum to count as democratic.

In none of its areas, academic or social, does a democratic curriculum expect all students to arrive at the same learning in the same way. Much of what goes on in a democratic curriculum is comprised of distinct and occasionally quite dissimilar learnings of individual students and small workgroups. Yet it is taken for granted that from all these efforts together, from the different paths and resources, a core of shared learning will emerge and be expected of everyone. Students will be responsible to each other and to the teacher as the legally and morally responsible adult to help create this common core of learning and to come to know it well. They will also take away from their efforts some things they have learned deeply and enduringly that their peers have not.

An example of how democratic curriculum-making depends on the quality of relationships between teacher and learners and among learners is provided by MacKay's (1997) essay about "nurturing dialogue and negotiation in the primary classroom." In the spirit of the democratic culture of curriculum, MacKay attempted to make a radical departure from her approach to curriculum in prior years, an approach that she considered "child-centered," but, in fact, she realized, had neither centered control in the children as individuals nor in them as members of a classroom learning community. She reflected on her practice:

My classroom was organized around areas for math, reading, writing, art, science, blocks, and dramatic play. We sat in circles. I let the children talk. I went home at night and spent hours cleverly connecting thematic units. If we were studying frogs, we read frog books, sang frog songs, did frog math, made frog art, wrote frog stories, and observed real frogs, until we completed the "What We Have Learned About Frogs" on our KWL chart and moved on to our next topic. Slowly, painfully, this year I realized that by organizing and connecting everything we did for them, I was denying the children opportunities to work in ways they were perfectly capable of working. Even if the idea for the frog theme had been generated by the children's genuine interest in frogs, I had taken away any hope for a true democratic experience by proceeding to make all the plans for their work—denying them the opportunity to participate meaningfully in the decisions that would affect their learning. (p. 20)

It is clear that originally MacKay skirted around the possibility of her children significantly composing their own learning. They had negligible control over the ideas and questions of interest, methods, and objects of study. She did not take the democratic teacher's role of facilitation, guidance, support and encouragement, coordination, and final arbitration; nor she did not allow her children to play the defining elements of this role for themselves and for their peers.

Ultimately, in MacKay's account, she cast aside the "false choices" she had given her children in favor of authentic choices over learning they could make for themselves—as individuals and with each other. Each child's learning was to find its way into a place within the nexus of what the class was learning as a whole—becoming ultimately this classroom community's shared core of knowledge. Growing up in support of this open-ended determination of curriculum was an infrastructure MacKay referred to as an "arrayed repertory" of resources offering many possibilities. The repertory included:

all the available materials at any of the areas in the room or in the school, ideas born from the children's stories or other literature, and also any ideas or materials the children brought from home. It remained important for me to help the children make connections with each other.... I began to perceive group activities as opportunities to expand the group's repertory instead of opportunities for me to inject my own thematic agenda.... We focused as a whole group on tools which would expand the available repertory and enhance the children's individually chosen areas of work. (p. 22)

MacKay also found ways "in which to problematize and question those [personal] choices together" so that they became the basis of the curriculum.

Democratizing the curriculum meant to "truly negotiate the curriculum with the children" and by the "children among themselves." MacKay concluded that the "patterns of our relationships" around all learning and "reflecting upon those relationships over time" became "the very stuff of the curriculum." And "our fates [were] bound together in dialogue." The teacher thus becomes, as Kelly (1994) has termed it, a "catalyst for collaboration."

The relationships of democratic association MacKay created for her children fostered their growth as mutually responsible learners; they were responsible to themselves to find a primary course of personally significant learning and to assist the meaningful learning of others. Through this reciprocal engagement, points of intersection and common focus were discovered, and the class together fashioned a core of shared knowledge.

The force of root values and principles in the democratic culture of curriculum decisively affects the character of learning for individuals and the entire classroom community. Teachers and students alike are deeply engaged together in the enterprise of seeking to discover, understand, and create. They aim to employ their learning in the service of further knowledge and appreciation, creative expression, and worthy action in human society, the living world, and the physical domain.

## BELIEFS AND PRACTICES: CONTENT AND CONTEXT

All the preceding examples in this chapter show in one way or another how democratic curriculum moves beyond the boundaries of the usual school subject areas into the sort of dynamic and varied inquiry undertaken in the formal disciplines of knowledge. As Beane (1997) points out, the school subjects are "institutionally based representations of disciplines" that "deal with a boundaried selection of what is already known within them" (p. 39). The disciplines assume a particular lens (or analytic orientation) on the world and favor certain investigatory techniques by which to interpret phenomena. Yet within these disciplines, the range of specific topics addressed, questions posed, and methods employed is generally quite wide and their boundaries of disciplined inquiry are quite fluid; thus, heightening the curriculum's democratic potential because of the freedom of inquiry and the multifaceted nature of knowledge.

Many of the most salient instances of the democratic culture of curriculum are from the social studies and humanities, or from integrated curriculum studies. This is not surprising in view of the primary orientation of this culture to the political and social dimensions of knowledge. Studies of the social world are thus natural candidates for this curriculum, perhaps focused on the activity of making knowledge within a community of scholars or lay people.

The Center for Study of Responsive Law offers the curriculum, *Civics for Democracy: A Journey for Teachers and Students* (Isaac, 1992). The curriculum intends to bridge "the gap between classroom and community experience" so that students may become—in the present and the future—"skilled citizens" who practice civics to "overcome apathy, ignorance, greed, or abuses of power in society at all levels." "Participatory civics for democracy requires knowledge of history, understanding of civic rights and strategies, and sharing in a growing civil culture of regular participation" (p. v). *Civics for Democracy* provides stories of students who have worked for positive change and citizen movements: civil rights, labor, women's, consumer, and environmental movements. Also included are descriptions of the techniques of participation: direct actions, citizen lobbying, action in the courts, ballot initiatives, and uses of the media. Finally, possible activities for students to undertake in their schools or communities are sketched out. The concept of civic participation assumed in this curricular content obliges all citizens to work to create conditions for association, communication, and commitment that foster open, inclusive, responsive, and fair deliberation crucial to a vital democracy.

In addition, historical events may offer rich opportunities to consider the nature of democracy. As a case in point, the democratic curriculum would study the American Civil War as a period of intense struggle over the course of society and governance—testing the "great experiment" in democracy. It is a crystalline case for curriculum to come to grips with the perpetual controversies of democracy expressed in conflicts great and small.

Central topics in the democratic curriculum, such as the Civil War, are well served by democratic deliberation because they require careful gathering or generation of knowledge, thorough explanation, and insightful interpretation. As topics are pursued in that manner, a fund of knowledge will reveal itself in numerous ways: how a student frames a problem, searches for related information, uses reference materials and data bases, seeks diverse viewpoints, judges the strength of arguments, interprets primary documents, adjudicates competing interpretations, creates arguments, and weighs alternative course of action (Parker, 1997).

Gerzon (1997) argues that, indeed, conflict is at the heart of democracy. Conflict gives democracy its vital pulse, albeit a pulse that can race out of control. The core challenge of citizenship, according to Gerzon, is learning to engage well in conflict. He believes that the most controversial issues for the American school curriculum—such as sex education, creationism, multicultural literature., school prayer, and the religious content of holiday music concerts—can become appropriate topics for study.

Accordingly, Parker (1997) views the school as an unsurpassed forum for providing opportunity both to learn democratically and to discover how to live democratically. There are many classroom and schoolwide issues that call for community decisions: rules of conduct, administrative and logistical matters, allocation of resources to extracurricular activities. How can these decisions best be made? Parker calls for developing what he terms the "deliberative arts" of democracy. Among these arts are the many facets of joint problem-solving—listening as well as talking, grasping others' points of view, and using the common space to forge positions with others rather than using it only as a platform for expressing opinions (p. 32).

Nonetheless, many teachers have substantially democratized curricula in the sciences, mathematics, and technology, and have employed content material from trade books, news sources, and historical documents (Beyer, 1996b; Sehr, 1997; Wood, 1992). A school can choose to both open the math, science, and technology courses more to the activity of the related disciplines, to applications to the everyday world by trained professionals and practitioners, and to the experience of nonspecialists with mathematical, scientific, and technological knowledge and skills.

We imagine a scenario that demonstrates the richness of a democratic curriculum in mathematics, sciences, and technology: the math curriculum would encompass a rich core of knowledge, including accounts of major historical developments in the ways in which people have used mathematics. Teachers would encourage understanding that knowledge is neither static nor uncontested by showing how fresh discoveries in the world of mathematics are now commonplace—such as the invention of non-Euclidean geometry, differential calculus, and discrete analysis.

Their colleagues in the sciences could explore similar achievements, such as Copernican astronomy, quantum theory and relativity. In addition, teachers would emphasize contemporary theoretical debates that are fueled by continuing research discoveries, such as whether plants can produce food in the absence of light, if life exists on Mars, and how likely it is that dinosaurs were warm-blooded.

All math, science, and technology courses would also invest a good deal of time introducing students to applications of this knowledge by non–research professionals and technical specialists: people like engineers, accountants and actuaries, forensic chemists, environmental analysts, pollsters, transportation planners, and others. Finally, the courses would offer a number of detailed cases on the use and non-use, understanding and misunderstanding of mathematical, scientific, and technological principles in the every day lives of people who are professionals or technical specialists in these areas.

Content cannot be considered apart from process. In democratic curriculum, it is important for all students to be aware of what others are doing; that, in other words, there is full (democratic) communication among the projects as they develop. Students can learn from each other and from the teacher, getting needed advice on how to proceed, information about useful resources, and suggestions on how they might best represent and convey what they had learned through their models, writings, and artifacts. It's also very important to note that all learners have equal opportunity to participate in all forms of learning: model-building, fact-finding, analyses, and summary discussions and writings, although individuals may concentrate on one or several these activities.

The learning in which they engage is comprehensive, thorough, and insightful because it springs from and is organized around powerful questions, issues, and problems meaningful to all, singly and collectively. Because this is a community whose members are invested in learning, many resources, methods, and perspectives are brought to bear: Through the core of shared knowledge held by the whole classroom community and the unique personal achievements of each individual, what is gained is so much the richer and deeper.

In an important sense, democratic knowledge and curriculum arise in the free, open, inclusive, and responsive communication that is the lifeblood of democratic society. In the democratic culture of curriculum such communication into, within, and across the formal disciplines and corresponding realms of the everyday social world makes possible a full exchange of ideas, imagination, understanding, and purpose. Knowledge rises, extends, changes direction, and falls under the force of evolving consciousness and occasionally transformed understanding.

The content of learning is also shaped by the interpretive context in which it occurs, and often has the reciprocal effect of reshaping that context in ways that participants might not have envisioned. Democratizing curriculum and education means, in its broadest sense, connecting learning in the classroom with the use of knowledge in settings near and far. It is in this sense of a democratic curriculum that Kelly (1997) suggests the descriptors, "outreach-oriented" and "connectionist." By the former term, Kelly means an advocacy of "school learning which is authentic; that is, learning which, in a disciplined way, addresses problems and an audience beyond the school." By the latter, he refers to teaching and learning that is "multi-dimensional, interdisciplinary, context-conscious. This relational vision of teaching and learning integrates the head, the heart, and the hands" (p. 8).

Among the intended areas of learning in a curriculum may be that of the social life of the classroom itself. Teachers consider the analysis of classroom relationships and values an important goal. To this end, they use classroom meetings, the definition of rules and expectations, peer mediation of conflict and adjudication of disputes, and, not infrequently, the creation of a classroom constitution. Of greatest concern is how such classroom regularities as decision-making procedures, status systems, affective relationships, and social control processes presently shape or could possibly influence the varieties of experience and learning that might arise, especially through the curriculum (Beyer, 1996; Goodman, 1992; VanSickle, 1983).

Formal education has long been acknowledged as preparing young people for life beyond the school, in the present and in the future as young people become adult workers, community members, heads of families, and citizens. In the Deweyan view of education, learning as the reconstruction of experience—especially those experiences that relate to future adult roles—cannot take place outside of a shaping context of social arrangements and activity. The democratic culture of curriculum, therefore, takes foremost a social and political stance to learning in classrooms and schools and in all matters of curriculum.

## BELIEFS AND PRACTICES:
## PLANNING AND EVALUATION

It is not unreasonable to consider planning and evaluation the center of the democratic culture of curriculum. This curricular culture assumes no preeminent content but considers planning as a process at the heart of its functioning. Democratic curriculum is constantly in a state of formation; knowledge and learning are continuously reconstituted out of the deliberations that constitute planning and evaluation.

Deliberation is democratic to the extent its participants associate freely and widely and communicate openly and fully. Participants are those individuals who are affected by these deliberations, primarily the teachers and students. Ideally, all participants would have equal power and resources, and indirect participants, (e.g., teachers' aides, administrators, community members), have some claims on the deliberative process. To be sure, there is a legitimate differentiation in authority between teachers and students, and often indirect participants are insufficiently recognized. The process, therefore, must be constantly monitored and calibrated to avoid imbalances and neglect.

Democratic deliberation turns on the shifting balance of mutuality and diversity. Participants assume some irreducible differences and conflicts but have faith that other participants will do their best to find common ground. Above all, planning and evaluation within a democratic culture of curriculum must be entirely open and inclusive, deeply creative as well as critically-minded, and ever alert to those emerging intersections of value and interest that might grow into commonalities of thought and action.

Teachers are, by legal authority and professional training, more than strictly equal partners in planning and evaluating the curriculum. In addition to their own interests and judgments about the direction and content of the curriculum, they must represent the policies and voices of those in the school organization and surrounding community who have a stake in the curriculum.

Curriculum planning might involve many stakeholders in a deliberative process that widens the concept of planning from a linear model of goals and objectives to broad and inclusive discourse about the nature of knowledge, instruction, and community. A multitude of questions could be asked about, for example, an elementary language arts curriculum: What is good literature? What proportion of material should come from each of the major literary genres, for example or, better—how much from the traditionally under-represented or non-Western traditions? Should curriculum be chosen for breath of coverage or for depth? Should complete sources be utilized rather than excerpts? What should be the roles of direct instruction, experiential activities, community-based learning, and direct contact with working authors? How much planning should be oriented to the families and communities the school serves? Is it important to know about the languages other than English spoken there, and the various religious, social, family, and aesthetic values and practices observed? Is it important to ensure that the children's developing literacy is directed to understanding the roots and possible resolution of issues before the local community? Do children who come with different strengths need to be treated differently in respect to their learning—assisted or guided more than others at some times or in some areas?

Students can be key players in curriculum planning and also work with the larger community. Wigginton (1988) discusses the role of students in planning and producing a magazine for a Foxfire project involving the use of the community as a primary source for their learning and of the content represented in the final products. Such democratic curriculum planning takes into consideration understanding of the community's needs and interests. What Wigginton claims for Foxfire projects would be true in principle for many forms of democratic, community-based learning, service learning, action or advocacy learning, community cultural or historical studies.

Students not only can participate meaningfully in planning the curriculum, but also in conducting evaluation of their own learning and that of peers. Brodhagen (1995) emphasizes: the importance of students setting goals for their learning over both the short and long term; frequent checks by teachers of their classes' ongoing progress; unit and quarterly reviews of the quality and effectiveness of activities undertaken by students and teachers; the roles to be played by students, teachers, parents; and the collaborative assessment of each student's achievements over the designated grading periods. VanSickle (1983) notes the positive effect on classrooms when students not only instruct and advise one another, but also when they participate in formative evaluations of one another's success in academic and social realms, such as constructive participation.

Evaluation seeks to confirm that students are fulfilling their dual responsibility of engaging in the path of most meaningful personal learning and making their learning available to their peers. In this way, a common core of learning and knowledge is forged, but it does not constrain substantial learning of a strongly personal nature. In the democratic culture of curriculum, evaluation and planning are situated right in the midst of the classroom locale: the "small public," so to speak, that the classroom constitutes. Evaluation is focused first, therefore, on learning and the learner, but is broad enough to encompass other curriculum matters. Multiple methods and focuses used in authentic and effective evaluation of student learning can be expanded upon to address specific curricular questions concerning teaching and teachers, content and resources, and context and environment (Neill, et al., n.d.).

For example, a teacher in a traditional subject area (not an integrated, fluid curriculum) would invite students to play a key role in determining class activities, to continue to evaluate these activities, to negotiate the pace of moving through the text, and to decide how much homework was needed in order to help all students to be successful.

As the democratic culture of curriculum gives such great importance to participatory governance and collaborative decision-making at all times, planning and evaluation assume a pivotal role: to set the conditions under which the other defining beliefs and practices concerning teachers, learners, content, and context are enacted. The reciprocal nature of planning and evaluation is critical as well. Certainly, evaluation is essential to understanding how well we have done what we set out to do, but good planning is necessary to imagine what we might do in future efforts from what we have learned from our past and present.

## DILEMMAS OF PRACTICE

Teachers wishing to build a democratic culture of curriculum in their classrooms face a number of dilemmas or predicaments. Schools have not generally been showcases of, or laboratories for, democratic practice; there are numerous formidable institutional forces in place to counter or undercut teachers' attempts to become strongly democratic in the practice of curriculum. Not the least among these is the typically hierarchical nature of decision-making in schools. In many senses, teachers are considered simply to be agents of higher seats of authority. It is not within teachers' purview, according to this ideology, to make significant decisions about curriculum, either independently or in concert with their students—or, for that matter, with any other stakeholders or interested parties such as colleagues, parents, or community members. So the first constraint is the predominant institutional culture of official authority over curriculum.

For teachers who wish to push the current boundaries of authority in order to become more democratic, there is the reality of what students have come to expect about the way schooling is supposed to operate. The longer students have been in school, the more likely they are to have adopted the conventional beliefs and assumptions about authority over the curriculum. Students can become quite suspicious when offered the possibility to participate in a significant democratic experiment in their classroom. There is need to span the wide and deep chasm between the authority usually attached to the teacher's role compared with that of the students'. It is easy for teachers, especially when they are new to classroom democracy, to unintentionally subvert democratic principles via habits that die hard and are often difficult even to recognize. A process of extensive re-socialization is generally necessary for teachers and students alike.

Putting democracy into practice requires time and energy that may appear to be irrelevant or wasted to the "real" task at hand. The premium placed on deliberation and collective decision-making in the democratic culture of curriculum can seem, even to the teacher, to be more than is really needed. And, in fact, a truly thorny dilemma for teachers is to find a viable balance between planning and evaluation activities and study activities. To be sure, there is a tripartite responsibility to be fulfilled: individuals to self, the classroom group to the core knowledge of its community, all participants to the available knowledge and perspectives of the larger world—especially those likely to be less visible or less acknowledged.

Beyer and Liston (1996) and Parker (1996b) point to the need to locate deliberations over curriculum planning and evaluation in a broad context of a range of stakeholders who are invested in the breadth and quality of education that young people receive. It is the power of such deliberations, the authors argue, that gives rise to an education that is developmentally appropriate, morally sensitive, culturally relevant, academically rich, and linked to what lies beyond the school. But these authors also acknowledge the great difficulty and usual failure to bring representatives of stakeholder groups into serious curriculum deliberations. Teachers must help build curriculum from what matters to young people and to all these constituencies. They must exercise, as well, their own commitments and sense of responsibility to the multiple approaches to knowledge in and beyond the academic world and to the knowledge held within society's many communities and cultures.

All this coordination of experience, interest, and purpose depends upon sustained and ordered interaction conducted in the democratic spirit as well as by democratic precepts. Learning how to balance and allocate time, especially how to invest heavily in the earliest phase of a curriculum development in order to reap increased learning later, is a teaching skill that is acquired only with arduous experience.

Teachers who manage to forge democratic curricula for their classrooms often stand out as rather peculiar in their schools. If not alone—and it has proven important for teachers not to feel or be alone in their endeavor—teachers who work democratically frequently see themselves in a decided minority in their schools. They may be the object of spoken or silent resentment or dismissal for their natural "popularity" with students or thought somewhat irresponsible for their concern with students' ideas, intentions, and capability for self-direction. Democratic teachers often find themselves asking for resources beyond textbooks, opportunities to modify the daily schedule, and support to move learning into settings outside their classrooms. For their expansive attitudes toward alternative sources, modes, instruments, and ends of learning that a democratic curriculum may engender, teachers should be prepared to face the consequences of traditionally more narrow-minded and hierarchical institutions.

## CRITIQUE

The democratic curriculum of culture is oriented to the political and social dimensions of the educational process and invites critique that focuses on purposes or aspects of schooling that are seen as undervalued in the democratic culture. Such critique would argue that no classroom can sufficiently approach the conditions of a viable small-group democracy; the classroom can have relatively little autonomy or sovereignty and does not distribute authority among its members nearly equally enough. As a result, in trying to establish a local community of knowledge and learning, this curricular culture can be charged with failing to nurture student and teacher individuality and not introducing students enough to those specialized areas of knowledge that comprise the highest levels of formal education. Finally, the democratic culture may be seen as too feeble to seriously challenge the conditions of inequality or injustice in a society whose force continually corrodes those insufficient attempts to remedy them.

It is certainly true that the classroom can never be anything close to a sovereign small-group democracy. Teachers have significant ascribed and legal authority over students. Perhaps more important, the curriculum is not really an open proposal. Through tests, guidelines, specification of textbooks and other resources, and direct oversight, the curriculum of any classroom will be substantially determined; at best, the mandated curriculum will be diluted, amended, or deflected in certain of its components. Given the reality of schools (high teacher–student ratios, steep workloads, limited resources), it is practically impossible for the democratic curriculum to validly accomplish it primary aims: significant individual preference in learning, critical awareness of the larger world, and shared participation in a core of highly valued knowledge.

In fact, the latter aim is best sought through a curricular culture, the orientation of which is not one so broad or so nonacademic as the democratic culture. The democratic culture, in its broadest reach, serves the philosophy of general education. In its narrower terms, the culture may serve a comprehensive social studies or humanities program. But it cannot begin to address induction into the specialized bodies of knowledge and communities of scholars that is concern of formal education at its most advanced levels. Students who participate in the democratic culture may be quite ill-equipped to take their studies further.

On another score, by presuming that the curriculum should revolve around a constructed core of shared knowledge, the democratic culture forfeits the opportunity to stimulate authentic individual growth, especially of learners, but not inconsequentially for teachers either. The goal of optimizing personal development cannot coexist with any pretense toward a curriculum which requires something of everyone in common.

Finally, any attempt at local democracy will surely wither in the face of anti-democratic forces—overt and implicit, great and small—from the larger society that also permeates the institution of schooling. By far, the better lessons in democracy would be had by systematic inquiry into the conditions of inequality, injustice, and exclusive privilege that undermine attempts at strong democracy in any locale or at any level of contemporary society. While classroom and school social conditions and those of the surrounding community may prompt learning and even supply cases in point for study of the concrete failings of democracy in everyday institutions, it would be highly self-deceptive to believe that any classroom could reinvent itself so thoroughly as to become an example of democracy worth studying.

In sum, the role of the classroom is to provide a venue for learning about the most noble trials of democracy, wherever and whenever they have existed, and to intelligently uncover the shortfalls of modern institutions that only pretend democracy. It is hardly the responsibility or the potential of classrooms to become micro-democracies.

## REFERENCES

Apple, M., & Beane, J. (Eds.). (1995). *Democratic schools.* Alexandria, VA: Association for Supervision and Curriculum Development.

Barber, B. (1984). *Strong democracy.* Los Angeles: University of California Press.

Bastian, A., Fruchter, N., Gittell, M., Greer, C., & Haskins, K. (1985). *Choosing equality: The case for democratic schooling.* Philadelphia: Temple University Press.

Beane, J. (1997). *Curriculum integration: Designing the core of democratic education.* New York: Teachers College Press.

Beane, J., & Apple, M. (1995). The case for democratic schools. In M. Apple & J. Beane (Eds.), *Democratic schools* (pp. 1–25). Alexandria, VA: Association for Supervision and Curriculum Development.

Beyer, L. (1994). The curriculum, social context, and "political correctness." *Journal of General Education, 42*(3), 1–31.

Beyer, L. (1996a). Introduction: The meanings of critical teacher preparation. In L. Beyer (Ed.), *Creating democratic classrooms: The struggle to integrate theory and practice* (pp. 1–26.). New York: Teachers College Press.

Beyer, L. (Ed.). (1996b). *Creating democratic classrooms: The struggle to integrate theory and practice.* New York: Teachers College Press.

Beyer, L., & Liston, D. (1996). *Curriculum in conflict: Social visions, educational agendas, and progressive school reform.* New York: Teachers College Press.

Brodhagen, B. (1995). The situation made us special. In M. Apple & J. Beane (Eds.), *Democratic schools* (pp. 83–100). Alexandria, VA: Association for Supervision and Curriculum Development.

Brodhagen, B., Weilbacher, G., & Beane, J. (1992). Living in the future. *Dissemination Services on the Middle Grades, 23*(9), 1–6.

Carlson, D. (1997). *Making progress: Education and culture in new times.* New York: Teachers College Press.

Cremin, L. (1961). *The transformation of the school: Progressivism in American education, 1876–1957.* New York: Vintage.

Darling-Hammond, L. (1996). The right to learn and the advancement of teaching: Research, policy, and practice for democratic education. *Educational Researcher, 25*(6), 5–17.

Dewey, J. (1916/1966). *Democracy and education.* New York: Free Press.

Dewey, J. (1938). *Experience and education.* Bloomington, IN: Kappa Delta Pi.

Gastil, J. (1993). *Democracy in small groups: Participation, decision making, and communication.* Philadelphia: New Society.

Gerzon, M. (1997). Teaching democracy by doing it. *Educational Leadership, 54*(5), 6–11.

Gibboney, R. (1994). *The stone trumpet.* Albany: State University of New York Press.

Goodman, J. (1992). *Elementary schooling for critical democracy.* Albany: State University of New York Press.

Isaac, K. (1992). *Civics for democracy: A Journey for Teachers and Students.* Washington, DC: Essential Books.

Kelly, T. (1994). Democratic empowerment and secondary teacher education. In J. Novak (Ed.), *Democratic teacher education: Programs, processes, problems, and prospects.* Albany: State University of New York Press.

Kelly, T. (1997). Perspectives on democratic pedagogy and selected educational innovations. *Democracy and Education, 11*(3), 7–12.

MacKay, S. (1997). Planting the seeds for a critical pedagogy by nurturing dialogue and negotiation in the primary classroom. *Democracy and Education, 11*(3), *18–31.*

Mansbridge, J. (1983). *Beyond adversary democracy.* Chicago: University of Chicago Press.

Neill, M., Bursh, P., Schaeffer, B., Thall, C., Yohe, M., & Zappardino, P. (undated). *Implementing performance assessments: A guide to classroom, school, and system reform.* Cambridge, MA: The National Center for Fair & Open Testing.

O'Connor, T. (1993). Looking backward to look forward. *Democracy and Education, 8*(2), 9–16.

Parker, W. (1996a). Introduction: Schools as laboratories of democracy. In W. Parker (Ed.), *Educating the democratic mind* (pp. 83–100). Albany: State University of New York Press.

Parker, W. (1996b). Curriculum for democracy. In R. Soder (Ed.), *Democracy, education, and the schools.* San Francisco: Jossey-Bass.

Parker, W. (1997). The art of deliberation. *Educational Leadership, 54*(5), 18–21.

Pateman, C. (1970). *Participation and democratic theory.* Cambridge: Cambridge University Press.

Public Education Information Network (1985). *Equity and excellence: Toward an agenda for school reform.* St. Louis: PEIN.

Reese, W. (1986). *Power and the promise of school reform.* Boston: Routledge & Kegan Paul.

Sehr, D. (1997). *Education for public democracy.* Albany: State University of New York Press.

Tarcov, N. (1996). The meanings of democracy. In R. Soder (Ed.), *Democracy, education, and the schools* (pp. 1–36). San Francisco: Jossey-Bass.

VanSickle, R. (1983). Practicing what we teach: Promoting democratic experiences in the classroom. In M. Hepburn (Ed.), *Democratic education in schools and classrooms* (pp. 49–66). Washington, DC: National Council for the Social Studies (Bulletin No. 70).

Wigginton, E. (1988). What kind of project should we do? *Democracy and Education, 3*(1), 1–9.

Wood, G. (1992). *Schools that work: America's most innovative public education program.* New York: Dutton.

# 8

# Confronting
# the Dominant Order

**Mark A. Windschitl**
*University of Washington*

**Pamela Bolotin Joseph**
*Antioch University Seattle*

*Education as a force for social regeneration must march hand in hand
with the living and creative forces of the social order. In their own lives
teachers must bridge the gap between school and society and play
some part in the fashioning of those great common purposes which
should bind the two together.*
—George Counts, 1932, *Dare the School Build a New Social Order?*

Ms. Garrison teaches a block course of English and social studies for
sixth graders in a middle school serving a diverse, largely working- and mid-
dle-class community in a moderate-sized city. One fall, while thinking about
how to approach the required Central American unit of study, Ms. Garrison
noticed an article in the local newspaper about Jennifer Harbury, a Har-
vard-trained lawyer who for some years worked to assist immigrants from
Central America, including refugees from the Guatemalan civil war.

Ms. Garrison learned that Harbury became involved in the struggle of native people and other "campesinos" for justice from the nearly feudal agrarian conditions and oppressive central government. Harbury eventually married freedom fighter Commander Everardo. His disappearance in combat led Harbury to attempt to elicit information from the United States government about her husband's fate. She eventually charged that Everardo was captured and tortured by a Guatemalan army colonel on the payroll of the Central Intelligence Agency of the United States.

When Ms. Garrison read about Jennifer Harbury's hunger strike to call attention to her need for information about her husband, the story touched her heart and she thought it would similarly touch her students as well. She recognized that Harbury's story showed the very human and personal side of conflict and struggle, which generally have been portrayed in textbooks only in limited and very abstract political terms, unrelated to emotions and experiences that her students could understand.

Ms. Garrison designed her Latin American curriculum unit around the people, events, and issues surrounding the Harbury article. Her students studied in detail the lives and circumstances of the people categorically called "guerrillas," "campesinos," and "Indians," and learned about the dire material conditions under which the people struggled and their voicelessness in public affairs. Her students also learned about the strength of the people's determination, their dedication to attaining a better life, and their personal devotion to family, comrades, and neighbors. The unit developed further with a classroom visit by the reporter who wrote the original newspaper article and with a letter-writing campaign to the chair of the Foreign Relations Committee. The class also sent copies of those letters to Jennifer Harbury; the unit culminated in a classroom visit by Jennifer Harbury herself, who was touched by the students' letters on her behalf. Activities steadily flowed from one to another—taking the form of writing, discussions, and projects. Students engaged in combinations of artwork, background writing, collection of artifacts, and presentations by students to their peers and, occasionally, to their families and community members.

The introduction of this unit brought much uncertainty to Ms. Garrison. She was unsure initially about the worth of the guerrillas' struggle. She was uncertain about the wisdom of centering her curriculum on a topic of such political controversy involving a strident challenge to United States policy and the conduct of federal officials. And she was not convinced that the focus of her teaching should be on engaging students as directly as possible in such affairs, in preparing and encouraging them to become activists.

As the class moved further along with the unit, Ms. Garrison herself became involved in solidarity activities and became convinced of the rightness and importance of Jennifer Harbury's project, of the Guatemalan liberation movement, and of the challenge to American foreign policy and CIA operations. She no longer had qualms about teaching with the purpose of encouraging students to take action in making the world a better place.

What came forth in this period of time was a striking new direction in Ms. Garrison's pedagogy. She utilized the social terrain of the lives of her young adolescent students to name issues of fairness, justice, oppression, and freedom to correspond to what was presented in the curriculum's formal content. She also introduced a multitude of media—painting, collage, model, music, and sculpture—for students to more expressively capture the particulars of action, thought, and feeling that weave throughout the everyday lives and strivings of the people they studied. She worked to ground abstractions of social, economic, and political relationships and interests and make them comprehensible and laden with personal meaning.

At the end, Ms. Garrison believed that her students deeply understood as part of human existence the notions of justice, liberty, security, and dedication to cause—that her curriculum essentially addressed the question of what it means to be human, to live humanely, and to strive for the human rights of all. Ms. Garrison now declares that she is proud to be teaching through her curriculum the critical importance of activism and activists to the future of democracy and to the well being of all people.

This description represents the actual experience of an educator who transformed her role as a teacher and her curriculum work. Ms. Garrison's emerging goals and practice reflect many elements of the curricular orientation, "Confronting the Dominant Order."

Although the word *confrontation* customarily evokes images of discontent, assertiveness, and angry response, this chapter employs the concept of confrontation not as an arbitrary act with aggressive overtones but as reasoned action taken as a result of deep reflection. This kind of action, and the illuminated state of reflection that prompts it, rises from critical awareness of existing social, political, and economic conditions and the belief in the possibility that society can be transformed to bring about circumstances so that all people have the access to a free, fair, and humane life. Although we describe this curricular culture as "critical," in essence, we are guided by our understanding of it as a curriculum of liberation, arising from the multicultural, feminist, and critical pedagogies.

## VISIONS

"Confronting the Dominant Order" contains several visions, first of confrontation, and then of transforming individuals, schools, and society. But to explain these visions, we must first explain how advocates of this culture of curriculum characterize the dominant order and why it is necessary to confront it. The underlying view of this curricular culture describes a world in which there are imbalances of power and privilege brought about by social, political, and economic dynamics. Obstacles to freedom, liberty, and empowerment stem from unequal access to knowledge, resources, and opportunity—much of this connected to racism and other forms of discrimination.

Another conviction in this worldview is that oppressed people themselves unintentionally contribute to the perpetuation of unequal powers relationships. Acceptance of the existing social, political, and economic order may take the form of hopelessness in that people feel that they are controlled by "outside forces" and cannot imagine how they can come together and bring about change" (Greene, 1988, p. 25). Or acceptance may mean that people become satisfied with their situation, however limiting. The power dynamic that brings about this uncritical acquiescence is explained by the term *hegemony*.

> The concept of hegemony refers to a process in which dominant groups in society come together to form a bloc and sustain leadership over subordinate groups. One of the most important elements that such an idea implies it that a power bloc does not have to rely on coercion. (Although at times it does.... ) Rather, it relies on *winning consent* to the prevailing order, by forming an ideological umbrella under which different groups who usually might not totally agree with each other can stand. The key to this is offering a compromise so that such groups feel as if their concerns are being listened to ... but without dominant groups having to give up their leadership of general social tendencies. (Apple, 1996, pp. 14–15)

The hegemony of cultural influences—including popular culture, media, government, business, and science—persuades individuals that their constrained reality, the status quo, is normal and right. Individuals thus do not feel compelled to question their experiences or to ask if society's norms are just (Giroux, 1997, p. 12).

Among the cultural influences that maintain existing social, economic, and political relationships is schooling (Anyon, 1980/1994; Bowles & Gintis, 1976). Those who support "Confronting the Dominant Order" view education as a non-neutral enterprise in which traditional schools reproduce dominant societal structures. Some students acquire the knowledge needed for their successful admittance into dominant society, whereas others are denied this "cultural capital." The mechanisms of reproduction reside in classroom practices such as tracking (which is never liberatory and is unsupported by research in learning) and unequal access to resources such as books, technology, and excellent teachers.

Critical advocates have metaphors for traditional schools as banks or factories. Knowledge is deposited "as a gift bestowed by those who consider themselves knowledgeable upon those whom they consider to know nothing" (Freire, 1990, p. 58) and students are seen as products narrowly trained to be contributors to the workforce (Apple & King, 1983). Even when students resist the explicit and hidden curriculum that reinforces political, social, and economic values, they do not obtain a critical, self-conscious education that will prepare them to alter the cultural dialogue and bring about change.

The traditional ethos surrounding evaluation emphasizes control and uniformity. People external to the classroom create the testing standards and the tests, suppressing any meaningful evaluation strategies that should rightfully be based on intimate knowledge of young people. Teachers are "de-skilled"; their evaluation input is not necessary in this kind of schooling (Apple, 1982, p. 71). Standardized tests scores label students, often reflecting arbitrary allocations of social class, ethnicity, and other attributes (Cherryholmes, 1985, p. 64).

Schools and traditional foundations of knowledge embody institutional racism, classism, and sexism, often derived from the pernicious ideology of "essentialism"—sorting people as if they had innate abilities according to the group to which they belong, predetermining potential (or lack of) for achievement. By their femaleness women are stereotyped as emotional, superficial, or math-impaired. Other inferior characteristics are attributed to African Americans, Asian Americans, Latinos, and members of the gay community. Although popular culture and other social institutions serve to reinforce and perpetuate these limiting stereotypes, schools are one of the worst offenders, combining a pathological response to student differences and rigid institutional practices to sustain an educational underclass.

Accordingly, schools influence individual personality development. They reward students for learning subject matter, but not for questioning it, thereby working against the development of critical, autonomous, and confident learners. Schools also can limit learners' aspirations. Young people acquire very restricted understandings of their own identities and potentialities; they do not imagine themselves as effective, creative, or self-actualized (Wardekker & Miedema, 1997, p. 49). When these limited self-definitions become internalized, students, like other marginalized members of society, tend to express fatalistic attitudes toward their situation, a fatalism sometimes interpreted as docility.

Despite a worldview that harshly characterizes how schools limit learning and hope, advocates of "Confronting the Dominant Order" have visions of "what schools can do" (Weiler & Mitchell, 1992, p. 2). They believe that education can (and must) be redirected toward individual transformation and social action that changes the status quo. Transformation takes place as students learn to use their own intelligence to take control of their lives. It begins with understanding of the identity of self and recognition that individuals are shaped by their experiences with class, race, gender, or other socially defined identities; these realizations begin the process of empowerment.

Ideally, schooling should give each child the uncompromised opportunity to develop into a self-determining and rationally acting person by way of self-reflection, analysis, and criticism—all within an environment of mutual respect and trust. The possibility for self-determination must not be limited by material power, ideologies, or prejudice. The school provides opportunities for taking action to improve social conditions and students learn to see themselves as social, political beings with rights to access the legitimate systems of influence in schools, their workplaces, and their communities.

Empowerment is more than an individual or psychological event, it has a double reference: to the individual and to society. The freedoms and human capacities of individuals must be developed to their maximum, but individual powers are linked to democracy in the sense that social betterment must be the necessary consequence of individual flourishing (Giroux, 1993, p. 10). The ultimate aim for individuals working together is to build the kind of society that makes possible growth and development for everyone. Therefore, individual transformation leads to social transformation.

This culture endorses principles of personal liberation, critical democracy, social equality, and an acceptance of the political and partisan nature of knowledge, human learning, and the educational process (Aronowitz & Giroux, 1985; Banks & Banks, 1993). The primary purpose of education is to teach about the broader contexts of citizenship, shared political power, and the dignity of human life (Gay, 1995). Education provide students with the "knowledge, character, and moral vision that builds civic courage" (Giroux, 1993, p. 18). This curricular philosophy serves to break down the master narrative of Eurocentrism and penetrates the grand myth that the United States society is a homogeneous, unitary cultural system. As a pedagogical strategy, it recognizes that the democratic tradition is a worthy ideal, but an imperfect experiment and an unfinished agenda that is characterized by struggle within and between multiple groups (Gay, 1995).

Because traditional education lacks a language of possibility about how schools can play a major role in shaping public life (Giroux, 1993, p. 10), "Confronting the Dominant Order" requires that a new language be spoken—a language of critique, hope, and possibility. It calls for moral discourse in which the ideals of justice and compassion become the referents for all conversations, analyses, and actions.

## HISTORY

Although the notion of confronting the dominant order seems outside the mainstream of American educational tradition, we need to remember that confrontation and the expulsion of what was deemed a source of oppression—British curtailment of political and economic liberty—made a forceful presence in schooling and various educative agencies at the beginning of the American nation. "The real revolution," wrote historian Lawrence Cremin (1977) "had been essentially a matter of popular education" (p. 38). Committees of Correspondence, revolutionary pamphlets, newspapers, and sermons educated people about the need to confront and overthrow British rule. Furthermore, "teachers used the lectern to nurture ideas of independency, while students organized symbolic actions ranging from burnings in effigy to boycotts of tea" (Cremin, 1977, p. 38). After the revolution, education in the United States reflected the desire for "community" (Cremin, 1977, p. 87) and identification with conservative principles (Elson, 1964) as former revolutionaries sought to create and not overturn traditions; never again did confrontation of political and economic dominance typify American education.

Advocacy of curriculum for confrontation re-emerged in the 20th century, emanating from dissatisfaction with political, social, and economic conditions and structures. Social ferment of 1900–1920 in response to "a marked intensification of industrialization, immigration, urbanization, and bureaucratization" included many educational activities involving protest of existing conditions—literature, journalism, lectures, debates, study groups, and classes for adults. Moreover, curriculum for confronting the dominant order was taught to working-class children in Sunday schools organized by socialists who wanted to instill a respect for labor (Teitelbaum, 1998, p. 33).

The Great Depression of the 1930s brought doubt about the American economic system, and some prominent educators considered the role of schools for teaching about the need for change and promoting different political and economic values. Addressing the Progressive Education Association in 1932, George Counts galvanized the audience with his call to "face squarely and courageously every social issue, come to grips with life in all of its stark reality, establish an organic relation with the community, develop a realistic and comprehensive theory of welfare, [and] fashion a compelling and challenging vision of human destiny" (Counts, in Cremin, 1961/1964, p. 259). In the call for revamping society, Counts was "the Thomas Paine among early social reconstructionists" (Benne, 1995, p. xxii).

In the 1930s, although education with an avowed purpose of reforming society did not become a major thrust of progressive education (and certainly not of mainstream education), the ideas that Counts raised became the center of educational discussion in a small but important publication, *The Social Frontier*. The journal emphasized that schools should point out the excesses of the capitalist system and take the lead in rebuilding society. Many of the writers for *The Social Frontier* were "neo-Marxist," explaining social conditions along the lines of class struggle. Most importantly, the social reconstructionists writing for that publication examined how schools taught acceptance of social institutions (Giarelli, 1995), leaving an important intellectual legacy for more contemporary social theorists and educators. The journal also provided critique of its positions—for example, contributors frequently noted the problem of indoctrination (Giarelli, 1995) and the journal published dialogue that opposed neo-Marxist views of social conditions (see Dewey, 1936/1939).

During that time, also, a major curricular effort to confront the American economic system in the 1930s was the publication of a popular series of social studies textbooks for children and adolescents authored by Harold Rugg who believed that "the social studies should introduce students to controversial social, economic and political issues" (Carbone & Wilson, 1995, p. 65). Despite the fact that Rugg never argued for the end of capitalism, his espousal of a balance between planned economies and free enterprise and his emphasis upon class differences eventually caused him to be branded as a subversive (Carbone & Wilson, 1995, pp. 63–65, 68, 80). By the Second World War, Rugg's textbook series were pulled from schools.

Although some confrontation of social, economic, and political conditions within educative platforms occurred in the 1950s in response to the threat of nuclear war (Benne, 1995, p. xxiv), the social protest movements of the 1960s and early 1970s, such as the civil rights and Vietnam War protest movements, became real catalysts for re-visioning schools as instruments for social change. Efforts to educate young people (often by young people themselves) about social injustices occurred within freedom schools and "teach-ins" on campuses. In addition, critical analyses of education and schooling were written—for instance, Jonathan Kozol's (1967) grim exposé of urban schooling's inequality and racist educational practices. Clearly, at the end of this era schools were no longer viewed as neutral sites but as mirrors of social institutions as well as potential educative forums for analysis and contention.

Another sort of confrontation called into question traditional notions of knowledge and education; this was the philosophical movement known as postmodernism. This paradigm received some attention by the mid-20th century, and academic and societal acceptance by the 1980s; it remains an important theme in curriculum studies and educational research to the present day (Slattery, 1995). Postmodernism contested traditional intellectual authority (Doll, 1993), opposing the scientific, rationale view that the world is knowable, orderly, and controllable. Rather, it focused on the social construction of knowledge—individuals' personal interpretations of experience and interpretations as influenced by positionality—social class, gender, race, the chaotic and spontaneous aspects of experience, and artistic representations of reality (Slattery, 1995). Ultimately, the postmodern paradigm was an intellectual revolt against official knowledge—the basis by which dominant social groups made policy decisions affecting the lives of those not in power.

The feminist movement also challenged the nature of knowledge and education. Consciousness-raising groups in the latter part of the 1960s—influenced by earlier civil rights work and revolutionary political thought—led to women's studies courses and specific feminist literature throughout the next decades. Feminists called into question "the role and authority of the teacher, the epistemological question of the source of the claims for knowledge and truth in persona experience and feeling, and the question of difference" by recognition that women from different backgrounds—affected by their positions as influenced by social class, race, and ethnicity—have had diverse experiences (Weiler, 1991, p. 459).

Another powerful influence upon American social theorists and educators was the movement for popular education that put into practice the idea that people who are not part of the powerful elite can take control of their education and their lives. Brazilian educator Paulo Freire advocated education for "critical consciousness" to make it possible for disenfranchised people to create social change by understanding the social and economic forces that enslave them in his book, *Pedagogy of the Oppressed*, first published in 1973; it has become a basic text for "a critical method of instruction" (Spring, 1991, p. 149). Another educator who demonstrated how to teach for critical awareness was Myles Horton, who created Highlander Folk School. Although this school for adult education began in 1932, it was a mainstay in fostering dialogue about social change for many years and influenced educators of all levels (Ayers, 1995).

Throughout the 1970s and the following decades, the development of theory and practice labeled "critical pedagogy" became an umbrella for scrutiny of schools and society relating to treatment of women, people of color, and the working classes and the poor—although numerous social theorists and educators view feminist and multicultural pedagogy as counterparts rather than as subsumed by critical pedagogy. As a liberatory philosophy of education, critical pedagogy was shaped by various international theorists who determined that schools "seem to legitimize class inequalities" and explained how "education prepares the young for their place in a class-divided, sexist, and racist social order." Critical scholars also demonstrated that students resist the school environment and messages (both hidden and explicit) of schooling (Purpel & Shapiro, 1995, pp. 99, 105).

In recent years, curricular scholars such as Giroux, Apple, Greene, Purpel, and Shapiro—among many others—have written about the importance of using analysis as a platform to action, especially in creating a philosophy that encompasses hope (see Giroux, 1997, pp. 218–229). McLaren (1989) synthesized this vision of hope:

> Critical pedagogy resonates with the sensibility of the Hebrew symbol of "tikkun," which means, "to heal, repair, and transform the world.... " It provides historical, cultural, political, and ethical direction for those in education who still dare to hope. Irrevocably committed to the side of the oppressed, critical pedagogy is as revolutionary as the earlier views of the authors of the Declaration of Independence: since history is fundamentally open to change, liberation is an authentic goal, and a radically different world can be brought into being. (McLaren, 1989, p. 160)

Practitioners have joined together with a hope for a better world, such as in the National Coalition of Education Activists, to confront and change racism and intolerance in schools, while others have written about methodology needed to change classrooms to teach for equity and justice (see Bigelow, Christensen, Karp, Miner, & Peterson, 1994). Counts's question for educators, "do they dare to disturb the social order?," still resonates for those who champion a curriculum intended to confront the dominant order.

## BELIEFS AND PRACTICES: LEARNERS AND TEACHERS

In the critical culture of curriculum, learners are considered individuals with unique personal histories that are dynamic, rich with the respective influences of family life, peer relationships, and popular culture. These histories do not simply influence knowledge, dispositions, and interests—they form the interpretive lens through which students view the world. Learners bring with them into the classroom their cultural expectations, experiences of social discrimination or of privilege, life pressures, and their strengths in surviving (Wallerstein, 1987, p. 33).

Pedagogy is seen as a site of discourse among participants—teachers and students—whose identities are multifaceted, often contradictory, and always in process (Weedon, 1987). A "critical" culture means that teachers and students question how their personal identities as social beings influence their relationship with what is taught. This curricular culture values alternative ways of knowing the world, and the roles of aesthetics, emotion, and personal relationships in the creation of knowledge. Its vision casts knowledge as a value-laden social construction, comprised of equal status contributions from multiple cultural sources and groups (Gay, 1995).

There also is a role for rational thinking in this curricular culture, but knowledge as a set of universal, objective principals is not consistent with this culture's vision, nor is the view of knowledge-seeking as a value-free, dispassionate search for truth. Teachers and students not only work together to understand the content of the disciplines, but to examine how powerful mechanisms in society control their access to versions of knowledge, how these mechanisms control expectations and aspirations in individuals, and how individuals, in turn, may take action of their own to influence society. Together, teachers and students scrutinize the bedrock, taken-for-granted assumptions of education—the epistemological basis of subject matter; how knowledge is produced, interpreted, validated, and promoted; the purposes of schooling; and relationships among stakeholders in the educational enterprise.

The scrutiny of oneself and society leads to empowerment—the ability to think and act critically. When students are empowered, "they have knowledge of their social, political, and economic worlds, the skills to influence their environments, and humane values that will motivate them to participate in social change to help create a more just society and world" (Banks, 1992, p. 154).

Teachers are not seen as detached, classroom technicians; instead, they are "transformative intellectuals"—"engaged critics" who play an active role in shaping curriculum.

> They do not operate from an aloof perspective that legitimizes the separation of facts from values. The understand the nature of their own self-formation, have some vision of the future, see the importance of education as a public discourse, and have a sense of mission in providing students what they need to become critical citizens. (Giroux, 1993, p. 15)

Thus, teachers are "partisans, not doctrinaire." They believe something, say what they believe, and offer their beliefs to others in a framework that always makes it debatable and open to inquiry (Giroux, 1993, p. 15).

Teachers prudently reveal themselves to students so that learners are free to react to the personal history of the teacher. This is essential to stimulate dialogue—the primary vehicle for learning in the critical classroom. Dialogue in the critical culture often develops around profound personal experiences that are not necessarily shared by teachers and students. While teachers do not have the moral authority to speak for others whose experiences they do not share, they can speak—about and to—the experiences of racism, sexism, class discrimination, and other concerns as historical and contingent issues that affect public life (Giroux, 1993, p. 35).

Teachers have the responsibility to model and reinforce nonjudgmental responses, respond to student ideas and to not ignore or dismiss them when they are voiced, incorporate student experiences into their teaching and connect them where appropriate to the curriculum, show students that they are not alone and without help, and, ensure that students are confident and relaxed enough to voice their concerns.

Teachers may also try to stimulate and provoke a changed consciousness in students through vivid demonstration. One memorable example is third-grade teacher Jane Elliott's social experiment in her homogeneous (White) classroom in a small town in Iowa, in which the children began to grasp what it was like to face prejudice because of race. Her simulation allowed some children special privileges whereas others had restrictions in which they were forbidden the use of drinking fountains and playground equipment, were not allowed to play with children unlike themselves, and were continually reminded of their lack of intelligence—all depending upon whether the children had blue or brown eyes (Peters, 1987). Another provocative classroom account is Bill Bigelow's teaching of Columbus's "discovery" of America. Bigelow began by coming into class one day and absconding with a student's purse, announcing to the class that he had "discovered this purse." His students' disconcerted response became a catalyst for their thinking about unfairness. These high schoolers also became angry at the traditional textbooks' descriptions of discovery as Bigelow provided primary documents revealing the brutality of the European contact with indigenous peoples. Eventually, the students questioned all sources of knowledge, including the teacher's contributions, as they began to obtain a critical approach to learning and knowledge (Bigelow, 1989).

In addition to being provocateurs, teachers' tasks are to find out what the students know, to help them reflect on this knowledge, and to set it into a larger context in order to help them make connections (Freire, 1990). In turn, educators constantly modify their own knowledge through the reflections of the students. Learners—no longer docile listeners—are now critical co-investigators in dialogue with the teacher. There is a reciprocal process of dialogue so that students also educate teachers. "There are not teachers and students, but teacher–students, and student–teachers" (Freire, 1990, pp. 68, 59, 67).

## BELIEFS AND PRACTICES: CONTENT AND CONTEXT

This curricular culture understands content as the organized and systematic depiction to learners of the things about which they want to know more (Freire, 1990, p. 28). Through dialogue, the teacher "re-presents" that knowledge to students from whom it was first received—not as a lecture, but as a problem (Freire, 1990, p. 98). Investigations bring tentative viewpoints and answers that stimulate more questions, self-awareness, and an incrementally more conscious, mature, approach to these questions. The content thus renews itself.

Because many student-generated issues involve immediate and emotional themes, a structure is needed to temper anxiety and the articulation of resentments. Issues are recast as a concrete representation—in story, photograph, skit, collage, or song—with many sides in order to avoid polarizing points of view. These representations, called "codes," mediate discussions about topics that are too overwhelming or threatening to address directly (Freire, 1990, p. 106). The codes do not provide solutions, but are capable of prompting discussion about solutions and strategies from the class. Finally, the problems suggested will not be overwhelming, but should offer possibilities for group affirmation and small actions toward change. Action, or follow-through to the consequences of reflection is essential to learning.

Themes also play a significant role in the critical classroom. Themes are abstract terms that are anchored in people's common, lived experiences. Themes such as dominance and liberation, silence, and justice are investigated in relation to concrete experiences in the learner's world through such questions as: What are examples of dominance? What forms can silence take? How do people liberate themselves? Teachers and students can use photographs, drawings of people interacting, even "found objects" to be stimulants for dialogue. These objects can be cultural artifacts, advertisements, tools, toys, labels, clothing—anything that supports students' understanding of the environment.

This culture of curriculum de-emphasizes the compartmentalization of subject areas. Science, mathematics, and literature, for example, cannot be examined as stand-alone fields of study that remain uninfluenced by one other. Because social studies is a composite of several disciplines involving social constructions (e.g., political science, economics, history), it is easy to use conceptual frameworks from those disciplines to examine, for example, how funding for disease research is determined by politics rather than by science, or how female and African American contributions to literature have been systematically suppressed throughout American history.

This cycle of reflection and action is referred to as the *praxis* of knowing. Plans for action evolve from students' understanding of problems as well as from visions of better conditions. Students can practice taking action through in-class role playing and action competencies such as reporting a problem, filing a complaint, fighting for funding, or adopting an issue such as unsafe conditions around a neighborhood business (Wallerstein, 1987, pp. 42–43). As students test their analyses in the real world, they begin a deeper cycle of reflection that includes input from their new experiential base. Reflection and action are both necessary. Reflection without action is idle chatter, verbalism; action without reflection is simply action for its own sake (Freire, 1990, p. 77).

Not all of class time can be given over to the examination of the students' lived experiences; at times, the teacher will select specific content for students to examine. Freire believes that it is "unthinkable for a teacher to be in charge of a class without providing students material relevant to a discipline." He explains that "objects of study" should stimulate the teacher's curiosity. "They stimulate my curiosity and I bring this enthusiasm to my students. Then both of us can illuminate the object together" (Freire, 1987, pp. 212–213).

Content would include the social/historical products of revisionist scholarship as well as insiders' viewpoints. Attention is given to the historical and scholarly contributions of ethnic individuals and events rather than to the trivial, isolated, and exotic aspects of nondominant peoples (Banks, 1990; Hilliard, 1992, in Gay, 1995). Marginalized people, who have been silenced throughout history, are given voice and allowed to tell their own stories—challenging the "status quo" situation in which they have been represented as victims, servants to society, passive participants, second-class citizens, and imperfect imitations of male, European, Anglo models (Gay, 1995).

This curriculum is rich with primary sources—social commentaries, newspaper articles, personal memoirs, original artifacts, literary treatises, biographies, and artistic impressions—empowering learners to interpret historical events for themselves. Students learn how events are experienced by many different people; examination of multiple sources generates multiple realities. When original documents are not available to help students construct an unfiltered image of a particular discipline, commercial textbooks may be one of the few print resources available to students; then, students must be taught to critically examine sources, becoming aware of both historical and social constructions, such as the economy of publishing agencies and forces outside of school (e.g., state governments) that sanction certain texts purveyors of legitimate knowledge.

The definition of "text" in the critical classroom includes anything that carries a message. Popular culture is a serious object of study because it is suffused with text and exerts a powerful influence on the ways students mediate, relate, resist, and create their own cultural forms and forms of knowing (Giroux, 1993). Instruction also consists of helping students how to read critically; for example, Kohl, in his essay "Should We Burn Babar?" (1995), suggests that children can become conscious of classism and racism, even in apparently benign animal stories. Students also can be taught to imagine how to challenge and resist dominant versions of the text. Simon (1992) describes teaching *The Merchant of Venice* by including an interpretation of Shylock in a performance in the Yiddish theater—not as an anti-Semitic caricature, but a character showing defiance of anti-Semitism (pp. 101–120).

Although the classroom environment is a crucible for dialogue, expression, and even confrontation, a sense of community and trust must first be created. When students describe "good classes" in this curricular culture, they talk about places where construction of meaning happens in a context that honors supportive relationships, previous experiences, and multiple cultural and linguistic realities. Furthermore, the good classroom is a forum for critical analysis of the world that allows for the further development of solutions (Rivera & Poplin, 1995, p. 237). Similarly, topics and techniques are welcomed that honor feelings as well as the intellect: role-playing, simulations, drama, song, and poetry, readings, journals, brain-storming, and classroom celebration (Belenky, Clinchy, Goldberger, & Tarule, 1986, pp. 77, 194).

## BELIEFS AND PRACTICES:
## PLANNING AND EVALUATION

In this curricular culture, teachers seek to invest the students in their own learning by involving them as coauthors of the curriculum. It is believed that learners are competent to play a role in course development; and, in doing so, they join with teachers in knowing the joys and difficulties of intense intellectual activity (Shrewsbury, 1987, pp. 8–9). Teachers invite students to generate ideas, to negotiate subject matter, and to find resources outside the school setting as part of the learning process—for example, entering the community to gather documents, conduct interviews and make observations. Curriculum development stems not out of students' trivial preoccupations, but from an informed sense of "What should I be paying attention to here?" (Giroux, 1993, p. 14).

Planning begins with teachers discovering concerns that run through learners' conversations. Teachers try to situate themselves in the students' culture—to comprehend their literacy, aspirations, the stuff of their daily lives, while taking into account their students' cognitive and emotional states. To identify themes, teachers listen attentively to students, not only during class, but during breaks and outside the classroom.

Because curriculum constantly evolves from student issues, teachers cannot measure fulfillment of predetermined objectives or test outcomes. Evaluation in a problem-posing environment concerns examining a broad spectrum of student's abilities to articulate issues, generate their own learning materials, redefine their views of the world, and take risks to act in their daily lives. Through a variety of means, teachers try to continually ascertain if students understand the root causes of problems, whether student action on problems are effective and, especially, what special insights learners gain about themselves and the groups of which they are members.

These determinations cannot be made solely using terminal assessment techniques, but rather by qualitatively evaluating the ongoing work of students. Whether or not critical insights are being realized by learners is evidenced through discussions, role-plays, presentations to the class, oral arguments, position papers, letters to support social action, and other products of inquiry. Group work can be evaluated and honored as the product of a collective of learners rather than being parsed into individual components for "scoring." The purpose of evaluation is to provide feedback about communicative skills, content knowledge and, above all, critical insights about the content. Teachers evaluate not only processes of reflection but also the action taken by learners in the action–reflection–action cycle; their continuous evaluation functions as a guidance process as well as an indicator of accomplishment. Evaluation can take several forms: narratives from the teacher, written self-critiques by students during the reflection process, and interviews and observations by the teacher, by peers, or by community members who have been affected by student attempts at transformative action.

In the critical culture, assessment is conducted in the best interests of the students. It means providing guidance to learners for the purposes of opening a universe of possibilities for their future and as a means of supporting critical thinking and powers of reflection. Evaluation rewards creativity and encourages diversity. As in the design of instructional experiences, evaluation takes into account the individual students' life experiences and identity. And in contrast to traditional evaluation that so often marks the dead end of a unit of study, critical evaluations are a springboard for a continuing and more complex cycle of reflection–action–reflection.

## DILEMMAS OF PRACTICE

We begin with the obvious when considering dilemmas of practice in "Confronting the Dominant Order": teaching radical curriculum—challenging cherished premises and myths about society—is not only an unpopular stand, in many places it would be anathema. Without a community that tolerates political activism and without the support of administration, teachers, usually, would not feel safe to "disturb the social order." Even in a more sympathetic environment, teachers and students may find that exposing and objecting to unequal power relationships within their own schools may meet with resistance; it is one thing to challenge politics in Guatemala and quite another to confront the decision-making process one one's own "turf."

Still, even when teachers find themselves in situations that are not hostile to confrontational and liberatory pedagogy, their task remains difficult. A radical vision of the world calls for investigations of racism and classism, and works for fundamental changes in values and institutions. Can those who have not understood the experience of being marginalized develop empathy for those who have been oppressed? Can people with privilege work against their self-interest? Members of dominant social groups are more than willing to believe in the American dream and consider as true that the dream is readily available for all. Only with great difficulty can we teach to suspend individuals' beliefs about deeply imbedded social misunderstandings and myths, about a "democratic story about itself that is so enveloping and sentimental" (Shor, 1996, p. 23).

Teachers also are likely to discover that learners resist doing critical analysis (Ellwood, 1993; Shor, 1996). Students often have little experience in such thinking or social action, have no language to imagine the concepts of this curriculum, bring "no transformative agendas to class;" furthermore, "old habits die hard" (Shor, 1996, pp. 19–27). Critical theorists fear that the oppressed, who have adapted to the structure of domination in which they are immersed, often become resigned to it; they prefer the security of conformity in a state of familiar "unfreedom" to the unfamiliar situation produced by freedom and the implications it carries for personal responsibility (Freire, 1990, p. 32).

Furthermore, the essential elements of "Confronting the Dominant Order" (dialogue followed by individual and group actions) are dependent upon many factors: internal class dynamics (stemming from length of time students have been together in class, if they are from the same or different linguistic backgrounds, and their level of trust), students' understanding of the barriers to change, internal feelings (level of self-confidence created through problem-posing, through other life settings, and prior roles and experiences in their cultures), and support mechanisms of students' families, communities and work environments (Moriarty & Wallerstein, 1983).

Another impediment to this curricular culture may be the circumscribed worldview of teachers themselves. Often, school administrators and teachers are silent to each other and to the students about racial segregation, racism, and sexism (Lave, 1996, p. 160). Many teachers are not even aware of privilege and oppression in their own lives. How can they hold serious conversations with children about such pervasive yet unperceived phenomena? (Rivera & Poplin, 1995, p. 235). Although awareness of teachers' own positions and biases could develop from teacher education, it is not likely that colleges of education will support such a "radical shift" in teacher preparation (Purpel & Shapiro, 1995, p. 113).

Finally, literature about this culture of curriculum reveals a discontinuity between theory and guidelines for practice in K–12 education; there have been myriad arguments about theory, but sophisticated dialogue about method has been scarce. Despite substantial accounts of critical pedagogy curriculum (Bigelow, 1988; Davidson, Hammerman, & Schneidewind, 1997; Lee, Menkart, & Okazawa-Rey, 1998) and some thoughtful attempts to combine theory and practice, especially application of Freirean critical pedagogy (Frankenstein, 1992; Peterson, 1991; Rivage-Seul, 1987), the question of whether or not the critical approach can be developed in the direction of a viable program of instruction has not been satisfactorily addressed. Moreover, deliberation about the nature of curriculum and pedagogy has not been brought to the "area of public concern and public debate" by critical theorists (Bell & Schniedewind, 1987; Kampfer, 1978; Purpel & Shapiro, 1995, p. 111).

## CRITIQUE

Critique of "Confronting the Dominant Order" raises many issues emanating from the variant ideas within this curricular culture, its pedagogical implications, and its worldview. Several of these concerns reflect long-standing differences among proponents of this curricular culture. Issues have been raised as well by advocates through their own self-reflection; for those who propose critique of education and society, it has been reasonable for them to question their own purposes and practices.

The first element in our critique pertains to the theoretical complexity of this curricular culture. Although the differences among the critical, feminist, and multicultural pedagogies are often simply a matter of emphasis, in several ways these three contributing philosophies are incommensurate. Feminist theorists claim that the goals of liberation and political transformation espoused in critical pedagogy are not attainable without exploring one's own privileged position and the existing conflicts among the oppressed groups themselves; they also call into question the privileged position of White male

theorists (Weiler, 1991; Weiler & Mitchell, 1992) and recognize the importance of students' feelings of connection along with the concepts of family,
friendship, nurturing, and goodness (Rivera & Poplin, 1995, p. 233). Critical theorists associate the roots of racial domination with capitalism (and its
elaboration as a world system) and see the problem of racial inequality in
schooling subsumed under the general rubric of working-class oppression,
whereas multiculturalists view racism as a separate, more powerful dynamic
(McCarthy, 1988). There are inherent tensions among feminist, multicultural, and critical perspectives that thwart portrayal of this culture as a congruent whole. Even within each of feminist, multicultural, and critical
pedagogies there are ideological differences or unresolved tensions (see
Garcia, 1994, pp. 86–87; Rivera & Poplin,1995, p. 223).

The varying explanations of social dynamics, ideas about practice, and ultimate goals make imagining consistent pedagogical practices that remain
true to theory a daunting task. Clearly, this culture of curriculum calls for "living" with tensions inherent in dialectic thinking, fluid explanations of social
phenomena, and the complications of human interaction; it demands that
teachers be intellectuals who can grapple with complexity. This outcome is
questionable in light of American society's apathy to radical social reform, the
pursuit of quick fixes as educational solutions, and the frequent proce-
dure-oriented approaches suggested in teacher education.

The second component of this critique comes from response to the question: Should "Confronting the Dominant Order" be the singular curricular
orientation for children and adolescents? To this question, we give a mixed
answer. First, the idea of infusing curricula with critical analysis, concern for
identity, and social action surely elevates education to a moral and intellectual
enterprise. However, we have quandaries about what becomes left out (the
null curriculum) when concepts in academic subjects are chosen to "fit" into
this paradigm.

A critical approach to teaching subject matter does not necessarily provide
students grounding in a discipline because it may not teach the conceptual
frameworks and skills for learners to become thoroughly competent (see
Frankenstein, 1992). Likewise, students exposed only to this curricular culture can miss the joy of learning associated with the creation of knowledge
and deep mastery of a domain. Although proponents of the critical culture
may not make the claim that it is the only viable approach to curriculum, we
certainly think it is reasonable that content (be it mathematics, science, or literature) as a vehicle for critical analysis and for revealing privilege and oppression, must at least teach learners to understand certain content
fundamentals. Teachers cannot neglect the task of helping students become
literate by instead spending most of the teaching time on political analysis
(Freire, 1987, p. 212).

In other ways, the content of this curricular orientation may limit students' attainment of cultural capital, of a full, rich education that gives them "an even playing field," the means and competence not just to enter but to confront the dominant order. Grounding learning in the students' own life experiences is desirable in any educational system, but making it the de facto curriculum closes doors that students may not realize should be opened. Furthermore, we question if featuring popular culture as a vehicle for mediating student learning may be a mere capitulation to the shallow, immediate interests of children as consumers. The critical culture seems to circumscribe a null curriculum that disparages, by its absence, the classic works of literature, science, and the arts as culturally bound constructions with questionable validity and of little relevance to the students' own life situations. We are concerned about the logic of those holding this extreme position and realize that some critical curriculum workers would say that classic works may take their place alongside the suppressed and unrecognized contributions of authors, scientists, philosophers, and artists from the nondominant cultures—that emphasis is properly reapportioned to the classics, not denied them.

Finally, many aspects of "Confronting the Dominant Order" have a distinctly negative character (Wardekker & Miedema, 1997). This curricular culture's emphasis on inequities, dominance, distortion, and grossly imperfect social situations provokes unsettling quandaries: Does the critical culture crush hope and reinforce young people's despair? Does its harsh economic explanations of self-interest provoke cynicism? Can students resist the pessimism that they may feel when they cannot easily change the world? Moreover, does attention to power differences within this curricular culture become a barrier to community? Can young people who are acutely aware of political, social, and economic inequities imagine working with others across class, race, and gender borders to create a just and humane society?

Educators who themselves see the worth of the critical culture have some doubts about the imposition of their values and a negative worldview on young people (Ellsworth, 1989). Their qualms mirror the long-standing debate among social reconstructionists about indoctrination (see Dewey, 1936). For example, a new elementary teacher writes that "although I regard myself in many ways as a critical [pedagogue], I see the students' needs and interests as paramount over my own and see my role more as a provider of background and support, rather than as the general marching my troops into the fray of social struggle" (class journal). Ellwood (1993), then a high school teacher in an urban classroom, writes about imposition of the teacher's worldview on students, poignantly asking, can we really look through our students' eyes?"

I have gradually begun to see how invested many of my students are in the classic American dream.... I was reminded that my students must hold fiercely to the conviction that they can make it.... Still, I did not entirely understand that some students saw social critique as threatening, and why. Have I at times fed feelings of despair in some young people by asking them to examine society critically? Critical pedagogues might argue we should encounter such despair by mobilizing our students to action.... if you accept my argument that the classroom is an imperfect democracy with the teacher retaining a degree of power that cannot be denied, must we not also accept the possibility that we will push our students toward analyses that are not empowering after all? (Ellwood, 1993, pp. 76–77)

The opportunities for misapplication of critical pedagogy are many. Students can come away from this kind of experience with the sense that everyone is oppressing them, that every form of authority is constrictive, that all codified knowledge is relative, suspect, and of little personal value. Young students who begin their critical understanding of the world by being introduced to concepts of fairness and equality can be baffled by the particulars of what constitutes practices of unfairness. If some classmates come from more economically advantaged families, are they the oppressors? Is it always bad when someone has more of something than someone else? Determining who is oppressed and in what way requires that students consider in-depth triangulations of values, circumstances, and theoretical explanations; can young learners think with such complexity rather than choosing simple condemnation?

Also, the fact that many students do not share the same ethnic, social, racial, and linguistic backgrounds as their teachers may lead to cultural incongruencies in the classroom, which can mediate against actualizing curricular goals. Incompatibilities are evident in value orientations, behavioral norms, and expectations, as well as styles of social interaction, self-presentation, communication, and cognitive processing (Bennett, 1990; Gay, 1991; Spindler, 1987). The classroom sharing of experiences can lead to a sense of commonality, but in settings in which students come from differing positions of privilege, the sharing of experience likely could cause resentments and defensiveness rather than build solidarity. In these circumstances, a collective exploration of experiences leads not to a common knowledge based on sameness, but to the tensions of articulated differences (Weiler, 1991).

In conclusion, the greatest concerns about this culture of curriculum are its complexity and negativity. Is there so much emphasis on the intricacies of theory that this culture remains outside the imagination of most educators? Do ideas about difference eclipse conversations about how to accomplish egalitarian schools and a just and humane society? Does pessimism overshadow hope? Can proponents of "Confronting the Dominant Order" articulate a vision that can enter public discourse and initiate curriculum change? Without the articulation of a clear, convincing, and confident vision, we believe that this culture of curriculum will be doomed to its label as "radical" and disregarded, rather than being viewed as a viable alternative for education.

## REFERENCES

Anyon, J. (1980/1994). Social class and the hidden curriculum of work. In J. Kretovics & E. J. Nussel, (Eds.), *Transforming urban education*. Boston: Allyn & Bacon.

Apple, M. (1982). *Education and power*. London: Routledge & Kegan Paul.

Apple, M. (1996). *Cultural politics and education*. New York: Teachers College Press.

Apple, M., & King, N. (1979). *Education and control in every day school life*. In M. Apple (Ed.), *Ideology and curriculum* (pp. 27–63). London: Routledge & Kegan Paul.

Apple, M., & King, N. (1983). What do schools teach? In H. Giroux & D. Purpel (Eds.), *Moral education and the hidden curriculum: Deception or discovery*. (pp. 82–99). Berkeley, CA: McCutchan.

Aronowitz, S., & Giroux, H. A. (1985). *Education under siege: The conservative, liberal and radical debate over schooling*. Hadley, MA: Bergin & Garvey.

Ayers, W. (1995). Popular education: Teaching for social justice. *Democracy & Education 10*, 5–8.

Banks, J. (1990). Citizen education for a pluralistic democratic society. *The Social Studies, 81*, 210–214.

Banks, J. (1992). A curriculum for empowerment, action, and change. In K. A. Moodley (Ed.), *Beyond multicultural education: International perspectives* (pp. 154–170). Calgary, Alberta: Detseling Enterprises.

Banks, J. A., & Banks, C. A. (1993). *Multicultural education: Issues and perspectives*, (2nd ed.). Boston: Allyn & Bacon.

Belenky, M. F., Clinchy, B. M., Goldberger, N. R., & Tarule, J. M. (1986). *Women's ways of knowing*. New York: Basic Books.

Bell, L., & Schniedewind, N. (1987). Reflective minds, intentional hearts: Joining humanistic education and critical theory for liberating education. *Journal of Education, 169*, 55–77.

Benne, K. D. (1995). Prologue: Social reconstructionism remembered. In M. E. James (Ed.), *Social reconstruction through education: The philosophy, history, and curricula of a radical ideal*. Norwood, NJ: Ablex.

Bennett, C. (1990). *Comprehensive multiculural education: Theory and practice* (2nd ed.). Boston: Allyn & Bacon.

Bigelow, B. (1988). A new kind of classroom: Critical pedagogy in action. *Rethinking Schools, 3*(1), 4–5.

Bigelow, B. (1989). Rediscovering Columbus: Re-reading the past. *Rethinking Schools, 4*(1), 1, 12–13.

Bigelow, B., Christensen, L., Karp, S., Miner, B., & Peterson, B. (1994). *Rethinking our classrooms: Teaching for equity and justice*. Milwaukee, WI: Rethinking Schools, Ltd.

Bowles, S., & Gintis, H. (1976) *Schooling in capitalist America*. New York: Basic Books.

Carbone, P. F., Jr., & Wilson, V. S. (1995). Harold Rugg's social reconstructionism. In M. E. James (Ed.), *Social reconstruction through education: The philosophy, history, and curricula of a radical ideal* (pp. 57–88). Norwood, NJ: Ablex.

Carnoy, M. (1974). *Education as cultural imperialism*. New York: Longman.

Cherryholmes, C. (1985). Theory and practice: On the role of empirically based theory for critical practice. *American Journal of Education, 94*, 39–70.

Cremin, L. A. (1961/1964). *The transformation of the school: Progressivism in American education 1876–1957*. New York: Vintage.

Cremin, L. A. (1977). *Traditions of American education*. New York: Basic Books.

Davidson, E., Hammerman, J. K., & Schneidewind, N. (1997). Education for equity: Acting on critical consciousness. *Democracy & Education, 12*, 39–42.

Dewey, J. (1936/1939). Educators and class struggle. In J. Ratner, (Ed.), *Intelligence in the modern world: John Dewey's philosophy*. New York: Modern Library.

Doll, W. E., Jr. (1993) *A post-modern perspective on curriculum*. New York: Teachers College Press.

Ellwood, C. M. (1993). Can we really look through out students' eyes? An urban teacher's perspective. *Educational Foundations, 7*, 63–78.

Ellsworth, E. (1989). Why doesn't this feel empowering? Working through repressive myths of critical pedagogy. *Harvard Educational Review, 59*, 297–324.

Elson, R. M (1964). *Guardians of tradition: American schoolbooks in the nineteenth century*. Lincoln: University of Nebraska Press.

Frankenstein, M. (1992). Critical mathematics education: An application of Paulo Freire's epistemology. In K. Weiler, & C. Mitchell, (Eds.), *What schools can do: Critical pedagogy and practice*. (pp. 237–264). Albany: State University of New York Press.

Freire, P. (1987). Letter to North American teachers. In I. Shor (Ed.), *Freire for the classroom: A sourcebook for liberatory teaching* (pp. 211–214). Boynton, Cook, Heinemann.

Freire, P. (1990). *Pedagogy of the oppressed*. New York: Continuum.

Garcia, E. (1994). *Understanding and meeting the challenge of student cultural diversity*. Boston: Houghton Mifflin.

Gay, G. (1991). Culturally diverse students and social studies. In J. P. Shaver (Ed.), *Handbook of research on social studies teaching and learning* (pp. 145–156). New York: Macmillan.

Gay, G. (1995). Mirror images on common issues: Parallels between multicultural education an critical pedagogy In C. Sleeter & P. McLaren (Eds.) *Multicultural education, critical pedagogy, and the politics of difference* (pp. 155–189). Albany: State University of New York Press.

Giarelli, J. M. (1995). *The Social Frontier* 1934–1943: Retrospect and prospect. In M. E. James (Ed.), *Social reconstruction through education: The philosophy, history, and curricula of a radical ideal* (pp. 27–42). Norwood, NJ: Ablex.

Giroux, H. (1985). Critical pedagogy, cultural politics and the discourse of experience. *Journal of Education, 167*, 23–41.

Giroux, H. A. (1993). *Border crossings: Cultural works and the politics of education*. New York: Routledge.

Giroux, H. A. (1997). *Pedagogy and the politics of hope: Theory, culture, and schooling, a critical reader*. Boulder, CO: Westview.

Greene, M. (1988). *The dialectic of freedom*. New York: Teachers College Press.

Hilliard, A. G. (1992). Why we must pluralize the curriculum. *Educational Leadership, 49*, 12–14.

Kampfer, D. (1978). Theorie-praxis-verhaltnis. In C. Wulf (Ed.), *Wörterbuch der erzichung* (pp. 585–588) Munich: Piper.

Kohl, H. (1995). Should we burn Babar? Questioning power in children's literature. In *Should we burn Babar? Essays on children's literature and the power of stories*. New York: New Press.

Kozol, J. (1967). *Death at an early age: The destruction of the hearts and minds of Negro children in the Boston public schools*. Boston: Houghton Mifflin.

Lave, J. (1996). Teaching, as learning in practice. *Mind, Culture, and Activity, 3*, 149–164.

Lee, E., Menkart, D., & Okazawa-Rey, M. (1998). *Beyond heroes and holidays: A practical guide to K-12 anti-racist, multicultural education and staff development*. Washington, DC: Network of Educators on the Americas.

McCarthy, C. (1988) Rethinking liberal and radical perspectives on racial inequality in schooling: Making the case for nonsynchrony. *Harvard Educational Review, 58*, 265–279.

McLaren, P. (1989). *Life in schools: An introduction to critical pedagogy in the foundations of education*. New York: Longman.

Moriarty, P., & Wallerstein, N. (1983). *Teaching about nuclear war: A positive problem-posing strategy*. San Francisco: Catholic Archdiocese (Commission on Social Justice).

Peters, W. (1987). *A class divided: Then and now*. New Haven: Yale University Press.

Peterson, R. E. (1991). Teaching how to read the world and change it: Critical pedagogy in the intermediate grades. In C. E. Walsh (Ed.), *Literacy as praxis: Culture, language & pedagogy*. Norwood, NJ: Ablex.

Purpel, D. E., & Shapiro, S. (1995). *Beyond liberation & excellence: Reconstructing the public discourse on education*. Westport, CT: Bergin & Garvey.

Rivage-Seul, M. K. (1987). Peace education: Imagination and the pedagogy of the oppressed. *Harvard Educational Review, 57,* 153–169.

Rivera, J., & Poplin, M. (1995). Multicultural, critical, feminine and constructive pedagogies seen through the eyes of youth: A call for the revisioning of these and beyond: Toward a pedagogy for the next century. In C. Sleeter & P. McLaren (Eds.) *Multicultural education, critical pedagogy, and the politics of difference* (pp. 221–244). Albany: State University of New York Press.

Shor, I. (1996). *When students have power: Negotiating authority in critical pedagogy*. Chicago: University of Chicago Press.

Shor, I., & Freire, P. (1987). *A pedagogy for liberation*. South Hadley, MA: Begin & Garvey.

Shrewsbury, C. M. (1987). What is feminist pedagogy? *Women's Studies Quarterly 15,* 6–14.

Simon, R. I. (1992). *Teaching against the grain: Texts for a pedagogy of possibility*. New York: Bergin & Garvey.

Slattery, P. (1995). *Curriculum development in the postmodern era*. New York: Garland.

Spindler, G. D. (1987). *Education and cultural process: Anthropological approaches*. Prospect Heights, IL: Waveland.

Spring, J. (1991). *American education: An introduction to social and political aspects* (5th ed.). New York: Longman.

Teitelbaum, K. (1998). Contestation and curriculum: The efforts of American Socialists 1900–1920. In L. E. Beter & M. W. Apple (Eds.), *The curriculum: Problems, politics, and possibilities* (2nd ed.), pp. 34–57. Albany: State University of New York Press.

Wallerstein, N. (1987). Problem-posing education: Freire's method for transformation. In I. Shor (Ed.), *Freire for the classroom: A sourcebook for liberatory teaching* (pp. 33–43) Portsmouth, NH: Boynton, Cook, Heinemann.

Wardekker, W. L., & Miedema, S. (1997). Critical pedagogy: An evaluation and a direction for reformulation. *Curriculum Inquiry, 27,* 45–62.

Weedon, C. (1987). *Feminist practice & postructuralist theory*. Oxford: Basil Blackwell.

Weiler, K. (1991). Freire and a feminist pedagogy of difference. *Harvard Educational Review, 61,* 449–474.

Weiler, K., & Mitchell, C. (1992). *What schools can do: Critical pedagogy and practice*. Albany: State University of New York Press.

# 9

# Reculturing Curriculum

**Mark A. Windschitl**
*University of Washington*

**Edward R. Mikel**
*Antioch University Seattle*

**Pamela Bolotin Joseph**
*Antioch University Seattle*

> ... to restructure is not to reculture.... Changing formal structures is
> not the same as changing norms, habits, skills, and beliefs.
> —Michael Fullan, 1993, *Change Forces*

We began this book believing that it could help educators approach curriculum through a deliberative framework that would lead to greater awareness of their own goals and practice—daring to hope that our structure for understanding curriculum could enter the public discourse if readers used it in school and community forums. We imagined that we could create a platform for inquiry, for clearer understanding of what is chosen, practiced, evaluated, and valued within classrooms and schools. However, as we continued to write and deliberate, we saw that our framework could be more than a heuristic (a means of learning);

rather, we began to consider its potential for stimulating reflection and encouraging action leading to reform.

This chapter reflects ongoing conversations among authors as we discussed the classification, sequence, content, and application of the concept of curricular cultures. It is organized by questions, the ones we have asked each other, the ones that our students have asked us, and those we anticipate our readers might have after reading the previous chapters.

## Don't All Classrooms and Schools Already Contain Cultures of Curriculum?

All classrooms and schools reveal cultures in the sense of having norms, values, beliefs, practices, stories, and power relationships. In contrast, ordinary classroom and school cultures lack the unifying visions that characterize what we call "cultures of curriculum." A culture of curriculum is different from a real culture in that it makes its beliefs and aims explicit, open to scrutiny and evaluation.

In the existing school cultures, most formative beliefs remain unstated (Heckman, 1987, p. 67); curriculum is influenced by "folk pedagogies" (Bruner, 1996) that are composed of incoherent, deeply imbedded beliefs about what is normal; these convictions generally are left unexamined. Moreover, many curricular practices are generated from ad hoc decisions, often in response to competing demands from various constituencies rather than from articulated beliefs. With the exception of some alternative schools in public systems and independent schools, the cultures of schools seem bereft of vision and appear to simply perpetuate largely unexamined norms, habits, values, and goals. Therefore, belief systems in most schools are difficult to articulate, examine, and change.

But scholars suggest that despite occasional enactments of contradictory impulses, such as child-centered education (Cuban, 1993), classroom cultures have not been diverse; there has been a typical and deeply entrenched culture of classrooms and schools in 20th-century America. In Goodlad's study of more than 1,000 classrooms (1984), he found an "extraordinary sameness" of learning environments featuring "bland, repetitive procedures of lecturing, questioning, monitoring, and quizzing" (p. 249). In *The Ecology of School Renewal*, Heckman (1987) described recent prevailing conditions of American classrooms: "Most teachers talk most of the time; students sit, listen, do seatwork, and take tests. This occurs for approximately 85% of the 75% of the class time devoted to instruction." Heckman went on to say that the studies of contemporary classroom cultures are similar to a study done at the turn of the century (p. 70).

Thus, in the majority of schools, the classroom culture had been one of coping and compliance, where teachers control students' intellectual activity to ensure uniform exposure to the curriculum and maintain discipline, as students play the role of unquestioning, passive learners. This prevailing culture was not necessarily unsystematic. Indeed, many teachers depended on the regularities of curricula fashioned and organized by external intellectual authorities, inflexible models of instruction, and a narrow definition of learning. These limited vehicles of teaching and learning represented some of the most consistent and persistent phenomena known in the social and behavioral sciences (Sirotnik, 1983).

More recently, we see some modification of the teacher-centered landscape (Cuban, 1993). Educators, gravitating again toward student-centered instruction, adopt partial strategies that include establishing classroom learning centers, using various forms of cooperative learning, and incorporating project or problem-based learning—these activities typically integrated into a core of otherwise teacher-centered practices. Most teachers, however, limit students' participation in curriculum, denying them full partnership in planning of content and choice of learning activities.

Classrooms with more student-centered activities do not necessarily signify coherent cultures of curriculum. Such classrooms do suggest, however, that modifications are emerging from the historically monolithic culture of schooling. Still, any deviation from the traditional structure is recognized as a special event. They are experiments—risky exceptions to the day-to-day business of schooling. Events—such as empowering students to make meaningful curricular choices, developing poignant humanistic themes, or integrating class work with other subject areas—challenge the entrenched practices and hierarchies of power.

The existence of this coping culture is particularly noticeable in large studies which overlook individual educators and the worlds that they make. We realize, however, that teachers have never functioned as automatons; they weave their own expertise, interests, cultural knowledge, values, and responsiveness to individual students into the structures and routines of the prevailing culture of schools. Classrooms and schools were—and still are—combinations of default and desire. There may be more richness of experience in them than is revealed in the distillate of wide-scaled studies, but their sum and substance have not been visionary.

## Should Only One Culture of Curriculum Exist in a Classroom or in a School?

To answer this question, we must first point out that several of the six curricular cultures we describe share similar assumptions. There are overlapping beliefs and practices across various cultures, including goals for students (e.g., the development of autonomy), philosophies of curriculum development (e.g., the importance of drawing from a established body of knowledge), the roles of teachers (e.g., awareness of students' interests), and assumptions about learners (e.g., their active engagement in learning and their experiences as the bases for curriculum selection). Thus, two learners may be working in the same way with similar subject matter and perhaps being similarly assessed despite the fact that they are in separate classrooms reflecting two different cultures of curriculum.

But we recognize that similar practices within various cultures of curriculum can stem from very different visions. Telling examples include multicultural education, cooperative learning, and technology because they illustrate how similar methods can be employed for very different aims and how like means may lead to profoundly different ends:

The multicultural curriculum represents a cacophony of content, practices, and goals across cultures. It readies students for a workplace that includes colleagues of other ethnic backgrounds and prepares for competition in a global market; as well, it encourages learning from others' perspectives, appreciation for one's own cultural identity, preservation of cultural traditions, and the development of critical perspectives to understand and confront racism. Cooperative learning can be identified with several cultures of curriculum. It has been adopted in some classrooms because it encourages cooperation for the workplace, in other classrooms because it facilitates the construction of knowledge, and in others because it fosters democratic decision-making or draws out students' voices to create dialogue with others. Finally, technology in classrooms is a tool for business, can provide access to cultural knowledge, enables self-directed learning and communication with others, and be a powerful medium for social action.

Conversely, we realize that some practices fundamental to one curricular culture may hardly seem feasible to incorporate into another. Students in the critical culture, for example, are not likely to make sense of curriculum intended to help them learn to obligingly operate in a work world—unless it involves questioning the very premises of worker–employer power relationships. Similarly, a constructivist approach to learning traditional wisdom may result in a group of students who have such different constructions of the canon that any sense of a common body of knowledge is lost amidst a sea of personal interpretations.

Notwithstanding, we have seen how educators create hybrids because they believe that commingling elements of different curricular cultures meet a community's needs. In New York City, Central Park East High School included themes relating to critical inquiry in a core humanities curriculum and also fostered emergent curriculum stemming from students' interests (see Meier, 1991; Wood, 1992/1993); in Washington state, the Tulalip Indian Tribal School developed a curriculum incorporating Native language and traditions with Montessori constructivist methods.

The above examples prompt further questions: When we integrate two or more curricular cultures, which elements of one culture can be meaningfully transposed into the other? As long as beliefs from two curricular cultures are neither contradictory nor preemptive, it seems reasonable that they are, to a degree, transposable from one culture to another. A good deal of reflection and planning would be necessary to understand which components would be in harmony, which would be incompatible, and overall, what would be lost by attempting a hybridization. Or can we create composites knowing that we will have to work with inherent tensions—for example, inquiry stemming from themes about power relationships when studying the canon and work education?

We believe that it is a mistake to try to create a hasty amalgam of curricular cultures. If educators try to be all things to all learners, promising a potpourri of outcomes from all classroom cultures, the effort is likely to result in a morass of incongruous educational practices. When content and learning activities are used for multiple but unrelated purposes, they contribute to an ad hoc curriculum that has little significance to learners or teachers.

Whether or not it is desirable for a student to experience total immersion in only one curricular culture is open to debate. We can conceive of some scenarios for several curricular cultures coexisting within a school, but these would arise from deliberated design, not because of short-term goals or "ad hoc-ness." For instance, a school community may be concerned that a singular vision held by all would not generate healthy challenges to beliefs and practices. The school staff could create a laboratory setting by trying out several curricular cultures in different classrooms—creating an intellectual climate of inquiry for research and evaluation. In such a situation, visions and practices would have to be made explicit; students and teachers would study their experiences of living with several curricular cultures. A school might also create a sequential plan, based on perceived needs of children and adolescents, to expose learners developmentally to different cultures for several years at a time, perhaps a constructivist primary education, a democratic middle school, a critical culture for high school. The idea of sequence would make more sense if the selected curricular cultures did not suggest discordant visions and values.

We see advantages in having the same classroom culture consistently present across the classes of a learner's school day. However, many of the same issues about the benefits of a single coherent culture in the classroom pertain to the question about a unified, schoolwide approach to curriculum. A culture of curriculum would have a great impact on the lives of students if its beliefs and practices were consistently present across the range of school subjects and sustained throughout the educational career of the learner. For students trying to participate functionally in several different cultures in a single school day, there is little continuity across subjects, and, over years of schooling, they cannot clearly envision the goals of learning. Undoubtedly, a school community devoted to the same vision and working to create and maintain congruent practices would produce far less dissonance for learners and teachers. Additionally, community members and parents could clearly understand the school's educational mission.

If this culture continues over the entire school career, its subtle but powerful belief system will exert its distinctive influence. Learners then will come to have certain expectations of themselves and their teachers and shared understanding of the nature of knowledge, schooling, and the community. Only after students experience prolonged engagements in these cultures will they internalize notions of "what learning is good for," who has authoritative knowledge, or what the relationship should be between students and teacher.

Today, only preparation for work and survival seems to get a serious and sympathetic hearing, especially on the secondary level where business has had such a strong voice in shaping national and state reform legislation. Particularly at a time when the ubiquitous American culture (though legislation, public opinion, and popular culture) singularly sanctions education for getting a job, students and teachers will need explicit affirmation of alternative visions to believe that other curricula can be embraced.

## What Difficulties Are Encountered When Creating a Culture of Curriculum?

The emphases on survival, anxieties about making the grade, preoccupation with short-term planning, and a lack of encouragement for visioning suggest to us that creating a culture of curriculum in the contemporary educational climate is a struggle. In the prevailing culture of schools, the curriculum is driven by a body of incentives and disincentives rather than by visions. Furthermore, we should never underestimate the power of the status quo order to maintain itself.

Coherent, articulated cultures of curriculum cannot arise without some measure of deliberate change from the current culture of schooling. Too often, institutional text (Pinar, Reynolds, Slattery, & Taubman, 1995)—testing, procedures, and classroom management—characterizes most conversations around curriculum. Change is difficult because educational practices are rarely subject to critical internal and public reflection beyond those related to efficiency in maintaining the status quo. Participants in existing school cultures seem fixated on short-term goals such as getting through a unit of instruction, preventing disarray in the classroom, perhaps even "getting more kids involved in learning," but these are not premised on deeper ideals that extend beyond the immediacy of the classroom walls or the three o'clock bell. Shapiro pessimistically concludes,

> One looks in vain in the discourse of teaching "excellence" for a concern with education as a potentially powerful vehicle for the renewal of a culture of active and meaningful citizenship; one in which education has a principal role in nurturing

the skills, values, and commitments necessary to a culture in which individuals care about, and participate in, the making of a society that is just, compassionate, and free. (Shapiro, 1998, p. 54)

Educators' lack of vision may be a consequence of predominant conversations about school improvement, national and state testing, benchmarks, curriculum alignment, and systemic initiatives that shape discussions about reforms. Such mandates often create compliance pressures on teachers who face dominated from above (Hill, 1995). "The teachers' natural response ... will be to avoid taking initiative and to concentrate on ways to protect themselves in the face of bureaucratic scrutiny" (Knapp, 1997, p. 231). As well, these propositions do not communicate a clear vision, do not lead teachers toward their own understanding of congruent practices and ultimate aims, nor invite critique.

Persistent institutional conditions also thwart efforts for innovation and limit the possibility for real change. Schools have cultural regularities that inhibit teachers' interactions with peers and other professionals which might serve to stimulate professional growth and reflection about teaching practices. Some critics of schooling believe that teachers have become "more and more viewed as technicians—called upon to implement classroom objectives that are tightly controlled and defined by others higher on the administrative chain of command" (Purpel & Shapiro, 1995, p. 109).

Such a role increasingly precludes the involvement of teachers from any real authority for decision making in the school. It robs them of the opportunity to think creatively about how they teach or what it is that should be taught. And it denies them. the moral and political significance of what they do.... The 'deskilled' teacher is required to teach with little consciousness or conscience about the fundamental values that he or she is trying to initiate in the classroom. (Purpel & Shapiro, 1995, p. 109)

Furthermore, in contrast to other professions, teachers spend most of their day not with colleagues but with children; they have a great deal of autonomy in the determining the details of the classroom, but teachers typically are enclosed in their own classrooms with little chance for exposure to new ideas. Teachers instead depend on their memory of their own days as students, putting into action the conservative, familiar images of what is proper, possible, and efficient in a classroom setting (Russell, 1993).

New teachers entering the profession—dealing with an almost unmanageable array of responsibilities—rely on a combination of available past images and specific survival techniques to guide their thinking. Cuban (1993) describes this initiation:

[F]acing the complicated practices of establishing routines that will induce a group of students to behave in an orderly way while learning subject matter that the teacher is still unfamiliar with, the teacher is driven to use practices that he or she remembers seeing used or that veterans advise using. By taking such advice, entrants absorb through a subtle osmosis, the school's norms and expectations about what it takes to survive as a teacher. The folklore, occupational gimmicks, norms, and daily teaching reinforce existing approaches rather than nourish skepticism. (p. 254)

Another obstacle to developing a culture of curriculum in a classroom or throughout a school relates to the norms surrounding the traditional organization of the curriculum. Walled classrooms, class periods, and distinct academic departments persist because they seem "normal" (part of the folk pedagogy of education) or because they are convenient, and thus innovation (such as curriculum integration) appears unfeasible.

Perceptions about the nature of subject matter also discourage the adoption of particular curricular cultures; it is presumed that certain curricular cultures are subject-specific. For example, apprenticeships in the community, home economics, or mathematics often exemplify the training for work and survival culture; the critical culture is more likely to be part of the history or social studies classroom rather than the biology lab.

Another way in which the "real" culture of schools perpetuates itself is through the tendency of traditional educators and the public to disdain any kind of curriculum work not part of the status quo, that which seems "abnormal." Caricatures abound when other alternatives are mentioned (no doubt, reinforced by popular culture). For example, curriculum that calls attention to power relationships among people or groups of people are branded as radical and dangerous; child-centered approaches as nonacademic, sentimental, or indulgent; alternative schools as "hippie" or anything-goes; and a vigorous humanist education as "elitist." Albeit, even the prevalent curricular culture of preparation for the workplace receives stereotypical treatment from critics who assume that only a narrow, uncritical education devoid of intellect must occur. Caricatures may contain some truth, but they are overly simplistic and certainly not useful in curricular discourse leading to imagining alternatives.

## What Are the Benefits of Creating a Culture of Curriculum?

The benefit of creating a culture of curriculum lies in the power of a publicly conscious, unifying vision. A clear vision guides the articulation of goals, standards, and ideals, brings together ideas and desires, and becomes the catalyst for change. When a culture of curriculum exists, the learning experience reflects a rationale with intention and purpose. A thoughtful body of beliefs, then, serves to cohere what would otherwise be a succession of classroom activities with little integrity. In ordinary cultures of classrooms and schools, a distinct and meaningful vision is not required.

Educational reformers point to the force of a special vision in the process of successful change whereas the absence of such vision has been noted as a major obstacle to school reform. Through the ethnographic study of the institutions of schools and the nature of school change, Staessens and Vandenberghe (1994) understand that it is vision that separates schools with distinct curricular cultures from schools with status-quo cultures. These researchers depict vision as a core component of school culture, as a "goal-consensus" grounded in the daily interactions of school participants. Individual classrooms, likewise, can assume a distinctive culture with a vision conveying the overarching general sense of what sets this culture apart. Its participants would hold an associated stock of images of exemplary practices, underpinned by their defining beliefs and values. Such goal consensus has a cognitive dimension, representing a rationality of articulated aims and conscious consensus. But, vision also has a "cathectic" dimension; the school culture becomes invested with emotional and intellectual energy (Staessens & Vandenberghe, 1994).

Focusing on significant change across schools as institutions, restructuring reveals the difficulty of escaping persistent regularities of school practice. A leading analyst of educational change, Michael Fullan, claims that even the best-intentioned, well-resourced, and most highly concentrated efforts cannot succeed in bringing about meaningful change without transforming the culture of schooling. It is the culture of schooling that casts light on the distinctive nature of practices: "changing formal structures is not the same as changing norms, habits, skills and beliefs" (Fullan, 1993, p. 49).

We are left, however, with the unsettling question: "Do beliefs matter?" Westheimer (1998) states that "many researchers and reformers maintain that what is important [for transforming schooling] is that beliefs are shared," yet he doubts that analysts of restructuring care "whether the beliefs that are shared are worth sharing." Perhaps any coherent culture of curriculum would improve the status quo, but Westheimer asks us to consider: "What kind of world should we strive for?" Insisting that we must look hard at school cultures to see if "marginalized voices are heard" and if they "reflect ideals of participatory and egalitarian communities," Westheimer concludes that "purpose matters" (pp. 139, 142). Similarly, we realize that aims require critique.

## How Might the "Cultures of Curriculum" Framework Guide Curricular Change?

We believe that major educational change comes from individual commitment and through the efforts of people who share similar goals and values. But first, individuals and coalitions must articulate a clear representation of their vision. Then, a cycle of scrutiny and reflection must occur to assess not only the outcomes but the worth of chosen goals in light of new knowledge, research, or changing social conditions.

In the prevailing culture of schooling, teachers have little time and support for taking these first steps—reflection and deliberation. Purpel and Shapiro (1995) describe what needs to happen to change this situation: "Teachers need to be encouraged to reflect on, and understand, the broader human and social purposes of what they do and to make decisions about what and how they teach in the light of their commitments to attain these purposes" (p. 110).

We propose that the framework of *Cultures of Curriculum* provides a lens for self-scrutiny, a process by which individuals can contemplate their ultimate aims and means of accomplishing them. We believe that individuals need to name their visions and assumptions, look for irreconcilable conflicts that would make it impossible for them to "do it all," and eventually to characterize the culture of curriculum that best describes their beliefs and values.

We encourage reflection about visions and practices to begin in teacher education and to be revisited by individuals throughout their careers. Inquiry and reflection about curriculum work should become habitual, so individuals stay attuned to their "call to teach" (Kohl, 1984) and continually ask themselves if they are working to realize their ideals.

TABLE 9.1
**Beginning a Conversation: Examining Beliefs About Curriculum**

| Focus | Explanation | What Are Your Beliefs? | How Should These Beliefs Be Reflected in Practice? |
|---|---|---|---|
| Visions | Ultimate purposes of education | | |
| Students | Students' needs and how they learn | | |
| Teachers | Role of teachers | | |
| Content | Subject matter and its organization | | |
| Context | Environment of the classroom and school | | |
| Planning | How curriculum should be planned and who should be involved | | |
| Evaluation | How students should be assessed and the curriculum evaluated | | |

We are not suggesting, however, that naming one's culture of curriculum should be the sole objective of inquiry. The chosen culture of curriculum also must be held up to scrutiny. Individuals must recurrently engage in critique, questioning if their visions, assumptions, and practices reflect naiveté or conclusions based on research and evaluation. Have they, for example, learned from students what learning has meaning, or, have they questioned if the environment of the classroom and school supports their goals? Scrutiny means a constant examination of visions and practice and the articulation of the relationship between them.

Accordingly, all cultures of curriculum need to be revisiting periodically to assess their timeliness and vitality. These cultures should not be perceived as static, but as dynamic or evolving because belief systems are acted upon by historical events, societal change, scholarly discoveries, and transformative moral discourse. We do not suggest that these six cultures of curriculum are infinite. For example, we perceive aspects of holistic education—making the spiritual connection of individuals to the natural world and ecology the primary purpose of education (Moffett, 1994)—as an emerging curricular culture. Also, "Connecting to the Canon" may evolve as the teaching of non-Western as well as Western cultures (Nussbaum, 1997).

Nonetheless, *Cultures of Curriculum* can be starting point for dialogue with colleagues and community members. The framework for eliciting visions and beliefs can be utilized with teachers, parents, community members, and students as they discuss curricular changes or initiate alternative schools. We can imagine a forum in which people sit in a circle and share their visions for the purposes of education or their beliefs about how students learn best. Or a facilitator could start with beliefs or visions, asking participants to (literally) take a stand of support or opposition along a line—illustrating a continuum—drawn on the floor.

The discussion would continue so that people could further understand the nature of their beliefs about curriculum and articulate their values. The participants who focus only on the short-term goals of instruction would be urged to imagine the political, social, and moral consequences of education; those who think broadly of education leading to changing or sustaining a particular social vision must be encouraged to deal with pedagogy. Through a more articulated framework, participants then could work to understand not only what culture best describes their understanding of curriculum, but how their positions are similar and different from others. Because cultures are not isolates, participants may discover shared social visions but see different pedagogical means for attaining their visions. Or they may agree about instruction, but assume very different social and political ends.

We anticipate several possible outcomes of such dialogue. Articulation of beliefs may inspire conversations about pedagogical goals and practices, political, moral, and social issues. Those of like mind may begin planning how they can create an environment to support their goals. It may be possible, too, that people who have not talked to each other before, or who have assumed that there are profound differences among them, could discover what assumptions and visions they might hold in common—a good starting point for further conversations and collaboration. We imagine that even dissonance would produce insight as people learn from each other, are challenged, and develop clearer and perhaps modified articulations of their beliefs.

The danger, of course, is that these conversations may produce disturbing discord in which participants find that they have drastically different goals; lines may be drawn, and people may learn that some of their positions cannot be compromised and a community or school would be faced with the dilemmas of how to accommodate conflicting visions. But in the long run, vigorous public discourse about meaningful pedagogical, social, and moral issues would challenge the prevailing culture of "business as usual" in which beliefs and practices go unexamined.

Ultimately, however, no culture of curriculum can exist where the institutional structure of a school is incongruent with its vision, beliefs, practices, activities, and values. Thus, a culture of curriculum that challenges the status quo obligates its adherents to strive through coalitions, platforms, and policy against the givens of the school as a non-visionary set of short-term goals and institutional practices.

There are organized efforts of several types that support teachers and schools in creating the kinds of curricular cultures that challenge the current cultures of compliance and coping within the institutional status quo of schooling. Some of these have grown directly out of grass-roots efforts on the part of teachers and parents to reconstitute the existing culture and seek a variety of progressive goals. In this category we can locate activist networks such as the Institute for Democracy in Education (IDE), the Rethinking Schools Network, the National Coalition of Education Activists (NCEA), Network of Educators on the Americas (NECA), and the National Coalition of Advocates for Students (NCAS).

Other efforts have begun with a central organization, but seek to promote the building of individual teacher's and school's capacities for determining their appropriate educational path and the means and resources by which to pursue it. These efforts include the Coalition of Essential Schools, the Center for Collaborative Education in New York City, the New Standards Project of the Center on Education and the Economy, and the National Center for the Restructuring of Education, Schools and Teaching (NCREST). These projects offer visions of educational and school change philosophically broad enough to accommodate virtually any of the cultures of curriculum we have named.

While networks, coalitions, and associations are important to the support of deliberate transformation of curriculum and schooling, it is not only through shared ideologies that teachers and other stakeholders can assist one another. Any curricular culture, and especially those that promote a serious alternative to what currently dominates, requires an institutional infrastructure of appropriate resources, political legitimacy, and administrative authorization. Teachers need time, materials, facilitative schedules, access to learning sites and sources, and collegial relationships. It is to create these conditions that virtually all states and many school districts have themselves inaugurated programs of change and reform. While it is certainly arguable that most of these initiatives fall short of renewing schooling at the level of cultural transformation, they do at least implicitly acknowledge that their project is necessarily sociopolitical.

Thus we are aware that a platform for dialogue and reflection is just a beginning. But if we stimulate serious discourse about beliefs, goals, and congruent practice, we believe that we will can challenge the prevailing culture of schooling and the fragmentation caused by unexamined innovation—change for change's sake.

In conclusion, we have learned from writing this book that it is crucial to name a vision, to use it as a guide and as a beacon for new attainments. Vision is far-reaching in nature, emanating from the heart of the culture, giving significance to everything it encompasses. Vision is shared with passion by all participants, taking its shape and central place by being forged in a myriad of efforts over a long period of time. Finally, vision forces us to scrutinize the culture of curriculum that we create, continually moving us to work toward its actualization, constantly reminding us to compare the real with the ideal.

## REFERENCES

Bruner, J. (1996). *The culture of education*. Cambridge, MA: Harvard University Press.

Cuban, L. (1993). *How teachers taught: Constancy and change in American classrooms 1890–1990* (2nd ed). New York: Teachers College Press.

Fullan, M. (1993). *Change forces: Probing the depths of educational reform*. New York: Falmer.

Goodlad, J. (1984). *A place called school*. New York: McGraw-Hill.

Heckman, P. (1987). Understanding school culture. In J. Goodlad (Ed.), *The ecology of school renewal: Eighty-sixth yearbook of the National Society for the Study of Education, Part I* (pp. 63–78). Chicago: University of Chicago Press.

Hill, P. T. (1995). *Reinventing public education*. Santa Monica, CA: RAND Corporation, Institute on Education and Training.

Knapp, M. (1997). Between systemic reforms and the mathematics and science classroom: The dynamics of innovation, implementation, and professional learning. *Review of Educational Research, 67*, 227–266.

Kohl, H. (1984). *Growing minds: On becoming a teacher*. New York: Harper & Row.

Meier, D. (1991). The kindergarten tradition in the high school. In K. Jervis & C. Montag (Eds.), *Progressive education for the 1990s: Transforming practice* (pp. 135–148). New York: Teachers College Press.

Moffett, J. (1994). *The universal schoolhouse: Spiritual awakening through education*. San Francisco: Jossey-Bass.

Nussbaum, M. C. (1997). *Cultivating humanity: A classical defense of reform in liberal education*. Cambridge, MA: Harvard University Press.

Pinar, W. F., Reynolds, W. M., Slattery, P., & Taubman, P. M. (1995). *Understanding curriculum: An introduction to the study of historical and contemporary curriculum discourses*. New York: Peter Lang.

Purpel, D. E., & Shapiro, S. (1995). *Beyond liberation and excellence: Reconstructing the public discourse on education*. Westport, CT: Bergin & Garvey.

Russell, T. (1993). Learning to teach science: Constructivism, reflection, and learning from experience. In K. Tobin, (Ed.), *The practice of constructivism in science education*, (pp. 247–258). Hillsdale, NJ: Lawrence Erlbaum Associates.

Shapiro, S. (1998). Public school reform: The mismeasure of education. *Tikkun, 13*, 51–55.

Sirotnik, K. (1983). What you see is what you get: Consistency, persistency, and mediocrity in the classroom. *Harvard Educational Review, 53*, 16–31.

Staessens, K., & Vandenberghe, R. (1994). Vision as a core component in school culture. *Curriculum Studies, 25*, 187–200.

Westheimer, J. (1998). *Among schoolteachers: Community, autonomy, and ideology in teachers' work*. New York: Teachers College Press.

Wood, G. H. (1992/1993). *Schools that work: America's most innovative public education programs*. New York: Dutton.

# About the Authors

**P**amela **Bolotin Joseph**    This book represents a synthesis of my long-term fascination with the application of theory to life and practice. In some ways, I understand that this project probably began germinating several decades ago because of three wonderful courses that forever changed the way I understood the world: one in American pragmatic philosophy (taken as an undergraduate), where I began to look at the social and moral consequences of ideas and actions; another in graduate school, called "The Good Life," which applied philosophical conceptions to everyday life; and the first course for my doctoral professional sequence in the social studies (at Northwestern University), which introduced me to the study of culture. The concept of culture came as a bolt of lightning that eventually led to a dissertation, an interdisciplinary analysis of the role of emotion and culture in moral development and education. The dissertation also stemmed from my teaching experiences, especially how I encountered value conflicts (my own and with others) as a social studies and language arts teacher in middle school and high school.

I have continued to study moral education, but other areas that hold a strong interest are curriculum theory, the teaching profession, and the culture of schooling. The conception of this book also flowed naturally from my interests in history and the utilization of metaphor to understanding teachers' work and lives. I am the co-editor (with Gail Burnaford) of *Images of Schoolteachers in America* and I have published in *The Journal of Moral Education, Theory and Research in Social Education, Social Education, and The Journal of Teacher Education.*

I currently have the position of core faculty in the Graduate Programs in Education at Antioch University Seattle, generally working with experienced teachers. I teach courses in the curriculum field, history and philosophy of education,

175

qualitative research, alternative education, and moral education. Before coming to Antioch, I was a faculty member at National-Louis University and adjunct faculty at Northwestern University and Northeastern Illinois University.

While my four children were growing up, I was involved in public schools in a variety of ways as a parent and community member, including serving on a board of education and working with the PTA, community groups, and legislators for support of public education. More recently, I was on the site council for my children's high school and a community participant in that school district's curriculum advisory board. A catalyst for writing this book was my experience on that committee. While co-writing a report to the board of education on the new state reform legislation (based on Goals 2000), I suggested that we needed to describe how this legislation represents the curricular orientation of preparing for business; another committee member responded to my comment with, "Well, what other orientations are there?" It was then I realized the importance of public discourse for imagining alternative educational visions and not just that of dominant American culture.

My decision to write the chapter on the canon has, in many ways, paralleled my interest in religion, moral education, and the humanities. Although I have continually grown to appreciate the work done by those who teach to connect to their students to bodies of intellectual and moral knowledge, especially the search for personal meaning within a stimulating, intellectual course of study, I have had more passion for critique of this chapter than for its belief systems. The content chapter that was more "comfortable" for me was my collaboration on "Confronting the Dominant Order," because of the work I've done with students over the years, often introducing them to the ideas of critical, feminist, and multicultural pedagogies. The ideas in the critical chapter more closely mirror the ideals of my university—Antioch has a strong articulated mission of social justice—and my personal values.

**S**tephanie Luster Bravmann     My intellectual and personal lives have always been in delicate balance, each informing the other in ways that have shaped the individual culture in which I reside. My early schooling, especially at the Francis W. Parker School in Chicago, encouraged my quest to articulate and enact my beliefs about the intellect, social justice, and being a contributing member of society. An educational foundation of rigorous exploration and individual action for the benefit of the whole prompted me to pursue undergraduate work in literature, writing, anthropology, and social psychology. It also enabled me to productively interrupt my studies—for varying periods of time—to marry, travel and teach in West Africa, raise children, and in other ways participate in the world around me.

Teaching children from preschool through the secondary grades in inner city, urban, rural, public, independent private, and parochial schools, combined with work as a teacher in Ghana and Burkina Faso, provided me with a broad range of experiences from which to approach my doctoral studies. My academic work focused on the location of curriculum in the educational process and the constituent methods of those who mediate the curriculum for learners. A continuing interest in education in school and nonschool settings, and in the teachers and learners who transact the process itself, led to a dissertation investigating the role of mentors in the lives of those considered by dint of their accomplishments or potential to be particularly able individuals. This undertaking enabled me to rediscover my core belief in our need to somehow facilitate each person's own search for that which is most worthy in him or herself and in society and then to live a life steeped in that worth.

I am currently on the faculty of the Graduate School of Education at Seattle University, where I instruct both veteran teachers and those who educate children in venues outside of schools as they pursue their own masters and doctoral studies. Before beginning to work in higher education I was the general studies director and administrator of Seattle Hebrew Academy, the executive director of a not-for-profit agency, and the coordinator of school cooperatives in northwestern Washington State. Community undertakings through the years have included work with children who are homeless and with agencies providing services for marginalized children and membership on the Seattle Coalition for Educational Equity.

My participation in the conceptualization of this book project seems to have been a natural outgrowth of my academic and personal beliefs. The naming of things has always seemed to me to be a combination of the glib and the difficult—I truly believe that there is no single "right way" to educate because each of us, aside from our inherent equality in our humanness, is uniquely different and learns and lives in our own way. The concept of *Cultures of Curriculum*, when taken to encompass the full meanings of the word "culture," best expresses for me the task that I feel we have to accomplish. I am convinced that it is through individuals that our society will be healed; writing the chapter "Developing Self and Spiritf" provided me with a way to express at least some of the power that I feel an affirmatory approach can wield.

# Mark A. Windschitl
I approached this writing task as I do all my others, drawing on 12 years of experience in the middle school science

classroom for inspiration and examples. I taught in Des Moines, Iowa during this time, and I was constantly fascinated with how students learned, how they socialized in and out of school, and what courses their lives took after leaving the classroom.

As I moved on to graduate school at Iowa State University and was exposed to a wealth of curricular, social, and cognitive models—in particular, constructivism—describing the complexities of the educational enterprise, I came to fully appreciate my former teaching life and reflected back on it with a kind of altered vision. My interest in constructivism grew in subsequent years with more reading and reflection, eventually becoming a focus of my dissertation. I could see how constructivism could act as a logical bridge between the information-processing view of learning that supports traditional education and the more liberatory pedagogies.

Also, what permanently changed my conception of schooling was a year-long course in graduate school that emphasized critical, feminist, and multicultural theory. These powerful descriptive frameworks revealed and made clear to me what was invisible, unspoken, and suppressed in America today. I drew on these ideas in conjunction with my classroom experiences to help me contribute to the chapter "Confronting the Dominant Order."

Since receiving my doctorate in curriculum and instruction, I have investigated learning from many different angles, but always with an eye to how learners "make sense" of their worlds, often in spite of the teachers and curriculum. I am currently on the education faculty at the University of Washington in Seattle, and have written for *Phi Delta Kappan, Educational Researcher, Middle School Journal, Journal of Research in Science Teaching*, and other publications.

I will conclude by saying that the most powerful influences in my professional life have been my parents. My father has been a teacher and administrator for more than 35 years and my mother has served on the city council and for many years has been a vital part of my hometown community of Carroll, Iowa. My parents were the early authors of the narrative of my life and I hope that their steadfast belief in the humanistic side of education is faithfully communicated and passed on to the readers of this volume.

E dward R. Mikel          I came rather late to the academy, having earlier in my career briefly taught junior and senior high school social studies, been a program coordinator and evaluator at a national educational laboratory, and served as a research and evaluation specialist and division administrator with the St. Louis public school district.

The great themes and orientation of my professional career and civic life seemed to have been forged, however, in the political atmosphere of my early family. We were a family of modest, sometimes limited, means and very interested in politics in the old way: as partisan party loyalists and dedicated troops marshaled for electoral-governmental politics. My family and my parents' families before us were Roosevelt Democrats—spelled with both a capital and a lower-case "d." My political legacy was a deep, passionate faith in the role of government to try to make society better for those who found themselves disadvantaged, and a great deal of fractious contention among all constituencies over what that mission actually meant. For Democrats, and democrats, were constantly arguing with each other while coming together at pivotal moments to attempt to cull back the power of society's elite to have everything and to have it on their own terms.

I now understand that in an important way FDR merely saved American democracy for corporate capitalism. This sense grew in my experience in various modest roles in the civil rights and antiwar movements of the 1960s, the time of my own coming of age. It became increasingly clear to me that the primary constituencies of race, ethnicity, gender, and/or class could take effective action together against, or for, the significant laws and policies of government and society's defining conditions. Yet we seldom could agree on permanent analyses or overarching goals or hold together our specific campaigns and projects for very long. Broad temporary alliances were politically necessary, but primary affiliations gave us our core identity and sustained us over the long haul.

My study of history as an undergraduate in the late 1960s, especially the past and present story of southeast Asia, helped me gain perspective on the irreducibly multicultural nature of social life. Majoritarian oppressions are common in the history of democracy, and middling and have-not groups, divided along any of the major lines of cultural difference, have often sought to keep each weak so as to benefit themselves. In all respects democracy is highly textured and full of possibilities as well as problems. It has not been uncommon for parties, organizations, or nations to be moved by the liberal impulse to want to "improve" the lives of those suffering and dispossessed in the social scheme of things. But the implicit arrogance of such a perspective is self-defeating. There can be no "improvement" of any life that is not autonomously determined by those who live it. And certainly there is no democracy without autonomous members.

Especially since coming to higher education, teacher education more specifically, I have sought the democratic way to a fully multicultural and inclusive society through formal education. I am convinced it must begin in each locality, with democracy activated in immediate communities. Classrooms are the seedbeds of school, just as schools are seedbeds of society. Teachers and others who are in close touch with one another about progressive educational practice and policy can form broad networks for school and social change.

I have written the chapter "Deliberating Democracy" from the conviction that democracy, in its full range of workings and considerations, must spring up uniquely in every classroom. From across all these "embryonic democratic communities," however, comes a reaching out to the surrounding social world, intellectually and practically, through acts of the class group or of its members now or in their later lives. In this way, the spirit of democracy is renewed in each generation and the concrete hope of democracy rekindled for all places in this time.

# Nancy Stewart Green

My career goals have always been divided between, on the one hand, a certain inborn inclination toward the intellectual life and, on the other, my desire to oppose social injustice. The first inclination led me to an academic career in history and educational foundations, including teaching for 19 years at Northeastern Illinois University in Chicago. The second was fulfilled during the 1960s, when I managed a program of basic skills education for a War on Poverty agency, and in my work in the 1980s and 1990s with the Chicago Teachers Center, a part of Northeastern Illinois University that seeks to strengthen teachers and schools in the city of Chicago.

But even in my research and writing I was motivated by a desire to support the struggle of nondominant groups. My PhD dissertation reported on the effects of programs for first-generation college students in the YMCA Community College in Chicago; further research led me into women's educational history and a study of a public vocational high school (founded in 1911) for girls in Chicago. I have published in the *History of Education Quarterly, Chicago History, the Journal of Teacher Education*, and *Catalyst: A Journal of Chicago School Reform*, as well as in *Images of Schoolteachers in the Twentieth Century* and the *Historical Encyclopedia of Chicago Women*.

With this background, I approached the writing of the chapter "Preparing for Work and Survival" with some trepidation. Well aware of the critical condemnation of vocational education as a means of denying opportunities for upward mobility to working-class and minority students, I was also acquainted with sincere and dedicated teachers who seek practical hope for students alienated from the whole process of schooling. So I wanted to present as even-handed a portrait as I could of this curriculum, reserving my ire for the culture that limits choices for all its members.

# Quotation References

Bobbitt, F. (1926/1961). From the *Twenty-sixth yearbook of the national society for the study of education*. In L. A. Cremin, *The transformation of the school: Progressivism in American education 1876–1957* (p. 200). New York: Vintage.

Bruner, J. (1996). *The culture of education* (p. 67). Cambridge, MA: Harvard University Press.

Bruner, J. (1996). *The culture of education* (p. 88–89). Cambridge, MA: Harvard University Press.

Counts, G. (1932/1964). From Dare the school build a new social order? In C. H. Gross & C. C. Chandler (Eds.), *The history of American education through readings* (p. 375). Boston: Heath.

Fullan, M. (1993). *Change forces: Probing the depths of educational reform* (p. 49). New York: Falmer.

Dewey, J. (1916/1964). *Democracy and education* (p. 87). New York: Free Press.

Duckworth, E. (1996). *The having of wonderful ideas and other essays on teaching and learning* (p. 18). New York: Teachers College Press.

Fowler, B. (1930/1961). From "President's Message," *Progressive Education VII* in L. A. Cremin, *The transformation of the school: Progressivism in American education 1876–1957* (p. 258). New York: Vintage.

Freedman, S. G. (1990). *Small victories: The real world of a teacher, her students, and their high school* (p. 271). New York: Harper Perennial.

Hall, E. T. (1959/1970). *The silent language* (p. 166). New York: Fawcett.

Hutchins, R. M. (1953/1970). From *The conflict in education*. In J. W. Noll & S. P. Kelly (Eds.), *Foundations of education in America: An anthology of major thoughts & significant actions* (pp. 353–354). New York: Harper & Row.

Smiley, J. (1995). *Moo* (p. 386). New York: Fawcett Columbine.

# Name Index

# Subject Index

**DATE DUE**

DEC 2 9 2000

JUL 0 3 2006

MAR 2 1 2001

JUN 1 9 2001

JAN 0 2 2002

JUL 1 2 2002